Theocritus and Things

Ancient Cultures, New Materialisms

Series Editors: Lilah Grace Canevaro, University of Edinburgh and Melissa Mueller, University of Massachusetts, Amherst

Reconsidering the ancient world through the lens of New Materialism

From archaeological sites to papyri and manuscripts, we experience the ancient world through its material remains. This materiality may be tangible: from vases to votive offerings and statues to spearheads. It might be the text as object or the object in the text. The New Materialisms have transformed the way we conceive of the material world – but how and to what extent might they be applied to ancient cultures?

Books in this series will showcase the potential applications of New Materialism within Classics, giving us a new way to look at ancient texts, ancient objects and ancient world-views.

Editorial Advisory Board

Karen Bassi, University of California Santa Cruz
Ruth Bielfeldt, University of Munich
Jeffrey Jerome Cohen, Arizona State University
Diana Coole, Birkbeck, University of London
Katharine Earnshaw, University of Exeter
Milette Gaifman, Yale University
Jonas Grethlein, University of Heidelberg
Graham Harman, Southern California Institute of Architecture
Brooke Holmes, Princeton University
Mark Payne, University of Chicago
Verity Platt, Cornell University
Alex Purves, University of California Los Angeles
Michael Squire, King's College London
Miguel John Versluys, University of Leiden
Nancy Worman, Barnard College, Columbia University

Books available:

Amy Lather, *Materiality and Aesthetics in Archaic and Classical Greek Poetry*
Lilah Grace Canevaro, *Theocritus and Things: Material Agency in the* Idylls

Visit our website at edinburghuniversitypress.com/series-ancient-cultures-new-materialisms to find out more

Theocritus and Things
Material Agency in the *Idylls*

Lilah Grace Canevaro

EDINBURGH
University Press

Edinburgh University Press is one of the leading university presses in the UK. We publish academic books and journals in our selected subject areas across the humanities and social sciences, combining cutting-edge scholarship with high editorial and production values to produce academic works of lasting importance. For more information visit our website: edinburghuniversitypress.com

© Lilah Grace Canevaro 2023, 2024

Edinburgh University Press Ltd
13 Infirmary Street, Edinburgh, EH1 1LT

Typeset in 10/14 Ehrhardt by,
Cheshire Typesetting Ltd, Cuddington, Cheshire

A CIP record for this book is available from the British Library

ISBN 978 1 3995 1749 2 (hardback)
ISBN 978 1 3995 1750 8 (paperback)
ISBN 978 1 3995 1751 5 (webready PDF)
ISBN 978 1 3995 1752 2 (epub)

The right of Lilah Grace Canevaro to be identified as the author of this work has been asserted in accordance with the Copyright, Designs and Patents Act 1988, and the Copyright and Related Rights Regulations 2003 (SI No. 2498).

Contents

List of Illustrations   vii
Acknowledgements   viii
Preface   x

Introduction: Material Agency   1

1. The Cup   11
   Material Ecocriticism: An Exercise in Listening   11
   Boundaries: Author, Genre, Tradition   23
   Oiko-criticism and Dark Ecology: Revisiting Hesiod's Farm   37

2. The Woman   44
   Material Feminism: Changing Nature   44
   Idyll 1: Ekphrasis and Materiality   48
   Idyll 2: Reading Bodies   66
   Idyll 15: Women's Work   81

3. The Fisherman and the Rock   91
   Idylls 7 and 21: Imagined Landscapes   91
   Idyll 23: Vital Stone   113
   Excursus: San Sperate   140

4. The Plaited Trap   146
   Idyll 1: Creative Matter   146
   Idyll 28: Emigration and Collaboration   155
   From Distaffs to Guineas   169

5. Beyond the Cup 178
    Idylls 6 and 11: His Monstrous Materials 178
    The Pipes Are Calling 186
    Slàinte 195

A Concluding Excursus: Marsden 202

Bibliography 211
Index Locorum 223
Subject Index 2??

List of Illustrations

2.1.	'Root of Evil', mural by street artist MP5, Mosciano Sant' Angelo, Abruzzo, Italy. Photo credit: MP5	56
3.1.	San Sperate, Sardinia. Photo credit: Lilah Grace Canevaro	141–2
3.2.	San Sperate, Sardinia. Photo credit: Lilah Grace Canevaro	143
3.3.	Giardino Sonoro, Sardinia. Photo credit: Lilah Grace Canevaro	144
5.1.	The Theocritus Cup, Paul Storr and John Flaxman. Photo credit: National Museums Liverpool	196
6.1.	Marsden Rock and Grotto, Marsden Bay, South Shields. Photo credit: Lilah Grace Canevaro	203
6.2.	Lot's Wife, Marsden Bay, South Shields. Photo credit: Lilah Grace Canevaro	206

Acknowledgements

This book began in a field in Exeter. The 'Poetic Places' workshop was co-organised with Katharine Earnshaw, whose knowledge of and enthusiasm for all things ecocritical shifted my materialism into a more environmental gear. I learned a lot from all the workshop participants: classicists, geographers, artists and farmers.

Mark Usher was one of those participants, and it has been in conversation with Mark that I have worked out many of the ideas in this book. His feedback has been as invaluable as his friendship. Mark's publications are a constant source of inspiration, as he paves the way not only for ecocritical thinking but also for diverse kinds of writing that bring the person through onto the page.

William Brockliss was another of the workshop participants, and offered extensive comments on this book. Will's own work on Homer's environmental imagery and Hesiod's dark ecology was foundational to this project, and his feedback has been characteristically perceptive and generous. Mark Payne's work too has been a cornerstone of my research for this book, and I am grateful for his comments on my manuscript. Mark's expertise spans Theocritus and Ecocriticism: he is truly The Expert, and I am incredibly lucky to have had the perfect sounding board. Thanks also to Richard Hutchins and Calum Maciver for their insightful comments on various chapters.

Melissa Mueller has been a constant reassuring and collaborative presence throughout this project. I have really enjoyed swapping chapter drafts, hashing out ideas and working together on the Ancient Cultures, New Materialisms series. I only hope I can do Melissa proud with this addition.

My thanks to National Museums Liverpool and artist MP5 for providing images, and to the Pinuccio Sciola Museum and the Giardino Sonoro in San Sperate, Sardinia, for the experience and the inspiration. When we visited San Sperate, our eldest son Layton was one and a half – he features on the book's cover, surrounded by singing stones. Thanks to Layton for being there from the start, and for still being my rock. But a lot has changed during the writing of this book, which is dedicated to both Layton and his little brother Guthrie. Thanks to Guthrie for the smiles, the stories and the wide-open spaces. This book is for my whole family, who loom a lot larger in my life than the specks at Marsden might suggest.

Preface

Material agency; human and nonhuman agency; lithic agency; entangled agencies; assemblages and networks of actors and actants; hybrid agents. This book takes up the calls of New Materialism, Material Ecocriticism and Material Feminism to multiply and redefine our understanding of agency, foregrounding a diverse range of agents including but not limited to the human. In so doing, it expands the cast of characters in our discussion of ancient poetry. Material Ecocriticism has been described as an exercise in listening – and it is to a series of underrepresented agents (women, nature, the nonhuman) in ancient Greek literature that this book urges us to listen.

In its drive to foreground material agency, this book takes its structure from the decorated cup in Theocritus' first *Idyll*. The woman courted by two men leads to a material-feminist analysis of Theocritus' female characters, with ekphrasis bringing us back to Pandora, forward to modern street art and into Gorgo and Praxinoa's material narrative. The old fisherman and his rugged rock guide us through multilayered imagined landscapes and to stories of stone, from archaic poetry to modern-day Sardinia. The boy plaiting a trap for grasshoppers instigates a material-ecocritical consideration of creation and creative matter that ranges from the distaffs of Theocritus and Erinna to the object-subjects of eighteenth-century it-narrative. The journey continues through Polyphemus' monstrous landscape to the world of the syrinx, the Theocritus Cup as a real-world art object and the entangled stories of Marsden Bay.

This book contributes to the literary-theoretical field of Material Ecocriticism, expanding its chronological remit, and explores its potential applications to Classics. It focuses on the poetry of Theocritus as a corpus that reveals the multiple entanglements between human and nonhuman agents, but its line of enquiry does not stop there. Material Ecocriticism can give us a way in to questions of the Anthropocene, of sustainability, of countering human narcissism. It can also give us new perspectives on hallmarks of literary-critical analysis such as genre, authorship and literary tradition.

The 'from below' reading offered by this book gives a new way in to the paradoxes of Hellenistic pastoral poetry. The material and environmental connections of this poetry are mediated by context (the urban backdrop to bucolic poetry, the literary sophistication of the *Idylls* paired with their deceptively simple subject matter, the artifice of the *locus amoenus*), but there *are* connections. This book reveals a detailed picture of material agency and a diverse cast of characters, human and nonhuman, in Theocritus' *Idylls*, showing that while the poetry might be paradoxical, it is not rarefied. And through a dark-ecological reading, it highlights the darkness that undercuts the idyll.

Introduction: Material Agency

THE FARMER ASKED for a volunteer. I stepped forward. Sit down, cross-legged, in the middle of the field, and see what happens, she said. Cautiously and curiously I did as I was told. Within seconds, a whole herd of cows had clustered closely around me, noses down, to investigate the seated interloper. The farmer explained that cows are very inquisitive animals, always trying to make sense of their environs; and that since they do not sit in such a position, they are fascinated by people who do.

The 2016 volume *Object Oriented Environs*, edited by Jeffrey Jerome Cohen and Julian Yates, charts the results of a session held at the forty-second annual meeting of the Shakespeare Association of America in St Louis in 2014. In the introduction ('An environing of this book'), the editors recount their conference experience: walking around the city ('peripatetic philosophizing', they call it), breaking out of the stuffy conference room and heading through a door marked 'Staff only, do not enter',[1] reflecting on the St Louis backdrop, from ancient mounds to the Gateway Arch. It is an exercise in porosity: in being open to academic material at the same time as to real-world, real-time materiality. Shakespeare and St Louis; theory and tourism. It is a shaking up: of the conference format, of what it means to introduce a book, of how to think in and about place.

My visit to the farmer's field was part of a two-day workshop in Exeter in July 2018. The topic of the event was 'Poetic Places: Material Ecocriticism and Classical

---

[1] 'You will have guessed that a story about race, privilege, and access unfolded here and was carried into what followed when we returned to the beige room': Cohen and Yates 2016: xx. Environing can lead to a reading from below, as I offer in this book.

Poetry',² and it was made up of exploratory presentations and discussions from and with a group of invited academics, work with local artist Laura Hopes and a walk at Quicke's Farm, Devon, guided by the remarkable Mary Quicke, a fourteenth-generation farmer (who also has a degree in English literature). The aim of the event was to encourage us to think about Material Ecocriticism and its potential applications to Classics, particularly through ancient hexameter poetry. To think about reading the physical world – materiality, nature, the environment – into and out of classical literature. And this is the 'environing of this book': its roots, its origin. At the roundtable session I gave a preliminary paper on Theocritus and stone (the basis for the second section of Chapter 3, pp. 113–40), and that's where the writing of this book began. But more than that, over the two days I learned much about new-materialist, material-ecocritical and environmental humanities approaches in a collaborative and unconventional context, and thought about the texts and world-views we were studying in very different ways. Texts and paratexts like the ploughed field and its margins. The palimpsestic landscape. The volatility and unpredictability of the land being an agentic reality across time. The sheer timescale of the land necessitating a long family memory, a multigenerational view, the deep time of the farmed environment outlasting a human lifespan. The unknown: even soil has so much about it that we do not understand. The animosities: Mark Usher, classicist and agriculturalist, advises me not to sit down in a field with his own Scottish Highland cows, or risk having an eye put out (they have horns and are not afraid to use them). Though we enjoyed each other's papers, all the participants agreed that walking through those fields, talking about farming as much as art as much as poetry – that's when the real work was done. As Cohen and Yates put it, 'environing is best done in company' – in my case, a company of texts, ideas, colleagues – and cows.

This book foregrounds a range of episodes from across the Theocritean corpus (broadly conceived) that question the dividing lines we draw between the human and more-than-human worlds. A bird tied to a wheel as a love charm. Dogs that dream of bread; fishermen dreaming of golden fish. Stones singing against boots. Death by falling statue. Material agency is a central concept in this book. It will be worth our while, then, to spend a little time picking apart this concept at the outset. The first step is to separate out and distinguish the capacity of agency from the human, to acknowledge it as a capacity of some kind shared by a variety of entities: from humans, to animals, to trees, to the weather, to rocks. This is the first step in countering 'the narcissism of our species', as discussed by Serenella Iovino.³

---

² Available at <https://poeticplaces.wordpress.com> (last accessed 29 November 2022). Organisers: Lilah Grace Canevaro and Katharine Earnshaw.
³ Iovino 2012.

An anthropocentric reading of agency is sticky; it is persistent. Supported by centuries of dualism in the wake of Descartes' schemata, it has long been buttressed by those conceptual divides of which our society is so fond (nature/culture; human/nonhuman). Similarly, it is affected by the strong pull of Kantian correlationism, which has come to reinforce the idea that objects and the nonhuman are blank screens for our anthropocentric projections. Yet this is where Classics can contribute to the posthumanist debate: in its attention to 'pre-humanist' sources.[4] It is in discussing a pre-Cartesian, pre-Kantian corpus of literature that theories such as New Materialism or Ecocriticism can really fall into place.[5] The use of 'modern' theory to analyse ancient texts cannot, then, risk anachronism, as it finds affinity. As Bruno Latour famously put it, 'We have never been modern'.

It is worth observing that a human-specific conception of agency tends not to stand up to scrutiny. As soon as we start asking the question 'is agency really unique to humans?', we immediately find ourselves having to shore up the borders of agency as a concept in order just to tread water, and circular arguments raise their ugly heads. Agency absolutely must involve intentionality, we say. And a tangible, recognisable intentionality, at that. Something we can *see* in operation. Preferably with a face or a voice behind it. It must be intrinsically linked with a subject. A subject in a very clear subject/object hierarchy. Which must inevitably be a human, right? Because what other clear-cut subjects are there? And it all hangs on our cognitive

---

[4] Goldhill (2020: 334) comments on this relevance of Classics to the posthumanist project: 'to go back before the historical moment of humanism to explore posthumanism is to discover – inevitably? – a pre-humanism, where the claim of the centrality and dominance of the human is not yet a given and where the interfolding of the human with its others is repeatedly performed both in aggressive disavowal and in equally assertive assumption'. This is 'a space of the "not yet" – which may not only be a chronological condition – from which to view the trajectory of the challenge of the post- of posthumanism'. Also in this vein is the volume *Antiquities Beyond Humanism*, which 'maps out the ground for a richer and more sustained encounter with Greco-Roman antiquity, excavating an ante-humanism that nonetheless does not seek any kind of return to a pre-humanist arcadia. The volume arises from a commitment to actively engage this ancient philosophical tradition as a powerful field through which to tackle some of the most urgent questions addressed by the New Materialisms and forms of post- and non-humanism.' 'Antiquity gives rise not only to a humanist tradition but also to lines of thought that are better understood as non-humanist' (Bianchi et al. 2019: 3).

[5] Particularly useful on correlationism as it has developed with and since Kant, especially its potential ecologically destructive effects, is Morton 2017. Morton discusses the correlationist 'gap' between beings, arguing that it forbids solidarity with nonhumans. He calls this gap 'the Severing', and posits instead the idea of interrelatedness: that beings are deeply reliant on each other.

processes. If we can spot the difference between a human and an object, if we have the capacity (from very early childhood) to distinguish between them and set them in a hierarchy, then there must be a fundamental divide that something as important as agency simply cannot cross.[6] We see evidence all around us of forces equal to or often greater than ourselves – hurricanes (discussed by Nancy Tuana in *Material Feminisms*); pollution and toxicity (the subject of many chapters in Serenella Iovino and Serpil Oppermann's *Material Ecocriticism*) – and yet we persist in our efforts to ring-fence agency as a uniquely human attribute. The best way to combat this conceptual stickiness and the ontological and ethical issues it raises is to redefine agency: most importantly, to open it up. To take away the immediate associations of intentionality and subjectivity, and see what remains. We are left with something far more expansive, far more encompassing – and far truer to our lived experience. Further, by changing the definition rather than simply mapping it across, we are not going against our instincts or our cognitive patterns. We are not claiming that human and nonhuman agents are the same, or that we should amalgamate everything under one rubric. Rather, we are adjusting our sights to a fuller spectrum of agencies: a richer tableau in which we are not necessarily always, uniquely, at the centre. Or at least, we are not there alone.

In attempting to define agency, we might profitably take our starting point from feminist theory, in particular 'Material Feminisms' broadly defined (for further discussion, see Chapter 2, pp. 44–8). Karen Barad's conceptualisation of agency, coming from a Physics perspective, is very apt here. In her book *Meeting the Universe Halfway*, Barad devises a rather abstract definition of agency that is suited to the task of reading multiple agencies across and between the human and nonhuman: a definition by which 'agency is not an attribute' but a '"doing"/"being" in its intra-activity'.[7] We shall explore the idea of intra-activity or intra-action further at the start of Chapter 2 (pp. 44–8), but for now it suffices to explain that this encapsulates the meeting of agencies halfway, the performative establishment of agency, the collaborative co-constitution of meaning between a variety of parties (not only the usually foregrounded human subject). Barad elaborates: 'Agency is not aligned with human intentionality or subjectivity. Nor does it merely entail resignification

---

[6] There is much evidence to show that we respond differently to animate agents and inanimate objects from childhood (Johnson and Morton 1991 demonstrated that newborns exhibit preferential tracking of face-like stimuli) or even earlier (it has recently been shown that this also applies to the foetus in the womb: Reid et al. 2017). The new-materialist paradigm becomes even more interesting against this backdrop, as it explores our enmeshment and entanglement with things which we instinctively recognise as different from ourselves.
[7] Barad 2007: 815.

or other specific kinds of moves within a social geometry of antihumanism.'[8] It is not that we are simply transferring notions of human agency to the nonhuman, adjusting parameters and 'resignifying' terms; rather, we are radically reconceptualising what agency is, and where it lies. This initial attempt at defining a key term enacts *in nuce* the theoretical and ontological recalibration espoused in this book. This can be seen in particular in a resistance to, for example, anthropomorphic readings of material phenomena in Theocritus' *Idylls*: ideas of human agency are not projected onto the nonhuman in a top-down fashion, but rather the meeting points between a variety of agents are considered in an entirely different and responsive way (see, for instance, the exploration of petromorphism in Chapter 3, pp. 113–40).

In its drive to let material agency take centre stage, this book takes its structure from an iconic object: Thyrsis' cup in Theocritus' first *Idyll*. But why Theocritus? First, the Theocritean corpus is a broad and porous one. Its literary experimentation, its Homeric and Hesiodic influences, its impact on Virgil, the questions it raises about genre and authorship: all of these make it the ideal place to explore ancient hexameter. The boundaries of Theocritean poetry and those of 'Theocritus' himself are unsettled and uncertain, compelling us to keep our readings open. And Theocritus' presentation of both urban and rural environments trains our readings specifically on people, landscape and material *realia*. We could look further within mime, or later pastoral poetry, or comedy with its proliferation of objects, and extend the arguments offered in this book. Theocritus is not *uniquely* suited to a material-ecocritical reading. Yet he does stand in a unique position, between imitation and imagination, between the real world and story.[9] His hexameter poetry is not simply epic, nor is it parody: it is a 'possible world',[10] and the attention to material agency in his poetry shows its connection to that world.

The Hellenistic roots of pastoral literature are inherently paradoxical. The elite patronage of Hellenistic poets. The urban backdrop for the composition of bucolic poetry (a backdrop that moves to the fore in others of Theocritus' *Idylls* and which, therefore, is never far away). The literary sophistication of the *Idylls* paired with their deceptively simple subject matter. The artifice of the *locus amoenus*. The types of materiality considered in this book often reflect and reflect on those paradoxes: a focus on ekphrasis, for example, or on creation and creativity. But in revealing a

---

[8] Ibid. p. 826.
[9] On 'the pastoral blurring of real and imaginary', see Segal 1981: 3–24 (quotation from p. 5).
[10] Fantuzzi and Hunter 2004: 141. See further p. 148: 'It is this selective mixture of idealisation and reality that distinguishes Theocritean "realism" from the idealised and/or imprecise description of the countryside and pastoral life that we find in the poems of his Greek imitators and in Virgil's *Eclogues*'. To what extent Theocritus' *Idylls* can be considered 'epic' is discussed by, e.g., Halperin 1983 and Cameron 1995, Chapter 16.

detailed picture of material agency and a diverse cast of characters in Theocritus' *Idylls*, this book shows that despite its paradoxes, this poetry is not rarefied. Its urban backdrop, its elite perspective and its 'ontological mystique' (that is, the irreducibility of the bucolic world's origins to either myth or reality alone)[11] do not negate its connections to materiality and material agency. Its material and environmental connections are mediated by context – but it is not *dis*connected. And while this challenges some customary approaches to Hellenistic poetry, it is not, I believe, a reading of Theocritus that goes against the grain. There are enough clues within the poetry to facilitate this reading, as we shall see. It is, rather, a 'from below' reading of Theocritus[12] – and that is what gives Material Ecocriticism its impact: the possibility of shifting our perspective, our world-view, and of decentring typically foregrounded agents and moving others to the centre or focusing on the margins. The poetry of Theocritus has been described as a complex multiplicity of voices, a polyphony, as frames and dialogues integrate various levels of narration.[13] What I hope to show is that there are many *kinds* of voices and agencies conveyed in Theocritus' poetry. Not all of them are elite; potentially, not all of them are filtered through the elite; not all of them are male; and not all of them are human.

Chapter 1 begins with the cup as an entangled entity, testing out ideas of anthropo-decentrism, affect and vital materialism through this single (yet not discrete) object. The cup leads into an introduction of this book's core theoretical underpinning: that of Material Ecocriticism. A nascent field, Material Ecocriticism can provide a way into big questions – about the Anthropocene, about countering human narcissism. With it we can ask new questions, but we can also revisit the pillars of literary-critical analysis such as genre, authorship and literary tradition, and shift our perceptions of them (see Chapter 1, pp. 23–37). This book starts from Theocritean materiality, but it also reaches back to Homeric and Hesiodic poetry in particular, considering the roots of *oiko*-criticism and viewing Theocritus' allusivity specifically in terms of the encompassing material narrative it generates. The final section of this chapter turns to Timothy Morton's dark ecology and highlights the darkness in Theocritus' *Idylls*.

---

[11] Payne 2007: 15.

[12] I borrow the term 'from below' from a set of historical approaches that focus on people's history, the perspective of ordinary people rather than leaders and elites. In these Marxist-inspired approaches there is an emphasis on marginalised groups. I am interested here in people's experiences on the margins – women, the working classes, emigrants – but I treat the idea of marginalised groups expansively as I move away from a strict 'people's' history and give weight also to nonhuman agents. It is for this reason that I use the term 'from below' rather than specifically 'people'. For an introduction to history from below, see Thompson 1966.

[13] See, for instance, Goldhill 1990.

There are flashes of pessimism that punctuate the *locus amoenus*, and it is compelling to note that these dark-ecological moments cluster around the margins – women, emigrants, labour. The pessimistic tone may have resonated with readers attuned to these charged issues of gender, class and belonging.

Chapter 2 takes its cue from the woman on the cup of *Idyll* 1, and its approaches from Material Feminism. Material Feminism is informed by the linguistic turn in Postmodern Feminism, yet advocates a return from it to material reality. It is characterised by a focus on nature, but from a new perspective. Material Feminists argue that rather than distancing ourselves from nature, we should change the way we think of nature altogether: and it is in this foregrounding of nature as actant that Material Feminism and Material Ecocriticism come into alignment (see Chapter 2, pp. 44–8). This first ekphrastic scene on Thyrsis' cup takes us into a discussion of Pandora's materiality, from Hesiod to modern street art. In the next section, I tackle ekphrasis as a central phenomenon, drawing on Bill Brown's 'Thing Theory' to approach ekphrasis not primarily as a rhetorical device but in terms of the force exerted by materiality, exploring what happens if we refocus on the object as object. With Material Feminism we also see a refocusing on the human body, and this exercise of 'reading the body' becomes a key paradigm in the third part of the chapter, in my reassessment of Theocritus' *Idyll* 2 and the symptoms of Simaetha. A narrative of the madness and, ultimately, futility of desire is written across the body of a bird, a crafted object, a network of human participants (willing or not), a variety of nonhuman agents and the symptomology of the female body. The fourth and final section turns to *Idyll* 15, an evident intertextual reference point for the ekphrastic description of the woman on the cup in *Idyll* 1 and an essential source for any consideration of Theocritean women. A focal point of my analysis is the ekphrastic description of the tapestries but, crucially, against the backdrop of the first part of the poem, in which a proliferation of material objects establishes a domestic and specifically female gendered environment. It is from this material situatedness that the agency and viewpoint of the female characters emerge, giving rise to a female narrative that the men misunderstand and that creates a gendered intermediality linking Theocritus' women with their Homeric counterparts. In this section I read *Idyll* 15 from below, offering a material-feminist analysis that reveals the labour behind the object.

Chapter 3 is generated by the next scene on Thyrsis' cup: that of the old fisherman on his rugged rock. At the start of the chapter, I focus on the idea of 'imagined landscapes', through *Idylls* 7 and 21. In *Idyll* 7, man is equated with natural environs, material with song and song with man. We see in operation a central nexus of this book – and it is particularly relevant to material '*oiko*-criticism' that this is triangulated through the poetry of Hesiod. It is Hesiod's initiation scenes that loom large here, leading us into a consideration of autobiography. This *Idyll*, with its subtle explorations of truth and fiction, lies and veracity, autobiography and storytelling, challenges us to disentangle real from imagined landscapes. The poem ends with what has been seen as a highly artificial *locus amoenus*: from a material-ecocritical perspective, listening to the nonhuman voices alongside that of the poet, we can reconsider the role played by nature in this polyphonic episode. *Idyll* 21 presents a strong connection between fishermen and their environs. Through a seaweed bed, a plaited hut, a leafy wall, they are anchored in the environment. This is the poet's imagined landscape – and through a fisherman's dream, we are transported to a secondary imagined world embedded in the first. We are propelled into the imagination of a character, prompting us to reflect on the processes of imagination and representation, and the role of materiality within them.

The second part of Chapter 3 focuses on lithic agency. I trace a connection between the fisherman and his rock to other human/lithic entanglements in the *Idylls*, and on to the wider span of geological time. To consider a range of questions about petromorphism (rocks do not take on our attributes: we take on theirs), lithic communication (stone may not speak, but it participates in the production of acts of language, of literature) and affect (we fear lithic agency, yet we are simultaneously drawn to it), I turn to *Idyll* 23: a poem which takes us from hearts of stone to murderous statues. This is to expand the idea of intermediality, now mapping not only parallel discrete objects but an entire material category. Moving on to the next scene on the cup, that of the boy sitting on a drystone wall, I zero in on the term αἱμασιά, following its Odyssean intertexts. This is to complement the standard comparison of the cup's vineyard with that depicted on the shield of Achilles – a comparison that is useful in articulating the enhanced vitality of the Theocritean ekphrasis, as while Homer reminds us of the shield's material details, preventing the landscape from achieving independent vibrancy, Theocritus by contrast has not only his characters but also the environs transcend their physical constraints. Chapter 3 concludes with an 'excursus', modelled on those offered by J. J. Cohen in his *Stone: An Ecology of the Inhuman*. It is a wander through the village of San Sperate in Sardinia, with reflections on the folding in of human and lithic agency afforded by mural and sculpture.

Chapter 4 delves more deeply into this final scene from the cup, particularly the boy's plaited trap, and takes up the idea of creation and creative matter. Drawing on Material Ecocriticism in tandem with cultural ecology and biosemiotics, in the first section I follow the links between human creativity and the creativity of nature. In this part of *Idyll* 1, we see an interplay between the ekphrasis of the cup and an *ekphrasis tropou*: a narrative of making. This leads us in the next section to

Idyll 28, a poem in which creation, and in particular the equation of material object and poetry, takes centre stage. Whereas in *Idyll* 1 two 'artefacts', the cup and the song, are judged equivalent and exchanged, in *Idyll* 28 two artefacts work in tandem towards the same goal, as we imagine the poem to accompany the distaff on its journey to Miletus. This poem offers an essential focal point for a material-ecocritical analysis, concerned as it is with entanglements (actor networks, even hybrid agents), both human and nonhuman creativity, and personification and anthropomorphism. In this section I work through the various equivalencies established in *Idyll* 28, such as that between the distaff and Theocritus (both emigrants) and that between the distaff and Theugenis (as creative collaborators), considering Jane Bennett's proposition that anthropomorphism can reveal isomorphism. A material-ecocritical approach would extend our attention beyond the isolated literary object to read systems and processes. This is to propagate relational new-materialist paradigms, in which people are only ever one component in an assemblage. *Idyll* 28 is a poster child for this approach, as the systems within it readily open themselves up to our reading. Various human and nonhuman agencies overlap towards a creative goal – and they are simultaneously linked back to raw material, to animals and the land. As a further extension, in the third section of Chapter 4 I discuss a range of comparanda, from Erinna to the eighteenth-century 'it-narrative', continuing to probe ideas of material agency and the animated object.

Chapter 5 returns to and reiterates the underlying theme of dark ecology, bringing the menacing landscape (and seascape) to the fore through Theocritus' monster, Polyphemus, in *Idylls* 6 and 11. Has Homer's Cyclops been 'neutralised' by Theocritus, or does he rather rupture the idyllic and train our attention on material threat? In the second section I then focus in on one specific object type: the syrinx, or panpipe. Emblematic of bucolic song, it is ubiquitous in the Theocritean corpus. But rather than simply accepting and therefore ignoring its presence, I highlight the syrinx as a focal point for reflection on the central nexus of this book, that between human, material and narrative. From freshly made, sweet-smelling pipes to moulding pipes denoting disuse, we have a range of instantiations of this motif that evoke a variety of material agencies, from the vital to the dark-ecological. Further, in *Idyll* 8 the pipes are offered as a wager in a song contest: as such, the song is reified in this constitutive symbol. And the pipes exert their material agency when they cut Daphnis' finger – a reminder of Heidegger's broken hammer, or the stone that stubs our toe. A Theocritean riddling epigram composed for dedication on a syrinx, and made in the shape of one, then draws out further the material aspect of this literary motif, and brings together the many strands of this book's material-ecocritical exploration. The final section (pp. 195–201) pulls our attention back to the cup, but this time to a nineteenth-century artistic rendering of it in silver gilt. An exploration of the choices made in this cup's design highlights the complexity, openness and entanglements of Theocritus' description, and the elite context of the cup lays bare the contradictions inherent in Hellenistic pastoral poetry. A Concluding Excursus then takes us to Marsden Bay for a final reflection on people, poetry and place.

| The Cup

Material Ecocriticism: An Exercise in Listening

καὶ βαθὺ κισσύβιον κεκλυσμένον ἁδέι κηρῷ,
ἀμφῶες, νεοτευχές, ἔτι γλυφάνοιο ποτόσδον.
τῷ ποτὶ μὲν χείλη μαρύεται ὑψόθι κισσός,
κισσὸς ἑλιχρύσῳ κεκονιμένος· ἁ δὲ κατ᾽ αὐτόν
καρπῷ ἕλιξ εἰλεῖται ἀγαλλομένα κροκόεντι.
…
παντᾷ δ᾽ ἀμφὶ δέπας περιπέπταται ὑγρὸς ἄκανθος,
αἰπολικὸν θάημα· τέρας κέ τυ θυμὸν ἀτύξαι.

A deep ivy-wood cup, sealed with sweet wax,
two-handled, newly made, still fragrant from the chisel.
High up on the rim winds ivy,
ivy sprinkled with gold flowers; and along it
twines the tendril rejoicing in its yellow fruit.
…
All around the cup is spread pliant acanthus.
A marvel for a goatherd to behold; a wonder to amaze the heart.
                    (Theocritus *Idyll* 1.27–31, 55–6[1])

---

[1] Throughout this book, all Theocritus text is that of Gow 1950 and all translations are my own, unless stated otherwise.

The first *Idyll* in the Theocritean collection begins with Thyrsis and the goatherd waxing lyrical about each other's music. The goatherd's piping is sweet like the sound of the pine; Thyrsis' song is sweeter than the water cascading down the rocks. One should be rewarded with a goat, the other with a sheep. From the outset of the poem, music and man and animal and nature find equations and equivalences. The cup is the prize promised for Thyrsis' song, and is equated with it. It is a created object that emerges from nature, yet remains part of it. It features people and their stories: a woman fought over by two men; an old fisherman; a boy guarding a vineyard. The people in turn connect back to their environment: the old fisherman beside the rugged rock he resembles, the boy sitting on a drystone wall; the fisherman hauling nets to catch fish, the boy plaiting a cage to catch grasshoppers. In the coming chapters I focus on each of these scenes in turn, offering a new reading through a focus above all on their materiality. In this chapter, however, I start from the cup itself: its composition, its entanglements. Theocritus' first *Idyll* is a poem in which man, material and narrative are inextricably enmeshed. In this chapter I introduce and begin to use a material-ecocritical approach, reading the cup not only as part of a poem, but as part of the physical world of ancient hexameter poetry. Theocritus tells a story; so does Thyrsis. But what is the cup's story? How can we explore, and where do we delimit, its network, its assemblage? And what happens when we follow the tendrils of ivy beyond the poem?

In order to open up our readings of the cup's characters (Chapters 2–4), it is important from the outset to allow the cup itself a degree of vitality,[2] should the description warrant it. Kathryn Gutzwiller in a 1986 article notes that 'the verb μαρύεται is a middle, indicating that the ivy "twines itself", and εἰλεῖται also connotes self-propelled motion'.[3] This 'twining' is wound into lines 30–1 with the repeated root ἑλ- in ἑλιχρύσῳ/ἕλιξ/εἰλεῖται. Richard Hunter, in his 1999 commentary on the poem, notes that on line 31 ἀγαλλομένα, 'rejoicing', the verb 'illustrates the genesis of one kind of "pathetic fallacy", for here the viewer shares the plant's "joy"'. There is an affective relationship set up between the object and the viewer, and that affect emerges not from the human but from the nonhuman party.[4] The tendril rejoices in its fruit – so we take pleasure in its description. Throughout this book I repeatedly resist the straightforward anthropomorphic interpretation (the tendril is behaving as a person), exercising instead the productive new-materialist paradigm of anthropodecentrism and asking what it means to the poet to write, and

---

[2] On Vital or Vibrant Materialism, see Bennett 2010.
[3] Gutzwiller 1986: 254.
[4] On objects and affect, see contributions to Telò and Mueller 2018.

to the reader to read, that an object is acting (or, in this case, emoting).⁵ First, as Hunter notes, there is an alignment – the plant feels joy, so we feel joy. To take this further, there is a connection – we feel closer to the plant, and to the cup it encircles. We are drawn into the assemblage, as not only are the song and cup equated with one another, but the cup also reaches out to us. With the repeated ἑλ- root the ivy is twined around the lines as much as the cup, putting the reader of the poem in a parallel position to the recipient of the cup. Then the affective dimension of the description urges us to think through the cup's materiality. It is made from wood and is decorated with ivy and flowers. It is a crafted object – but it retains the vitality of its natural materials. What difference does it make that this is wood and plant, rather than, say, stone or metal (like the Theocritus Cup in Chapter 5)? We return to stone in Chapter 3, with a discussion of its durability, intransigence, but also affect-laden properties. A key element of that discussion is the chronology of stone: its longevity that is almost incomprehensible to the ephemeral human, and consequently our misunderstanding of its supposed stillness. For now, we might draw a preliminary contrast with the relative immediacy of wood and plant-life. To put it simply, we can see the plant grow, live, respond. It is clearly a living thing – and so even after it is cut down and crafted, it is not unexpected that it might be described in vital terms. The wood and plants are responsive – the acanthus is pliant, ὑγρός, moulding to the vessel. The material even responds to the instrument of its creation, the cup being 'still fragrant from the chisel' – a detail that takes this description to a multisensory level. The plants seem to move and grow even as we read about them: winding, twining, spreading.

Hunter notes on lines 29–31 that 'the intricate word-order is mimetic of the interwoven plants; the anaphora of κισσός across a verse-division displays the curling ivy'.⁶ Once again, the materiality of the cup drives its description, as the interwoven

---

⁵ Brooke Holmes explores the use of pathetic fallacy in ancient literature, considering it in very similar terms to my own: as affect that operates across the human and nonhuman. See Holmes 2019 and forthcoming.

⁶ Hunter 1999 *ad* 29–31. On the allusion to *Homeric Hymn* 7.40–1 here see Gutzwiller 1986: 253–4. She writes (254): 'In the *Homeric Hymn*, that to Dionysus, the ivy is growing with supernatural speed; its twining about the mast and the blossoming of its fruit and flowers are a Dionysiac miracle. In *Idyll* 1 the ivy likewise seems alive and even has animate feeling, although it is carved ivy, chiselled in wood ... What Theocritus has done here is to recast a miracle, which was acceptable under the terms of archaic religious thought, into a description of an object of art, marvelous in that its motion suggests either supreme artistic workmanship or the naïve imagination of the goatherd.' There is a further interpretation, however: that the Dionysiac miracle is repurposed to depict, through art and poetry, the 'miracle' of nature.

tendrils are conveyed through interwoven words. Gow prints κεκονιμένος, 'sprinkled', in line 30, but the more strongly attested variant κεκονισμένος, 'intertwined' (from κονίζω), gives an even clearer sense of entanglement. Further, the repetition of κισσός shows Theocritus etymologising κισσύβιον, and in the process making it something more. A rustic cup becomes a highly ornate item, not through superimposed decoration in the first instance, but through the intricacies and complexities of its own material.

The multisensory nature of the passage takes it beyond purely visual description, and indeed this ekphrasis is lacking the expected markers: as Mark Payne notes in his article 'Ecphrasis and song in Theocritus' *Idyll* 1',

> Thyrsis is not invited to look at the bowl at this time, nor at any point during the ecphrasis. It is only when the song is over that the goatherd produces the object itself, and with a flourish invites Thyrsis to see if it matches up to his earlier description (149): 'Behold the bowl; see, my friend, how sweetly it smells.'[7]

We are prompted to think of the entire description in a different way. In his article 'Characterization and the ideal of innocence in Theocritus' *Idylls*', Gary Miles writes: 'We are not actually shown the bowl. We are presented a version of it as seen through the eyes of an inhabitant of the bucolic world';[8] in this analysis, imagination takes precedence over visual description. Representation comes to the fore. A still different way to approach the cup is through materiality. Shifting away from a treatment of ekphrasis in terms of visualisation and imagination, we might turn our attention rather to ideas of affect and vitality, granting the cup full agentic licence within its material-discursive narrative.[9] Payne argues: 'If the bowl only makes its entrance at the end of the poem this should remind us that the ecphrasis is more a response to a work of art than a description of one.'[10] It is the goatherd's response, told to elicit Thyrsis' response, engendering a response in the reader – and this is all conducted by Theocritus, himself responding to an imagined object. The substitution

---

[7] Payne 2001: 264.

[8] Miles 1977: 147.

[9] On the term 'material-discursive', see Iovino and Oppermann 2014: 8: the 'shared creativity of human and nonhuman agents generates new narratives and discourses'. On narrative, see Iovino and Oppermann 2010: 9: 'Material ecocriticism is a way to give … "narrative" a more ontologically complex meaning. "Narrative" in this sense means the way our interpretation is itself intermingled with what it considers, in a material and discursive way … the emanating point of the narrative is no longer the human self, but the human–nonhuman complex of interrelated agencies.'

[10] Payne 2001: 265.

of 'response' for 'description' is useful in that it points us towards a dynamic interaction with this object, rather than a static appreciation of it.

Without even discussing its ekphrastic decorations, then, the cup of *Idyll* 1 has already introduced key themes that will persist throughout this book, such as assemblage and entanglement, systems and interweaving, alignment and affect. These are intricate networks, and we need a framework to guide us through them – to help us keep in view the wood and the trees. Particularly useful is the approach of Material Ecocriticism, and it is to an introduction to this emerging critical field that I now turn.

Ecocriticism has long offered a way of considering the world with and apart from humanity. There is a strong ecocritical tradition within Classics, from Charles Martindale's 1997 chapter 'Green politics', to Timothy Saunders's 2018 book *Bucolic Ecology: Virgil's Eclogues and the Environmental Literary Tradition*. The current book is not separate from that tradition, and indeed certain concepts I explore, such as 'deep time' or 'dark ecology', are part of the conceptual language of Ecocriticism and Environmental Humanities more generally. And yet, the material turn has brought in its wake a form of Ecocriticism that is subtly different – more angled towards materiality, to reading the stories of matter more attentively. Material Ecocriticism emerges from the meeting point of Ecocriticism and the New Materialisms. Material Ecocriticism extends the vibrancy of New Materialism to open up readings of the entanglements between humans and nonhumans, and to see systems beyond the objects. It reifies the broad vista of Environmental Studies, decentring the human subject and offering a view of systems and objects that extends the world beyond the ecocritical word. As an interpretive lens, Material Ecocriticism proposes a less human-centred approach to literature, suggesting that literature emerges from the 'intra-action' of human creativity and the narrative agency of matter. The term 'intra-action' comes from the work of Karen Barad: according to material ecocritics, human agency meets the narrative agency of matter halfway, generating material-discursive phenomena such as literature (and literary criticism). This framework will encourage a focus on Theocritus' representation of material objects, phenomena and landscape as points of porosity between the poet and his environment, allowing materiality to draw us into Theocritus' world.

The core concepts of Material Ecocriticism are drawn from a range of scholars working in a range of fields. Barad, for instance, works with Quantum Physics. As Material Ecocriticism is a nascent field, it is simultaneously narrow and nebulous, with a small number of publications under its explicit rubric, but with many interconnecting strands from Ecocriticism, New Materialism and Material Feminism (see in particular Chapter 2, pp. 44–8), to name just a few areas. The approach has great potential, but is as yet underdeveloped. In a small number of publications, literary scholars have tested out interactions between Ecocriticism and New Materialism, one key example being the 2016 volume *Object Oriented Environs*, edited by Jeffrey Jerome Cohen and Julian Yates and focusing on Graham Harman's Object-Oriented Ontology (OOO). In an even smaller number of publications, scholars have tried to set out and synthesise this meeting point and its potential: this is more or less limited to the 2014 volume *Material Ecocriticism*, edited by Serenella Iovino and Serpil Oppermann. In the current book I work through some strands that are key to this approach, using them as heuristic tools to open up new readings of the Theocritean corpus.

But what is the point, to put it bluntly, in viewing ancient literature through the lens of this particular modern theoretical approach? There are many answers to this question, which I hope to offer over the course of the book. But a good starting point is to focus on that most daunting of concepts, the Anthropocene, and its relationship to Classics. The Anthropocene evokes questions of ethics, of technology, of sustainability, of the place of the human in relation to the nonhuman – all of which are aspects of a material-ecocritical analysis. This is something that was explored in the 'Classics in the Anthropocene' conference held at the University of Toronto in April 2019.[11] The opening and closing keynotes to this conference were given by Katherine Blouin and Brooke Holmes respectively, and both speakers made points that are of relevance to Material Ecocriticism and convey its importance. First, the idea of expanding the chronological reach of modern concepts, in order to enhance and nuance those concepts. On a basic level, Material Ecocriticism as a nascent field has limited coverage – and adding ancient literature to its purview can only serve to expand and enrich it. More forcefully, Blouin argues that the current 'truncated, modernity-focused approach to the Anthropocene illustrates the widespread, systemic lack of conversation between scholars of Antiquity – and everything pre-1500 for that matter – and the rest of the Humanities and Social Sciences'.[12] She claims that 'should the list of "novelties" brought about by the British Empire be submitted to socio-economic historians of the ancient world, the list would be reduced by a great, great deal'. There is a fair amount of *nihil novum sub sole* here, which as students of the ancient world we would do well to remember, and to remind others of. This goes hand in hand with the compelling compatibility of posthumanist theory and pre-humanist literature.

Second was the notion of 'risk', or the 'uncanny', central to our unstable and unsettling place within the Anthropocene (we are notionally its drivers, yet

---

[11] Not the only conference of its kind: more recently, University College Dublin hosted the 'Antiquity and the Anthropocene' conference (online, February 2021) and its sequel, 'Antiquity and the Anthropocene: Ancient Materiality' (online, December 2021).

[12] All Blouin quotations here are taken from Blouin 2019.

undeniably all at sea). As Blouin puts it, 'ancient stories have a lot to teach us about how our species approached the uncertainties of the world'. This makes the simple point of the didactic function of ancient texts – the 'learning from our mistakes' approach to history (and literature). Yet, in the specific light of concerns over the Anthropocene, it takes on a whole new resonance. It is in our moments of greatest uncertainty, of greatest *risk*, that we most need to look back. And in her examples Blouin focuses on passages that involve 'a diverse, intersectional array of (non-) human agents', connecting these with Bruno Latour on agencies and animation or animism. Material Ecocriticism, the New Materialisms – these are approaches concerned with questioning dichotomies, problematising boundaries, breaking down the barriers between the human and the more-than-human world. Approaches to the Anthropocene often adopt a similar questioning stance. And where better to look for teachings on this, than in a pre-Cartesian, pre-Kantian, often animistic, world? Ancient literature can provide routes through the uncanny by virtue of a standpoint less starkly coloured by entrenched dualisms. Further, Blouin makes the argument of bi-directionality. As well as using ancient models to guide us through modern uncertainty, we might also harness this moment of risk within the Anthropocene and its concomitant intellectual shake-up to reflect back on our approach to ancient thought. Blouin writes:

> This brief example poses the question of the limitations of current forms of historiographical writings and methodologies used by scholars working on Antiquity. Let's be real: What is valued as 'rationality' in western scholarship is nothing but a harnessed, period-specific type of subjectivity that goes back to the Enlightenment. Now given that Enlightenment scholars were themselves nourished by a particular set of (elitist, hegemonic, male, literary) representations of Antiquity, we find ourselves confined to a circular reasoning that excludes many voices from the equation, and thus provide a too limited set of epistemological models.

Blouin asks how our reading of the ancient sources might change if we were to step back from this rational tradition and instead acknowledge different types of agents, both human and nonhuman. She suggests that it is all 'a matter of making the way we approach the Earth, and our place in it, more in tune with and receptive to what the Earth, and our species, look like'. Reading literature has always been a way of finding understanding – of the human condition, of emotion, of behaviour, of thinking. But reading literature from the perspective of crisis, from within the grasp of the Anthropocene and the earth's decline, as a way of finding understanding? This necessitates a particular kind of tuning, and a particular interpretive lens.

In her talk, Holmes focused on sympathy in antiquity.[13] She shows that although sympathy can denote inter*personal* feeling – that is, between human subjects – in the way that we tend to understand it in the modern world, more often than not it indicates affective relationships between different natures: both human and nonhuman. It is a co-suffering that operates across a wider network. She speaks of distributed intelligences, and argues that the ancient sources are working through this just as fervently as are modern theorists or philosophers. Indeed, we are heading full circle: Holmes notes that contemporary scientific models of sympathy seem to be moving back towards ancient materialist notions. This materialist inflection of sympathy provides a window onto ways of thinking about a community that are cross-species and rather different from, say, the Homeric impression of a predominant polis model, with the gods mimicking human society and a pervasive anthropomorphism. Holmes argues that this more entangled model is present in the ancient sources, too – it has just been less noticed. In the climate of modern ecology, however, this is a model that should be brought out for our understanding of not only antiquity, but also modern society. Holmes reflects on the persistence of anthropocentrism in the history of ideas, the continually reasserted dominance of the human – but, as she points out, acknowledgement of anthropocentrism, or anthropomorphism, should not work to the exclusion of other more distributed approaches.

Holmes notes that ancient sympathy suddenly appears across a range of domains trying to make sense of the natural world in the late classical and early Hellenistic periods: 'The rapid efflorescence of sympathy in this period signals a multi-focal and multi-faceted engagement with the question of how non-human natures, including the parts of human bodies, relate to one another'.[14] In her chapter in *Antiquities beyond Humanism*,[15] she focuses on the Stoic philosophers, but for our purposes here we may note that this sympathetic 'efflorescence' had already surged by the time of Theocritus' poetic production and the focus on human/nonhuman relationality had already taken root. This is yet another reason for training the current analysis on Hellenistic poetry.

The exclusion of voices mentioned by Blouin leads me on to my next argument for the importance of new-materialist, and specifically material-ecocritical, approaches to ancient literature. The introduction of New Materialism to Classics was questioned in Edith Hall's celebrated blog *The Edithorial* and her chapter 'Materialisms

---

[13] Some findings are published in Holmes 2019; see Holmes forthcoming.
[14] Holmes 2019: 239.
[15] Ibid. pp. 239–70.

old and new'.¹⁶ This 'devil's advocate' position is a good place to start the process of figuring out exactly what the New Materialisms *do* bring to Classics. Hall accuses the New Materialisms of classism, because (she argues) they do not focus on labour: 'One aspect of new materialist aesthetic analysis that classicists would do well to resist is its retreat from, indeed often refutation of the relationship between *work* and matter'.¹⁷ In her critique of the New Materialisms via Jane Bennett, Hall summarises the new-materialist goal as: 'Human subjects need to be downgraded in our appreciation of matter'. And this is where the new-materialist balancing act becomes crucial. Proponents of this field by and large do *not* advocate downgrading humans, but rather support *up*grading the *non*human. Bennett asks: 'What counts as the material of vital materialism? Is it only human labor and the socioeconomic entities made by men and women using raw materials?' To which Hall responds:

> We have never yet paid remotely *enough* attention to the relationship between material things, human labor and socio-economics. We can surely *add* some of the vocabulary of 'vital materialism' to our interpretive toolkit when working within any academic discipline. But the idea that scholars of culture have already done a good enough job of thinking about labor is preposterous.

It must be pointed out, however, that Bennett and others do not claim that our thinking on labour is done – merely that we shouldn't focus exclusively on labour at the expense of all else. New Materialism in fact advocates this 'adding' of vocabulary – adding the material into discussions of human labour. Indeed, this is the very essence of the notion of 'assemblage',¹⁸ so central to many branches of New Materialism: the idea that humans are only ever one component of a complex system,¹⁹ and that we do

---

[16] Available at <http://edithorial.blogspot.co.uk/2018/02/why-latest-trendy-theory-in-classics-is.html> (last accessed 28 November 2022); see also Hall 2018.
[17] Hall 2018: 204.
[18] Assemblage and related terms: assemblage (Deleuze and Guattari 1980; Bennett 2010); network (Latour 2005); meshwork (Ingold 2011); phenomenon (Barad 2007); entanglement (Hodder 2021; Barad 2007).
[19] Object-Oriented Ontology is arguably the one new-materialist theory that resists this relational approach. There is an ostensible divergence between OOO's insistence that objects are withdrawn from human access and from causal interaction with each other, and systems theories that focus on relations. Yet I am inclined to follow Bennett (2012: 227) in her assertion that 'perhaps there is no need to choose between objects or their relations' – and indeed, she notes that even Harman sometimes slips into theories of relation (specifically: communication).

that system a disservice by prioritising the human over nonhuman actants. Hall takes Medea's robe as a case study, writing:

> The 'thingness' of this particular object is in my view wholly inseparable from the thousands of silkworms or sheep or cotton bushes or flax plants which produced them, but also from the several human working hands through which the fibers passed and the hundreds of hours expended on the labor.[20]

Though presented as criticism, this turns out to be a ringing endorsement of relational new-materialist theories. Despite the way in which it is set up, the labour-oriented perspective Hall advocates could easily fall under a new-materialist rubric, concerned as it is with both human and nonhuman actants working in tandem.

Hall's goal is to reinvigorate Marxist criticism, to explore 'the potential value of Marxist theory in the analysis of Greek tragedy, and its lamentable underdevelopment hitherto'[21] – a laudable aim, and an approach which Hall shows to have true merit. I take up this call throughout this book, showing that it is not at odds with New Materialism but rather intersects with it. For instance, in Chapter 2 (pp. 81–90) I offer a material-feminist analysis of *Idyll* 15 that reveals the labour behind the object.[22] In my exploration of drystone walls in Theocritus and Homer in the second section of Chapter 3 (pp. 134–40), I show how Theocritus mines the proto-bucolic scenes in the *Odyssey* but draws our attention to materials and process. In Chapter 4 I focus on creation and creativity, giving a cyclical perspective and using the example of plaited and woven products as originating with the land and animals and evolving, through a process that involves both human and material actors, into complex woven creations. And at the start of Chapter 5 (pp. 178–86) I consider Polyphemus and his landscape in terms of (men on the) margins. With a persistent focus on assemblages of the human and nonhuman, we reveal worlds of work behind the words. This resonates with Timothy Morton's 2017 book *Humankind: Solidarity with Nonhuman People*, which argues that 'Marxism holds out more promise of ways to include nonhumans than capitalist theory'.[23] Morton argues that the anthropocentrism usually found in

---

[20] Hall 2018: 208.

[21] Hall 2018: 204.

[22] I would note here that Material Feminism, a new-materialist approach to which I turn in Chapter 2, is explicitly linked with Marxist approaches by Alaimo and Hekman (2008: 9–10): 'The emerging theories of materiality developed in material feminisms are crucial for every aspect of feminist thought: science studies, environmental feminisms, corporeal feminisms, queer theory, disability studies, theories of race and ethnicity, environmental justice, (post-) Marxist feminism, globalization studies, and cultural studies.'

[23] Morton 2017: 6.

Marxist theory is not foundational to that theory, but can be dislodged. This results in a political philosophy of solidarity with the nonhuman. Marxism is thus expanded to include both people and things, and the environments in which they participate.

Hall also wishes to alert us 'to the possibility that the emergence of the new materialism is doing ideological work of a political nature, however hidden any agenda may be'.[24] My questions are: what is the ideology? What is the agenda? What is the political pay-off? And my answer would be that this agenda is as broad as are the approaches and tools of the New Materialisms. There is a certain ethical stance to many branches of New Materialism, as expressed by both Bennett and Iovino. As Bennett writes in an article of 2012, what is at stake in the turn to things in contemporary theory is 'how it might help us live more sustainably, with less violence toward a variety of bodies. Poetry can help us feel more of the liveliness hidden in such things and reveal more of the threads of connection binding our fate to theirs';[25] given its focus on poetry, this statement is particularly relevant to the current book. Bennett argues that many contemporary materialisms 'cut against the hubris of human exceptionalism'[26] – again raising the idea of levelling the playing field – and draws attention to the ecological implications of disrupting the subject/object hierarchical dichotomy: 'the frame of subjects and objects is unfriendly to the intensified ecological awareness that we need'.[27] As Iovino puts it in her 2012 article 'Steps to a material ecocriticism',

> The narcissism of our species is both material and discursive: humans, in fact, are not only in charge of the world but also of the word. The counter-story that a vibrant materialism hands to ecocriticism is an exercise in 'listening'.

This shows how new-materialist models of anthropodecentrism can be mobilised: to displace the human from centre stage, from assumptions of supreme power. Such ethical considerations are often conveyed with a sense of urgency, as the influx of New Materialisms have been attributed to 'the emergence of pressing ethical and political concerns that accompany the scientific and technological advances predicated on new scientific models of matter'.[28] More generally, it is my contention in this book that new-materialist approaches can give us new ways of looking at material agency *without* eliding the human. Displacing or decentring does not, in fact,

---

[24] Hall 2018: 205.
[25] Bennett 2012: 232.
[26] Ibid. p. 230.
[27] Ibid. p. 231.
[28] Coole and Frost 2010: 5.

necessitate elision or neglect, but rather entails more relational considerations that are not fully anthropocentric or narcissistic but are as open to the material environs as to human agents.

So who or what are the agents foregrounded in this book? They are both human and nonhuman; both animate and material; all playing roles in a material landscape. Within a broad material-ecocritical framework, I also draw heavily on the Material Feminisms through a recurring focus on gender. This gender emphasis, combined with a persistent focus on the natural environment, shows that new-materialist methodologies provide a way to give voice to underrepresented agents. And this is, I contend, part of the new-materialist agenda and ideology (and a refutation of Hall's 'classist' claims). Countering narcissism; decentring typical foci; bringing underrepresented agents to the fore: these are all approaches that, used well and effectively, have the potential to be mobilised more widely, in relation to (for example) class debates, slavery studies and so on. In my 2018 book *Women of Substance in Homeric Epic: Objects, Gender, Agency*, I used a focus on material objects to give voice to silenced women. In the current book I extend the remit of 'the material', engaging with the landscape and material environs as much as with individualised objects – and I extend the 'exercise in listening' to the female, but also to the natural, the pastoral, the bucolic.

Edith Hall is a pioneer in the study of Class and Classics – an as yet underdeveloped field, and one that urgently warrants our attention.[29] One of the aims of this work is to expand the cast of characters in Classics; to listen to a wider range of stories. This is showcased in Edith Hall and Henry Stead's 2020 book *A People's History of Classics* and their website's 'Archive of Encounters', both of which aim to present and amplify the lost voices of British working-class men and women who engaged with ancient Greek and Roman culture: 'By presenting their stories now … we hope that their example may inspire a more inclusive atmosphere for participation in classical culture across society today.'[30] Another work in a similar vein is the 2018 book *Classics in Extremis*, edited by Edmund Richardson. The cast of characters introduced in that volume are all 'marginal' figures who resist such a definition. Contributors to the volume argue for a decentred model of classical reception: one where the 'marginal' shapes the 'central' as much as vice versa – and where the most unlikely appropriations of antiquity often have the greatest impact.

---

[29] See Hall 2008; Hall and Stead 2020. These scholarly discussions resonate with the work being done by the Network for Working-Class Classicists, established in 2021. Available at <https://www.workingclassclassics.uk> (last accessed 8 November 2022).

[30] Available at <http://www.classicsandclass.info/about-us> (last accessed 8 November 2022).

Though both projects are trained on the reception of Classics, rather than the classical material itself, they are compellingly relevant to the current argument in that they are about broadening and decentring, about shifting our focus and our perspective. By expanding our cast of characters, by listening to more and different stories, by giving weight to the impact of the 'marginal', we enrich our study of the ancient world and our responses to it. The New Materialisms provide heuristic tools for listening to diverse stories, for widening our viewpoint beyond the typically foregrounded agents and protagonists. A corpus that includes the pastoral is pertinent to this enterprise: as Paul Alpers points out in his book *What Is Pastoral?* 'shepherds … fittingly represent those whose lives are determined by the actions of powerful men or by events and circumstances over which they have no control'.[31] By foregrounding the herdsman, the everyman, as a way of reflecting on power, pastoral effectively redistributes that power, through the democratising of narrative agency. Further, women and the nonhuman, though 'marginal' in anthropocentric (and androcentric) terms, are shown to shape that which is central as material agency takes centre stage.

Theocritus' poetry, along with much Hellenistic literature, has long been pigeonholed as elite, urban, far removed from the people it represents. My contention is that a reading of this poetry from below, a reading that reconnects with the land, that allows nature and materiality their agency, that foregrounds a wide array of agents and that sees objects and the labour behind them, can reappropriate that poetry for underrepresented groups. Theocritus' poetry isn't *just* elite – or it needn't be.

Boundaries: Author, Genre, Tradition

The aim of this book is to start a conversation – or, perhaps, to join one. In her essay 'Otherworldly conversations; terran topics; local terms', Donna Haraway refers to the 'stunning narrative and visual imagery of structural-functional complexity' in material phenomena.[32] In the introduction to their volume *Material Ecocriticism*, Iovino and Oppermann make clear that 'the term "conversation" here is not simply metaphor', as 'things (or matter) draw their agentic power from their relation to discourses that in turn structure human relations to materiality'.[33] There is a conversation going on – one with no boundaries of time, of space, of academic discipline. To return to Iovino's statement, 'the counter-story that a vibrant materialism hands to ecocriticism is an exercise in "listening"'. Pastoral poetry,

---

[31] Alpers 1996: 161.
[32] Haraway 2008: 71.
[33] Iovino and Oppermann 2014: 4.

connected to place and song, the natural environment and the political climate, is the place to begin this exercise.

Yet we needn't consider pastoral poetry as a strongly demarcated and individuated entity. Rather, in the case of Theocritus in particular, it is a genre as entangled as are its various agencies.[34] The poetry of Theocritus will be at the core of this study – but viewed from the perspective of the wider tradition of ancient hexameter poetry, including heroic and didactic types. I explore the permeable boundaries between 'genres', and in this I follow Martindale's 'Green politics' in viewing genres as processes, 'not as essences or ontological entities, things, but as discursive formations, contested, fluid, resisting even while inviting definition'.[35] I trace the roots of Theocritus' cup to Homer's nonhuman actants (adopting a new-materialist approach) and Hesiod's world-view (extending *oiko*-criticism). Further, I establish a broad conception of the Theocritean corpus. I am open to treating not only the explicitly bucolic *Idylls*, but also the ('urban') mimes, the pederastic poems and those that are heroic or mythological in tone and subject matter. In this I follow the approach adopted by Richard Hunter in his 1996 book *Theocritus and the Archaeology of Greek Poetry*, considering the Theocritean corpus as a whole and, crucially, a whole comprising many equally important parts.[36] I also treat those poems collected as Theocritean, even if they are now thought not to have been composed by Theocritus. There is a scholarly consensus that Theocritus initiated the bucolic mode, and Virgil gave generic, organisational and representational shape to it. As Paul Alpers writes of Virgil's impact, 'his consciousness of boundaries and differences preserves the consistency and coherence of that world'.[37] It is in the more fluctuating environs of Theocritus' world, and the boundaries of 'Theocritus' himself, that I am interested. The Theocritean corpus, with its literary experimentation, its Homeric and Hesiodic influences, its impact on Virgil, is the ideal place to explore ancient hexameter *in nuce*, and provides a perfect convergence with a literary-critical approach that blurs boundaries between human and nonhuman, person and place. Alpers says of the opening of *Idyll* 1: 'For many critics, these

---

[34] On the characteristic Hellenistic mixing of genres, see e.g. Harder et al. 1998 and Fantuzzi and Hunter 2004, Chapter 1.

[35] Martindale 1997: 108. Equally relevant to this study is Martindale's suggestion that 'aesthetics and politics (in this like genres) may be thought of as differential terms rather than ontological entities, in which case each term is necessarily present within the other, at however occluded a level' (1997: 120–1). The world as revealed through a material-ecocritical analysis of poetics and aesthetics is as political as it is environmental.

[36] Other scholarship that treats Theocritus' corpus collectively includes Thomas 1996 (especially 227–38); Stephens 2006 (see p. 92); Hunt 2011 (statement at p. 379).

[37] Alpers 1996: 154; for an ecocritical reading of Virgil's *Eclogues*, see Saunders 2018.

lines represent a landscape, while for others they represent two herdsmen in a characteristic situation'.[38] Alpers chooses 'herdsmen and their lives', and this governs the account he gives of pastoral poetry. In adopting a material-ecocritical approach, however, I resist the need to choose, and instead put people and landscape into one system, one vista of human/nonhuman entanglement. Alpers continues: 'poetic representations of nature or of landscape … answer to and express various human needs and concerns; *pastoral* landscapes are those of which the human centers are herdsmen and their equivalents'.[39] Viewing the poetry from a material-ecocritical perspective prompts us to shift away from this anthropocentric view, to decentre the human subject and level the playing field between people and their material environment.

As Christopher Schliephake writes in the introduction to his 2016 volume *Ecocriticism, Ecology, and the Cultures of Antiquity*, 'it would be worthwhile to reread the ancient texts from a perspective that reevaluates the presence of the nonhuman as an actant in its own right'.[40] This is not just about reception or response, nor is it about the anachronistic imposition of modern theory. Rather, it is about returning to the ancient texts with new heuristic tools, a new lens through which to approach our sources. Schliephake continues:

> The topic of how ancient authors dealt with these interactions [those between human and nonhuman actants] in their respective texts could be a fruitful area of research that would lead to further interdisciplinary exchange between classical studies and modern environmental philosophy. By starting from a close reading of the intricate rhetoric and linguistic structures of the ancient texts themselves, this approach cannot only evade the danger of replicating modern environmental concepts, but could uncover the ancient discursive modes of literary ecology. This will help in highlighting lines of continuation that shape humanistic thinking today; it will also bring to light a posthuman antiquity whose signs we only begin to understand.[41]

In approaching ancient pastoral poetry (and the broader corpus assimilated to its progenitor) through a material-ecocritical framework, we can bring to light elements of an ancient 'literary ecology'. In this book I always begin from a close reading of the poetry, and in this way conclusions are offered by Theocritus himself, not imposed

---

[38] Alpers 1996: 22.
[39] Ibid. p. 28.
[40] Schliephake 2016: 9.
[41] Ibid. p. 10.

from the outside. The idea of 'highlighting lines of continuation' is especially relevant to the approach adopted here, as it is not about mapping modern theory onto an ancient text and forcing a fit or equivalence, but rather tracing echoes, looking for resonances. What can we find in Theocritus' poetry that acts as a precursor to current ecological considerations? To material-feminist arguments? To material-ecocritical analyses? Or indeed, what can we find in Theocritus' poetry that offers resistance to current theorisations? Theocritus is considered to be a founding father of the bucolic genre. But are there also indications in his work of a 'posthuman antiquity' – an essence of a field with which we are grappling right now? In her Afterword to *Material Ecocriticism*, Iovino raises some further points of relevance to my own project here, and which link up with Schliephake's introductory remarks. She gives us an aim: 'to think ecocriticism not only beyond its canonical tropes, but also *before* its (tacitly normative) chronological borders'.[42] Shifting towards a material-ecocritical approach is one way of expanding Ecocriticism beyond its standard tropes, as the enhanced material inflection integrates the impact of the material turn, with its sustained emphasis on material agency within different paradigms.[43] And taking the exploration outside of the usual chronological borders is one way in which Classics can make a genuine contribution to these fields (New Materialism, Material Ecocriticism, Ecocriticism more generally). By expanding not only the cast of characters but also the range of texts and the extent of the chronological period studied through these lenses, Classics can both utilise the tenets of these fields and feed back into them in a productive way. Iovino also writes that 'ecocriticism provides new keys to rethink what has already been thought for centuries or millennia, starting ... with the imaginative and physical horizon of our being-in-the-world'.[44] Again, this takes on a slightly different cast with the specifically *material* ecocritical approach I adopt here, but the essential argument stands: that our 'being-in-the-world',[45] how we articulate this, explain it and *imagine* it, has forever been and continues to be explored, and that our understanding of it shifts with new approaches and new heuristics.

The idea of 'being-in-the-world' aptly brings together the material and the ecocritical, through the philosophy of Heidegger. Heidegger used 'being-in-the-world' (or, more accurately, its German equivalent 'in-der-Welt-sein') to dislodge binary terms such as subject, object, consciousness and world. Heidegger stands at the roots

---

[42] Iovino 2016: 311.
[43] For an overview of the material turn as manifest in recent books within Classics, see Canevaro 2019a.
[44] Iovino 2016: 310.
[45] Term from Heidegger 1996 (first published in German in 1927).

of Thing Theory and the differentiation between objects and things: when an object breaks down or its use is changed, it becomes present to us in new ways as a thing.[46] The quintessential example is the broken hammer: a tool that goes from object to thing as it sheds its social encoding and grabs our attention. So Heidegger is central to many branches of the New Materialisms. But his philosophy is also about place, and is characterised by ecological considerations. In the essay 'Building Dwelling Thinking', for example, he argues that building is really dwelling and cultivating, and dwelling is the manner in which mortals are on the earth.[47] The fundamental character of dwelling is sparing and preserving.[48] And to make the final connection between materiality, environment and poetry that interests us here, Timothy Morton summarises: 'Poetry *is* place, for Heidegger.'[49] Morton continues: 'There is an ideological flavor to the substance of Heidegger's description. It is a form of Romanticism: of countering the displacements of modernity with the politics and poetics of place.'[50] To what extent does this resonate with pastoral poetry?

Paul Alpers asks the question *What Is Pastoral?* Ken Hiltner asks *What Else Is Pastoral?* And the jury is still out. What both of these authors do is to trace pastoral literature back to its earliest examples, and to draw out trends and developments in the 'genre' as it grew and shifted. I use the term genre loosely here, as it is resisted by these scholars, as indeed pastoral literature itself resists such strict categorisation. Above, I separated out Theocritean pastoral from Virgilian, in that the latter is thought to be the more delineated – and yet this is not the full picture, as Martindale clarifies in his assessment of Virgil:

> The modern critical stress on the structural unity of the collection may serve to conceal the considerable variousness of its contents – the title it was in all probability given by later editors 'Selections' (Virgil's was *Bucolica*) serves to suggest that, certainly in comparison with the *Georgics* or *Aeneid*, it is fragmented as much as unified, composed as it were of chips from the writer's block. Indeed *Eclogue* 9 operates with what might be termed a poetics of fragmentation.[51]

---

[46] See the essay 'The Thing' in Heidegger 1971.
[47] Essay 'Building Dwelling Thinking' in Heidegger 1971.
[48] In this same essay he connects place with things, in the example of the bridge that makes the riverbank possible as a place (the bank wouldn't be a bank without a bridge), though as Morton comments, 'There is a tendency, then, for Heidegger to secretly be on the side of technology rather than of Being' (Morton 2008: 182).
[49] Morton 2008: 182.
[50] Ibid. p. 183.
[51] Martindale 1997: 120.

That 'fragmentation' stands at this literature's classical beginnings creates problems for attempts to reconcile a smooth, continuous and presiding narrative about a genre, its roots and its diachronic development. Pastoral literature is notoriously difficult to define and to analyse – and both Theocritus and Virgil might shoulder some of the responsibility for that. Similarly thorny is the topic of terminology: I have used the term 'pastoral', and the line between it and 'bucolic' is thinly drawn and, again, permeable. In his *Before Pastoral: Theocritus and the Ancient Tradition of Bucolic Poetry*, David Halperin argues that there are clear differences between the two terms, and in the case of bucolic he emphasises that it is not limited to poems about herdsmen, but is intrinsically connected to the broader remit of the dactylic hexameter: that we should really be talking about the bucolic subgenre of *epos*. I would agree that the wider hexameter tradition pulls its weight in this poetry, and that we cannot separate off bucolic from other genres – but in drawing such a stark distinction between bucolic and pastoral we risk enforcing clear boundaries where there are none.

Alpers deftly sidesteps the question of genre definition, arguing that 'pastoral is a literary *mode* based on what Kenneth Burke calls a *representative anecdote*'.[52] A representative anecdote is the 'central fiction' of a text – in the case of pastoral, Alpers posits that this 'is not the Golden Age or idyllic landscapes, but herdsmen and their lives'.[53] I raised this point above: that two different accounts of pastoral are prevalent, with the one focusing on landscape and the other on the characters within it. Alpers espouses the latter, and in doing so offers a fundamentally anthropocentric reading of Theocritus, and of pastoral more generally. In what ways might Material Ecocriticism change our views on the 'representative anecdote' of pastoral literature? What, or whom, is this poetry representing – of what, or whom, is it representative? Our first act as new materialists or material ecocritics is to decentre the human subject – to ask whether the herdsmen are the only or primary actants with which we need be concerned. It is my contention throughout this book that this is not the case: that art, that materials, that the land, that objects all have an agentic role to play in Theocritus' poetry, and that the human and nonhuman cannot be so easily disentangled or set in a hierarchy of agents. 'Herdsmen and their lives', then, is *not* representative of the materiality of these texts. We would do better to combine the two different accounts of pastoral (the landscape *and* the people) – or, more probably, to move away from these accounts altogether. To whom and for whom are the diverse agents in Theocritus' poem speaking? The from-below reading I offer in this book shows that they are not just speaking to the elites from a disconnected elite perspective, giving a detached aesthetic presentation of a *locus amoenus*. The environment

---

[52] Alpers 1996: ix.
[53] Ibid. p. x.

exerts its agency too, women have their own complex stories and back stories that link with the land and with class struggles (see Chapter 2 on Simaetha, pp. 66–81), objects have biographies that reveal raw material and process as much as finished product.

Alpers considers the relationship between earlier modes of hexameter poetry and Theocritus' *Idylls*: 'Theocritus's bucolics … were a conscious reduction of Homeric verse to the felt range and possibilities of poetry in a post-heroic, cosmopolitan world'; 'the self-awareness and wit with which pastoral poets scale down their verse is a way of reclaiming a degree of strength relative to their world'.[54] This is reflective of the duality of tradition and innovation key to Hellenistic literature in general, and the Theocritean corpus in particular. It is programmatic in that full consideration of these statements necessitates a corpus-wide approach to Theocritus' *Idylls*, like that which I adopt here. It encapsulates a common approach to pastoral: treating it as an application of mind to landscape, and focusing on its functionality. It is my intention here to shift our focus from functionality to materiality – and to open up our reading to consider the bi-directional relationship between the landscape and the mind,[55] taking our cue from the nonhuman as much as from the human. Through considerations of porosity and dark ecology in particular, we can see the force the environment exerts on the human.

As Martindale observes, politicising accounts of pastoral may be admiring, praising the poems for articulating a desire for simplicity and protesting against the evils of the city; or they may be hostile, criticising the poetry 'for concealing the realities and oppressions of rural life, in a way that serves the interests of the ruling class'.[56] But as we noted earlier in the chapter (pp. 18–23), the new-materialist and material-ecocritical lenses can train our attention on the world beyond the word (the environmental but also the political) in a way that *reveals* much about underrepresented agents. That uncovers and gives weight to agencies beyond those typically foregrounded (e.g. male or elite). By allowing materiality to draw us into Theocritus' world, we pay attention also to the politics of that world – but in a way that posits complex networks of agencies that include the non-elite and indeed the nonhuman.

One of the key case studies in Chapter 3 is the poem that appears in some collections as *Idyll* 23. It is included in some but not all collections of Theocritus' poetry, as it is thought not to have been written by Theocritus himself. Sometimes attributed to 'the school of Bion' and thought to be of a later date than the bucolic core of the Theocritean corpus, it is not our most straightforward case study from the point

---

[54] Ibid. p. 51.
[55] Lather 2021 has pioneered a bi-directional study of mind and matter, bringing together New Materialism and Cognitive Psychology to excellent effect.
[56] Martindale 1997: 117.

of view of authorship and authenticity. Yet it is exactly this uncertain dating and attribution that makes *Idyll* 23 perfectly suited to this material-ecocritical reading. Here I would like to use this *Idyll* and the discussions surrounding it to introduce a central material-ecocritical theme: that of porosity.

Hunter (2002) discusses *Idyll* 23 from the point of view of the commentator. What should we do with it? How should we present it, how should we analyse it? He draws our attention to a phenomenon or 'syndrome' by which the inauthenticity of a text (the imposter in an author's corpus) leads to aesthetic criticism, which leads to cursory commentating. This is the case with *Idyll* 23 as treated by A. S. F. Gow in his landmark commentary. As Hunter notes, Gow is right in labelling the text as 'grossly corrupt', but

> his personal distaste for the poem has produced a commentary which, to borrow his own words about the *Idyll*, 'is the least attractive of the whole corpus,' one designed in fact, in Glenn Most's words, 'to show that the text one is commenting on is not worth reading'.[57]

Hunter, by contrast, highlights the importance of this poem to (for example) anyone concerned with Latin elegy – and in Chapter 3 (pp. 113–40) I offer a reading of the poem through its lithic actants, giving the *Idyll* what I believe to be its poetic due, through a specific material-ecocritical lens. I revisit, too, Gow's aesthetic criticisms of the poem, to see whether my particular stony reading can overturn or at least mitigate his judgements.

In the current chapter, however, I would like to preface my reading of the poem and of others in the Theocritean corpus with a consideration of the question of authorship more broadly. Hunter writes:

> The large-scale commentator, like Gow on Theocritus, traditionally seeks to build up a picture of a poet and his or her language; the 'perfect' picture will be a closed circle, its circumference guarded by internal cross references and parallels, like the movie campfire protected by a circle of wagons. Problems of authenticity threaten the foundations of this approach: other poets, all those pseudo-Theocrituses and pseudo-Ovids, keep getting in the way.[58]

From this perspective, the corpus of a poet is to be a closed circle, a complete whole, a sealed entity. 'Outsiders' – the pseudos and [Theocrituses], the imitators and the

---

[57] Hunter 2002: 100–1.
[58] Ibid. p. 97.

accidental accretions – are a threat to the boundaries of that corpus. So scholarship seeks to shore up the boundaries, to perfect the picture and tighten the circle. This leads to the 'syndrome' Hunter diagnoses: the casting of aesthetic aspersions on the outlier. This is not to say that the disparagements are always undeserved. There is, after all, a reason we have the poetic corpora we do: it is not all down to chance, but often down to popularity, success, prestige, and these usually because of style, content – quality. So, in the main, our named classical corpora represent (at least some of) 'the best' of ancient literature. But we take this generalisation too far when we use it as a tool for selection and, ultimately, criticism. To quote Hunter again:

> The 'authorless' text (or that which is judged so) has, on the whole, received a cold reception from classicists; for reasons which lie deep in the heart of the history of the subject, classicists have, on the whole, never been very comfortable with the anonymous, and this anxiety may indeed surface in 'aesthetic condemnation.' ... There has perhaps been a feeling that such texts have 'slipped through the net,' i.e. through that process of *krisis*, of collecting and categorizing, of filtering and selecting, which lies at the very heart of the notion of 'the classical' and which scholars rightly trace back to their spiritual ancestors, the great figures of Alexandrian scholarship. However unfair it might seem, free-floating, 'anonymous' poems are cheating the system, and criticism will have its revenge.[59]

But what if we were to think a little less like uncomfortable classicists, and a little more like material ecocritics? What if, instead of shoring up and policing boundaries, we were to probe them? What if we were to allow them their porosity? The literary corpus is, after all, a body. Embracing material-ecocritical paradigms such as trans-corporeality can allow us to read 'Theocritus' within and around his own corpus: from bucolic to mime, the pederastic to the heroic; from clear attribution to pseudonym; from the core to the sidelines. Intertextuality through objects can help with this, giving us a way to map materiality across a diverse range of poems without fixating on authorship and authenticity. A stone is a stone is a stone, whether it is cast by Theocritus or [Theocritus] – and given its full force, it can hit just as hard.

This is not to say that authorship is an unimportant concern for a material-ecocritical reading. It is to say, rather, that authorship should not *curtail* a reading keyed into an approach that breaks down boundaries. This book takes Theocritus as its starting point and its core source base, but it takes the exploration of themes and ideas into other periods, genres, literatures, media. So too does it take Theocritus beyond the poems now thought to have been authored by him. The picture of

---

[59] Ibid. p. 91.

material agency that emerges from the *Idylls* is a coherent and consistent one, whether that comes from one author or many. *Idyll* 21, for instance, is now not attributed to Theocritus. But its connection between fishermen and their environs recalls the fisherman and his rugged rock in *Idyll* 1, and the imagined worlds it presents connect vividly with those of *Idyll* 7 (see Chapter 3, pp. 91–113). Similarly, the lithic agency prevalent in *Idyll* 23 can be found in the hybridity of the first *Idyll*'s fisherman and rock, or in the singing stones of *Idyll* 7 (see pp. 113–20 and pp. 111–13 respectively).[60] The poems of the Theocritean corpus, irrespective of authorship, offer similar or at least complementary treatments of the relationship between bodies and materials, and it is for this reason that we can feasibly conduct a material-ecocritical analysis of the corpus as a whole.

Intertextuality is a standard way of approaching ancient literature, and indeed in treating dense, allusive Hellenistic poetry it is a dominant approach. To give this fundamental methodology a new lease of life, in this book I advocate following not only textual but also material clues across the different texts.[61] Through a focus on objects we can see intertextuality operating not purely in formal terms, but as a more material phenomenon. Throughout the book I use the term 'intermediality': a simultaneously more expansive and more specific term than intertextuality.[62] As W. J. Thomas Mitchell succinctly put it, 'all media are mixed media'.[63] The objects and material phenomena I examine are those created by, within and for the purposes of a text. They are thoroughly literary things: products of literary imagination and encountered through textuality. The intermedial approach is useful here, as it offers a way for us to articulate the relationship between different media, within one medium. Literary objects are part of the literature; they are on the one hand inseparable from the narrative, language, character, poetics or any other number of facets of their literary construction. And yet, they have a material dimension to them. Though it is the text alone that is 'materially present',[64] the text can evoke the visual object. There is, of course, slippage between the two

---

[60] There are other Hellenistic sources whose stones we might study, in particular Posidippus' *Lithica*.

[61] See also Mueller (forthcoming) and her discussion of Sappho's material intertextuality: 'Sappho's incorporation of "Homer" into her lyrics can, in turn, be felt to be a more tactile, material process than our own literary critical terminology ("allusion," "intertext") would generally allow.'

[62] One theory of intermediality is that offered by Rajewsky 2005. For a fuller presentation of this approach, see Canevaro forthcoming b.

[63] Mitchell 1994: 5.

[64] Rajewsky 2005: 53. This is where Theocritus and, for instance, classical drama part ways – on props in tragedy, see Mueller 2016 and Stavropoulou PhD 2021.

media, in that a text is in itself a material object — but I would argue that the imaginative evocation and the structural and elemental imitation that lie behind the literary object warrant distinct consideration.

Ekphrasis is perhaps the most obvious starting point for tracking intermediality in ancient literature, and it will be a theme that comes up again and again in this book.[65] Though ekphrasis need not always be about artworks or objects,[66] in these instances things are put before our eyes as a verbal representation of a material object casts them into the limelight. Intermediality in terms of materiality embedded in literature is arguably most evident in such examples, as the descriptive language used emphatically evokes a multimedia context of artistic creation and appreciation. We *see* something of which we *hear* (or read): an imaginative experience that proves transportive. I would emphasise, however, that intermedial references centring on materiality are not limited to instances of ekphrasis. In tracking the interplay between text and 'image', between textuality and materiality within ancient literature, we should not confine ourselves to those instances put on poetic display — but rather consider the full material landscape presented to us by the poetry. This is because, in dealing with literary objects, we are *always* dealing with imaginative constructs: not only when they are flagged up in hyper-literary ways, but also when they are part of the poetic furniture. There are always choices being made, signs being constructed.

So far, I have focused on intermediality as a kind of *intra*textuality, in that I have been considering the relationship between different medial elements within a text. But this is just a starting point. Once we have established that there is intermedial referencing operating between literature and literary object, that is, the text evoking materiality, or the word evoking the world, we need not restrict our analysis to a single text. To expand our view, we might explore exactly what — or, indeed, where — we consider objects to be. Object-Oriented Ontologists like Graham Harman argue that objects always remain somehow foreign and elsewhere, just beyond reach; that objects are withdrawn from human access and from causal interaction with each other. This philosophical standpoint has its difficulties — particularly for objects represented by an author — but it does usefully point to a level of 'otherness' inhabited by things, a withdrawn ontological plane that can provide a superstructure bringing objects together between and across texts. And it is because of this superstructure

---

[65] For reference to intermediality specifically in relation to the shield of Achilles, see Squire 2013.

[66] We should distinguish, with Webb (2009: 5–7), between ancient and modern definitions of ekphrasis. While the modern definition tends to limit ekphrasis to the description of, specifically, a work of art, 'in the ancient definition the referent is only of secondary importance; what matters … is the impact on the listener' (p. 7).

that intertextuality and objects are already – indeed inevitably – thoroughly implicated with one another. To put it more prosaically and practically, and without risking placing both objects and history on a flat surface, we might note that even literary objects have a parallel material life, mapping (in some way, more or less directly as the case may be) onto the real world. As such, they exist outside the confines of one text, and so can move between texts, by virtue of their physical counterparts and their situatedness. Intertextuality through objects is an intermedial phenomenon *within the text*: but it is simultaneously something more, as it not only gestures to but really *connects* the literary with the material, the word with the world.

Let's return now to parameters and to boundaries. We have established this book's porous perspective on the Theocritean corpus and on 'Theocritus' himself, as well as its broad angle on the question of 'what is pastoral'. I would like to introduce two further insights from Material Ecocriticism that can give us new ways in to questions of tradition, of genre, of transmission – essentially, the fundamentals of classical literary analysis, cast anew. It is in such examples that we can see the novelty of the material-ecocritical paradigm at work; the refreshed and refreshing perspectives it can offer; the potential really to stand things on their heads.

The first comes from Hubert Zapf and his chapter in *Material Ecocriticism*, 'Creative matter and creative mind: Cultural ecology and literary creativity'. I return to this piece in Chapter 4 with a more sustained and specific analysis – but for now one element of Zapf's approach might be brought to bear on these wider themes. To offer just a glimpse of the general argument, Zapf combines tenets of Material Ecocriticism with Cultural Ecology and Biosemiotics, the latter being a field in theoretical biology which holds that 'human language is just the most recent evolutionary part of a vast global web of semiosis encompassing all living things – from the smallest cell to the most complex multicellular organism'.[67] Zapf argues that creativity is something that humans share with the nonhuman world, and that literary creativity operates in tandem with (as 'a self-reflexive staging and aesthetic transformation of'[68]) the creativity of material nature. We are surrounded by creative matter, to which our own creativity is linked. A particular point of interest is the following:

> In this very act of continually renewing cultural creativity, literature always remains aware of the former stages of its own evolution and of the deep history of culture-nature-coevolution, the biosemiotic memory that has been part of literature's generative potential from its very beginnings. Through imaginative transitions and metamorphoses between nonhuman and human life, natural and cultural

---

[67] Definition from Wheeler 2014: 71.
[68] Zapf 2014: 51.

ecologies, this evolutionary memory remains present in the symbolic forms and codes of literary creativity.[69]

This is a way in which we might productively link the very idea of literary tradition, and more specifically genre, with human/nonhuman co-existence. 'Continually renewing cultural creativity' – this could be a definition of the literary tradition. Tradition and innovation operate in tandem, with literature acting along a continuum that constantly changes and metamorphoses, all the while remaining 'aware of the former stages of its own evolution'. Let us return to the idea of pastoral literature. It is a genre, a mode, a 'discursive formation' (to repeat Martindale's formulation) – demarcated and delineated, yet porous and permeable and ever changing. And ever aware: self-reflexive, invested with 'evolutionary memory'. As Alpers puts it, 'when pastoral writing is properly understood, it can be seen to be far more aware of itself and its conditions than it has usually been thought to be, or even capable of being'.[70] The Theocritean corpus is, as established above, a showcase of multiple genres, drawing on a variety of literary traditions – and though the pastoral element may be the least long-standing (if we are to think of Theocritus as one of its initiators), it interacts with other generic affiliations that have clear evolutionary memory. Further, a self-reflexive approach to tradition is arguably at its most compelling in the Hellenistic period: a time of intense and explicit engagement with, and innovation on, literary tradition.[71] We might think of ancient hexameter poetry in its diverse discursive formulations as being almost a compendium of creativity – and of Hellenistic literature as a nodal point of 'imaginative transitions and metamorphoses'. Pastoral poetry, then, helps us to conceptualise the cross-domain mapping of literary creativity onto the creativity of natural ecology, because in its subject matter, its approach and its tone it draws us inexorably towards the connections between human and nonhuman, people and the land. If, as Zapf argues from the perspective of biosemiotics, all life is characterised by communication, then literature as an epitome of human communication becomes a way to access the more-than-human world.

From biosemiotics, too, Zapf takes the idea of improvisational flexibility as key to both natural and cultural creative evolution: 'Former layers of evolution remain present in later forms in a kind of biosemiotic deep structure, in which the new is always a "recycling" and adaptive readjustment of the old.'[72] As well as the more

---

[69] Ibid. p. 57.
[70] Alpers 1996: xi.
[71] See Fantuzzi and Hunter 2004.
[72] Zapf 2014: 53.

general theme of tradition, this brings to mind two specific aspects of the study of ancient texts. The first: the oral roots of ancient hexameter poetry. The oral tradition is perhaps the most compelling example of improvisational flexibility in poetic creation. Ideas of composition in performance; of tailoring to an audience; of absorbing and incorporating contemporary reference points – all point towards an evolutionary process. It is within this broader context that we can set the written literary production of subsequent ages: compositional methods may have changed, but new forms are still only layers in a composite picture of ongoing creative adaptation. The second aspect this 'biosemiotic deep structure' recalls is that of the textual tradition: textual transmission, and our 'discipline' of textual criticism. To combine these two aspects, orality and the transmitted text, we might look to initiatives like the Homer Multitext Project: a resource which allows the overlaying of different versions, stages and permutations of the Homeric texts, actively showcasing their 'deep structure'. But more generally, the transmission of a text, its shifts and phases, has correlates in the natural world. Indicative is the conventional representation of a textual history in a stemma: a family 'tree' of variants, with a complex network of branches tracing a text back to its roots.

The arboreal metaphor leads me to another: the geological. The life of stone will be explored further in Chapter 3, but it is never too early to introduce the work of Jeffrey Jerome Cohen, in particular his book *Stone: An Ecology of the Inhuman*. Cohen writes: 'Contemporary scholars of Genesis describe its narrative in geological terms, detailing strata, describing the sedimentation of multiple authorships, discordant stories, and alternative realities.'[73] But this is not a model necessarily restricted to biblical scholarship. He continues with reference to the fourteenth-century *The Book of John Mandeville*:

> The *Book* is also *geologic*, in the rocky triple meaning of that word: sedimentary (an accretion of multifold texts, amalgamating them into new forms), igneous (hardened after long movement into contours that make transit evident), metamorphic (ever changing, open to futurity, circling the world to meet and no longer recognize oneself). Each textual variant of the multiplex *Book* can be seen as a crystallization, a gem created from an ever-fluid, seismic narrative that does not cease to be a body in motion, ready for shifts to come.[74]

Cohen notes that this is not mere metaphor, as in the case of Mandeville the narrator's journey is actually characterised by lithic companionship. The geological is as

---

[73] Cohen 2015: 94.
[74] Ibid. p. 154.

much a character, a presence, an agent, as it is a metaphorical parallel. In Chapter 3 I return to this idea of lithic agents and show that stony nature can also be traced in the Theocritean corpus. But for now, it suffices to say that this possibility is open: and indeed this makes us rethink even the plant metaphor offered above. A persistent thread in Material Ecocriticism is the argument that metaphor is an emergent property of the entanglements between the human and nonhuman; that the operation of cultural and natural creativity in tandem, which we have discussed through Zapf's chapter, results in forms of communication and expression that draw the two together. I tackle this question in more detail in Chapter 4 – but here it is worth raising the possibility that we should let our attention be drawn to the natural domains of metaphorical expression, as they may well be participants in those very communicative acts. But to return to Cohen and his geological model: this can be mobilised more widely than Genesis or *The Book of John Mandeville*. Indeed, any textual tradition, and certainly the transmission of classical poetry, might be cast in these terms. Of particular interest in terms of archaic poetry is the idea of 'crystallization', a term often used to refer to the stage at which the oral tradition moved towards fixity and stability, but which Cohen's formulation shows to be just one layer among others. Further, it is interesting that Cohen's model invokes futurity, as well as the geological past. The seismic narrative is 'ready for shifts to come'.[75] Textual transmission is not a closed entity, a finished product. The family tree is still growing, with each edition an additional branch. In his book, Cohen deftly sets the human lifespan against geological or 'deep' time, contrasting our ephemerality with the longevity and durability of stone. And just as stone precedes and outlasts us, so the classical tradition not only stretches back in time, but also continues on as 'a body in motion'. Both natural and human creativity, then, outlive the individual human agent. A material-ecocritical approach not only counters generic human narcissism – I would argue that it also tempers illusions of academic exceptionalism. Recalling assemblage theory, we can think of Theocritus, and his readers, and his editors, and this book and its author – all as layers, as contours, 'ever-fluid' and 'open to futurity'. After all this transmission and interpretation, would Theocritus recognise himself?

Oiko-criticism and Dark Ecology: Revisiting Hesiod's Farm

A consideration of the broader tradition of hexameter poetry inevitably reflects on Theocritus' relationship with Homeric epic. This will certainly be a strong strand

---

[75] This can be linked back to biosemiotics: as Wheeler 2014: 72 puts it, 'Semiosis is always open-ended and, teleologically, future directed toward more complex and overdetermined formations.'

of the intertextuality through objects traced in this book, and is often at the heart of Theocritus' allusive and innovative poetics. And yet, Homer is not the only influence on the Theocritean corpus – nor is he necessarily the most relevant to a material-ecocritical project. Another point of departure is the poetry of Hesiod, and in particular the *Works and Days*, an archaic hexameter poem anchored in the land and focused on the *oikos*. This takes us to the root of the ecocritical part of our analysis in terms of both literary tradition and etymology. As Iovino notes, 'ecocriticism in general is a way to critically articulate the imagination of our *oikos*'.[76]

I return to biosemiotics, this time to Wendy Wheeler's article 'Natural play, natural metaphor, and natural stories: biosemiotic realism'.[77] In the final section, Wheeler zooms in from the general argument that natural and cultural creativity mirror (or co-constitute) one another, to the specific point that 'the development of literary meanings in narratives – which readers must *play* with to discover – imitates the processes of natural evolution'.[78] Natural play and literary play are related. This is a very interesting argument for a reading of Hesiod's *Works and Days*, a poem full of literary play of all kinds: from wordplay to riddles, from a multiplicity of narrative forms to parallel stories.[79] The *Works and Days* is made up of diverse narrative forms, and has often been criticised for its multiform structure. I maintain that the poetic strategies adopted in the poem work its audience hard, setting them on a search for meaning, for the lesson. The tough Iron Age life is modelled in Hesiod's challenging poetics. With Wheeler we might cast this as literary 'play' that mirrors natural play. The *Works and Days* is ostensibly about farming: about working the land and responding to the rhythms of nature. It is, of course, about so much more than this – but the central narrative is such that it points us towards the relationship between the human and the land. It is feasible, then, for us to trace a correlation between literary and natural play in this most foundational of *oiko*-critical texts.

In the vocabulary of evolution, there is a difference between natural *selection* and natural *play*. While selection acts to settle things, combination – which is integral to play – opens up new emergent possibilities, and as such it provides

---

[76] Iovino 2016: 310.
[77] Wheeler 2014.
[78] Ibid. p. 75.
[79] Canevaro 2015a argues that Hesiod's literary play is the perfect way to teach his audience to think for themselves. Canevaro 2018a and 2019b show how these mechanisms work from the perspective of cognitive psychology, specifically in terms of cognitive training and the complex cognitive task of anticipating audiences.

the basis for creative evolution in both biology and human culture.[80] I'm sure most readers would agree that Hesiod's *Works and Days* is an *un*settling poem. Whether we are perturbed by its elusive structure or confused by its riddles, lost in its multiple narratives or trying to make sense of its message, or just plain puzzled by all the parts of the plough, what is clear is that Hesiod opens up more possibilities than he settles. The audience is consistently offered multiple options, routes, choices; given one instruction in numerous ways; shown examples of a wide range of behaviours and paths. Hesiod does give us some angles on natural selection: the Myth of the Races, for instance, offers a diachronic, teleological narrative of humankind's development, and the overall narrowing of focus that can be traced in the *Works and Days*' trajectory points towards settlement.[81] And yet, the overriding impression left by the poem is one of emergent possibilities, of change and creative response.

Responsiveness is central to Wheeler's argument: that is, the capacity of nature and culture to react to one another, and to change and grow. Part of this is the responsiveness of cultural products, which Wheeler describes in this way: 'Poems, novels, paintings, and so on are not doctrinal advertisements for the promotion of whatever local virtues are currently approved; rather, they constitute relationships and serious demands for the light of other minds and room to grow.'[82] The 'serious demands' are particularly relevant to the *Works and Days*, in terms of the expectations the poem places on its audience to interpret and learn from it, and to Hellenistic poetry, with the interpretive demands made by its characteristic allusive poetics. These 'serious demands' do not operate only at the level of literary interpretation, however, but echo in lived experience. As the contributors to the 2016 volume *Ecocriticism, Ecology, and the Cultures of Antiquity* argue, antiquity too witnessed environmental problems, and responded to them. Alpers (1996) argues that pastoral poetry is not a vehicle of nostalgia, nor a utopian escape, but a mode that bears witness to the possibilities and problems of human community and shared experience in the real world. Hiltner (2011) offers an environmental reading of pastoral poetry that reconnects it with literal, and not just figurative, landscapes. He associates this 'mode' with moments of environmental change, specifically urbanisation, arguing that we only truly become aware of our environment when its survival is threatened. In this way, Material Ecocriticism is a situated theory – and pastoral poetry a situated mode. Tracing Theocritus' roots back to Hesiod as shepherd-poet takes on a

---

[80] Wheeler 2014: 77, drawing on Hoffmeyer 2008: 197.
[81] The narrowing of focus is both spatial and temporal: this has been explored in most detail by Clay (2003).
[82] Wheeler 2014: 78.

particular resonance in this light, as didactic poetry too is a situated genre, as argued by Donncha O'Rourke: 'didactic poems seem to coincide with the epistemic shifts which, according to Foucault, occur in periods of social and political reordering'.[83] Poems are not doctrinal advertisements. They do not have to *conform*, but can rather comment, critique. They don't have to promote approved virtues, but can question them. The demands on our interpretation are thus serious indeed, as we recognise that the relationship between word and world is dynamic and negotiated. All of this we must bear in mind if we are to consider Hesiod's world, or Theocritus' world: or the world of any other poet, for that matter.

I turn now to a model that is of key importance to this study of Theocritus' *Idylls*, but which warrants introduction through Hesiod's *Works and Days*. 'Dark ecology' was developed by ecocritic Timothy Morton. 'What is dark ecology? It is ecological awareness, dark-depressing.'[84] It is essentially an aesthetic response to difficult and entangled environments, a pessimistic reading of the human condition. It is a way of expressing the porousness of boundaries that so interests me here, and that is at the heart of Morton's work. When we realise that we are not even separate from our surroundings, let alone in control of them, how do we express that in literature?

In an article of 2018, William Brockliss effectively applies dark ecology to the *Works and Days*. He summarises the conclusions of his article:

> Morton's ideas can enrich our understanding of the Hesiodic *Works and Days*, which places emphasis on the difficulty of interacting with the environments of the Greek world. And while some passages seem to accord a privileged status to humans, many others stress the interpenetration of the human and the nonhuman, doing so in the sort of pessimistic tone that Morton associates with his dark ecological aesthetic.[85]

The 'interpenetration of the human and the nonhuman' is exactly my focus in this book, from Hesiod and Homer to Theocritus and beyond. Brockliss's analysis is

---

[83] O'Rourke 2019: 26. We might also follow Theocritus forwards, through Elizabeth Barrett Browning's *Sonnets from the Portuguese* 1:

> I thought once how Theocritus had sung
> Of the sweet years, the dear and wished-for years

These lines unite Barrett Browning and Theocritus in a 'human community' and 'shared experience', in the midst of the Industrial Revolution.

[84] Morton 2016: 5.

[85] Brockliss 2018: 1. See further Canevaro forthcoming a on Pandora and dark ecology.

particularly compelling in its consideration of an ancient audience's reaction to the dark ecology of the *Works and Days*. He argues that while modern readers, to whom the harsh environments of the Greek world are alien, might focus on the poem's more optimistic elements (construing Hesiod's advice as positive and constructive and human mastery over the landscape as ultimately achievable), ancient listeners would have focused on those passages that problematise distinctions between human and nonhuman, body and nature, and they would have followed the invitation to interpret these phenomena in a pessimistic way.[86] One important result of my study is the conviction that the 'pessimistic tone' we see in the *Works and Days* can be found in Theocritus' *Idylls* too, specifically in terms of materiality. This will come to the fore most prevalently in our consideration of lithic agency in *Idyll* 23 (Chapter 3, pp. 113–40). Stony actants take over the poem, and the fearsome stone exerts its effects on the narrative and our reception of it. A dark-ecological aesthetic can also be seen in the symptomology of a rejected woman 'othered' over multiple axes including class in *Idyll* 2 (Chapter 2, pp. 66–81) and the difficulties shared by emigrant people and objects in *Idyll* 28 (Chapter 4, pp. 155–69). It can be seen in the precarious labour and landscape of the fishermen in *Idylls* 1 and 21 (Chapter 3, pp. 91–113). Story worlds rupture, a fisherman begins to doubt even the seasons; as he questions everything, he leads the poem's readers to do the same. And in Chapter 5 (pp. 178–86) dark ecology comes in the monstrous figure of Polyphemus and his threatening land- and seascape. In terms of our reading of Theocritus' poetry from below, it is compelling to note that these dark-ecological moments cluster around the margins – women, emigrants, labour, the monstrous 'other'. The pessimistic tone may have resonated with readers attuned to these charged issues of gender, class and belonging.[87]

Pastoral poetry has overwhelmingly been viewed in terms of its *locus amoenus*. But what about these cracks in the pleasantry? The moments of disharmony between man and the land? Fantuzzi and Hunter claim that the Theocritean countryside 'is never a really wild countryside, a place of dangers and hardships, one quite inhospitable to humans; on the contrary, the Theocritean countryside is always peacefully under

---

[86] Brockliss 2018: 3.

[87] Morton 2008 uses the poetry of Jon Clare to work out his ideas of dark ecology. Clare is seen as a proto-ecological poet, and it is of relevance to my reading from below in this book that his is a working-class voice. His poems are about nature, but they are also poems of depression. In this article Morton concludes: 'the very feelings of loneliness and separation, rather than narcissistic fantasies of interconnectedness, put us in touch with a surrounding environment. I am calling it dark ecology, after Frost ("The woods are lovely dark and deep"), but also after Gothic culture, from *Frankenstein* to The Cure, a reminder that we can't escape our minds' (2008: 193).

human control'. This is, I argue, a conclusion born out of an anthropocentric reading of the poems. When we focus in on material agency, however, the Theocritean landscape becomes a whole lot more threatening. And through this reading we get closer to the priorities and realities of ancient readers. That literature can 'reflect a pessimistic conception of humans and of their place in the world'[88] takes on an even more compelling cast when considered in terms of these bucolic beginnings. In his 1981 book *Poetry and Myth in Ancient Pastoral*, Charles Segal sees the darkness in the Theocritean poems. For instance, in his reading of *Idyll* 1, he emphasises the disjunction between the scenes on the cup and the contents of the song, as amusing snapshots of country life contrast with the uncanny story of Daphnis, his unrequited love and his watery end. And Segal notes the 'ambiguous and sinister side' to the *Idylls* in the 'death by water' narrative pattern he traces across the corpus.[89] A material-ecocritical approach and particularly a dark-ecological reading clarifies these disquieting undertones in the *Idylls*.[90]

In the opening of the 2014 book *The Necropastoral*, Joyelle McSweeney defines its title: 'The term "necropastoral" remarks the pastoral as a zone of exchange, shading this green theme park with the suspicion that the anthropocene epoch is in fact synonymous with ecological endtimes.'[91] This is a book that approaches the new-materialist blurring of boundaries from a dark-ecological, pessimistic perspective: 'My necropastoral suggests that there is no wall between "nature" and "manmade" but only a membrane, that each element can bore through this membrane to spread its poisons, its Death to the other'.[92] McSweeney points to the cracks in the divides: 'For all the pastoral's shoring up of separations, and despite the *cordon sanitaire* it purports to erect between unhealthy urban strife and wholesome rural peace, we must remember that the premier celebrity resident of Arcadia is Death.'[93] The necropastoral pays attention to the borders, to the margins, and brings them to the centre, in that it is 'the manifestation of the infectiousness, anxiety, and contagion occultly present in the hygienic borders of the classical pastoral'.[94] Though McSweeney's book does not focus on ancient pastoral poetry, taking a tour instead

---

[88] Brockliss 2018: 4.
[89] Segal 1981: 48. On *Idyll* 1, see pp. 25–46; on death by water, pp. 47–65.
[90] Indeed, a focus on material agency may reveal *more* undercurrents than usually noted: the scenes on the cup, with their vital materiality, lithic agency and narratives across bodies and things, are not that far from uncanny themselves, and in *Idyll* 23 the 'sinister' water is eclipsed by stony threat (see Chapter 3, pp. 113–40).
[91] McSweeney 2014: 3.
[92] Ibid. p. 42.
[93] Ibid. p. 3.
[94] Ibid. p. 3.

around Wilfred Owen, Andy Warhol, Harryette Mullen, Roberto Bolaño, Aimé Césaire and Georges Bataille, it is important to note that the concept of the necropastoral does stem from her reading of antiquity. Owen might take the pastoral to the battlefields of World War I, bringing death to the forefront, but such dark avenues are opened up by his Greek and Roman predecessors.

2   The Woman

Material Feminism: Changing Nature

Material Feminism calls for what Bruno Latour termed a 'new settlement': a return from the linguistic turn in Postmodern Feminism to material reality, yet informed by the former.[1] In the introduction to their 2008 landmark volume *Material Feminisms*, Stacy Alaimo and Susan Hekman set out their goal: 'The new settlement we are seeking is not a return to modernism. Rather, it accomplishes what the postmoderns failed to do: a deconstruction of the material/discursive dichotomy that retains both elements without privileging either.'[2]

Both new-materialist approaches and Postmodern Feminism have focused on breaking down dichotomies. The New Materialisms foreground the material in order to disrupt entrenched binaries, dislodge agency from the human subject and level the ontological playing field. Similarly, postmodern feminists have argued that the male/female dichotomy informs all the dichotomies that ground Western thought, and they have argued that rather than moving from one side of the dichotomy to the other, simply reversing the privileging of concepts, we must deconstruct the dichotomy itself, to move to an understanding that does not rest on oppositions. However, material feminists argue that the male/female dichotomy is actually the one dichotomy Postmodern Feminism did *not* manage to deconstruct, instead just reversing the privilege and prioritising discourse. There is work still to be done. In 1985, Donna Haraway issued a call for a redefinition

---

[1] Though see Ahmed 2008 for a refutation of feminism's anti-biological reputation, and see also van der Tuin 2008 for a reaction to this refutation.
[2] Alaimo and Hekman 2008: 6.

of the material in discursive terms *without* repolarising in the opposite direction – and the Material Feminisms aim to revisit this call.³

Like the New Materialisms more generally, Material Feminism advocates a move from epistemology to ontology – or, with Karen Barad (2007), 'onto-epistemology'. Barad's agential realism, for example, explores the relationship between the material and the discursive, and takes as key concerns the nature of agency and the effects of boundaries. Hekman's 'new settlement' offers the model of 'disclosure' (taken from Barad), by which the world is not taken to be linguistically constructed (as in postmodern feminist thought) but rather *disclosed* by our portrayals of it:

> Disclosure entails that perspectives/concepts/theories matter – that they are our means of accessing reality. But disclosure also entails that we do not constitute that reality with our concepts, but rather portray it in varying ways. An important aspect of this understanding is that the reality, like the object in the photograph or the subject of the scientist's experiment, is agentic. It pushes back, it effects the result.⁴

Material Feminism, then, brings the 'attentiveness to things' that arguably was missing from Postmodern Feminism – and it also brings the valuable lessons from the linguistic turn, a (balanced) focus on the discursive that is missing from many of the New Materialisms.⁵

There are so many strands of feminism that Material Feminism claims to integrate, as an overarching paradigm. As Alaimo and Hekman put it,

> the emerging theories of materiality developed in material feminisms are crucial for every aspect of feminist thought: science studies, environmental feminisms, corporeal feminisms, queer theory, disability studies, theories of race

---

³ Hekman 2008: 86: 'With the hindsight of more than twenty years of feminist theory and practice, it seems fair to conclude that Haraway's project has failed. Instead of deconstructing the discourse/reality dichotomy, instead of constructing a new paradigm for feminism that integrates the discursive and the material, feminism has instead turned to the discursive pole of the discourse/reality dichotomy.'
⁴ Ibid. p. 112.
⁵ Term 'attentiveness to things' from Bennett 2010. My work on women and objects in Homer (Canevaro 2018b) can be cast as part of this material-feminist 'new settlement', in that it combines the material with the discursive. But I am not convinced I took the material side far enough to go beyond the post-modern balance in favour of discourse. The current book pushes further, following some of the tenets and methodologies of Material Feminism.

and ethnicity, environmental justice, (post-) Marxist feminism, globalization studies, and cultural studies.[6]

But the focus of this book draws me to one particular intersection: that between Material Feminisms and Material Ecocriticism. We have seen how Material Feminism relates to New Materialism more broadly. But how does it connect with Material Ecocriticism? How do these two fields, both mobilising new-materialist approaches but in relation to ostensibly different subjects, meet?

First, there is a focus on nature. Alaimo and Hekman note that mainstream feminism pursues a 'flight from nature', but they spot a problem with this approach: 'the more feminist theories distance themselves from "nature" the more that very "nature" is implicitly or explicitly reconfirmed as the treacherous quicksand of misogyny'.[7] Alaimo (2010) argues that there are actually more dualisms that persist in feminist theory than that of the material/discursive. She points out that in working to disentangle 'woman' from 'nature', feminist theory has been working within a dualism – and indeed she notes that feminist theory's most revolutionary concept, that of gender as distinct from biological sex, is predicated on the nature/culture dichotomy. Rather than distancing ourselves from nature, material feminists (along with environmental feminists, or ecofeminists) argue that we should change the way we think of nature altogether:

> Rather than perpetuate the nature/culture dualism, which imagines nature to be the inert ground for the exploits of Man, we must reconceptualize nature itself. Nature can no longer be imagined as a pliable resource for industrial production or social construction. Nature is agentic – it acts, and those actions have consequences for both the human and nonhuman world.[8]

It is in this foregrounding of nature as actant that Material Feminism and Material Ecocriticism come into alignment. This has important consequences for our reading of both nature and women in literature, and particularly for our reading of women in the Theocritean corpus (where the pastoral looms large). We can use some of the same heuristic tools to uncover the agency of both female characters and the natural environment, while being alerted by those very tools to the need to break down binaries and dichotomies. Simon Estok writes:

---

[6] Alaimo and Hekman 2008: 9–10.
[7] Ibid. p. 4.
[8] Ibid. pp. 4–5.

> Out of the welter of books and articles that have recently appeared relating to material ecocriticisms, human bodies have reappeared as the site and source of concerns about our changing relationship with the material world … They are … 'material narratives' about the way human corporeality is dangerously entangled within a complex of discourses and material agents that determine its very being.⁹

As with Material Feminism, we see in this description of Material Ecocriticism the combination of discourse and materiality. We also find a refocusing on the human body – and this is a further aspect that, as I will show, Material Ecocriticism and Material Feminism have in common. It is an interesting turn, from a new-materialist perspective. New Materialism works hard to decentre the conventional human subject; to level the ontological playing field; to move in disanthropocentric directions. But as the 'reappearance' of the body within fields under the broad new-materialist umbrella shows, a focus on materiality does not necessitate neglect of the human.

In her 2018 article on Alexander Pope's *The Rape of the Lock*, Elizabeth Kowaleski Wallace maps some of the tenets of the current New Materialisms back onto eighteenth-century thought – particularly connecting Jane Bennett's vital materialism with the long-standing vitalist tradition. By referring back to this philosophical standpoint as manifest in the eighteenth century, and by setting it in contrast to mechanism, Wallace can show its value in feminist terms, summarising: 'To feminist New Materialists in particular, vitalism offers an intriguing starting point from which the history of female materiality can be rethought'.¹⁰ She notes that

> the vitalists tended to be more progressive in their politics: their philosophy tended to resist hierarchal relations, seeing the world in terms of horizontal affinities, and this point has particular importance for gender … vitalism did tend to afford more agency not only to matter but also to what had been encoded as female.¹¹

In her context, she argues that 'Pope's satiric attack on vitalism, as well as his resistance to the idea of self-moving matter, has everything to do with his problematic rendering of his female protagonist'.¹² This supports my argument in this book, my rationale for combining the study of female and material agencies: the New Materialisms broadly conceived, including and in particular vital materialism, Material Feminism and Material Ecocriticism, can level the playing field, elevating

---

⁹ Estok 2014: 130.
¹⁰ Wallace 2018: 106.
¹¹ Ibid. p. 107.
¹² Ibid. p. 114.

underrepresented agents which comprise women as much as nature as much as material things. Ontological (along with gender) hierarchies are flattened in this refocusing. Wallace notes that, according to most critics (including those coming from a feminist perspective), 'Pope deprives Belinda of her full status as embodied human'; she is 'effectively muted and rendered ineffectual as a human being. Belinda is turned into *an object* without the capacity to act independently.'[13] But by probing and revisiting our (and Pope's) conception of the object, and therefore of the equation of the female with the object, Wallace questions this starkly hierarchical approach to both materiality and the female. She notes that critics have immediately defaulted to a non-vitalist understanding of the object as inert and passive. More nuanced is her argument: that Pope raises and acknowledges vitalist possibilities, just as he strives to contain them. So although the outcome is the same (Pope trying to contain Belinda's agency), the process is very different. It is not a simple equation between inert matter and passive woman: rather, *both* have to be argued for, as neither can be a given.

Idyll 1: Ekphrasis and Materiality

> ἔντοσθεν δὲ γυνά, τι θεῶν δαίδαλμα, τέτυκται,
> ἀσκητὰ πέπλῳ τε καὶ ἄμπυκι· πὰρ δέ οἱ ἄνδρες
> καλὸν ἐθειράζοντες ἀμοιβαδὶς ἄλλοθεν ἄλλος
> νεικείουσ' ἐπέεσσι· τὰ δ' οὐ φρενὸς ἅπτεται αὐτᾶς·
> ἀλλ' ὅκα μὲν τῆνον ποτιδέρκεται ἄνδρα γέλαισα,
> ἄλλοκα δ' αὖ ποτὶ τὸν ῥιπτεῖ νόον· οἳ δ' ὑπ' ἔρωτος
> δηθὰ κυλοιδιόωντες ἐτώσια μοχθίζοντι.

> Inside is fashioned a woman, with godlike artistry,
> dressed with cloak and headband. By her, two men
> with fine locks are contending with words,
> one from each side. But these things do not touch her heart,
> but now she looks to one man and smiles,
> now she turns her thoughts to the other. They, long
> dark-eyed from love, labour in vain.
> (Theocritus *Idyll* 1.32–8)

This is the first scene on the cup offered in Theocritus' first *Idyll*. The description begins with a contested placement marker: ἔντοσθεν. Inside what? Are the woman

---

[13] Ibid. p. 115, original italics.

and her suitors inside the cup, or inside the floral frame, or both?[14] The ambiguous marker has generated a discussion that feeds into our broader questions here. In Theocritus' *Idylls*, how are the human and nonhuman positioned in relation to one another?[15] Where are the boundaries? Are they clear? The opening of this passage encourages us to read across cup, foliage and woman, the spatial relationship between them left ambivalent, bringing them together in one enmeshed material narrative. It is this idea of entanglement that then feeds forward into the scene itself, with the woman surrounded by men (πὰρ δέ οἱ ἄνδρες; ἄλλοθεν ἄλλος; ἀλλ᾽ ὁκὰ ... ἄλλοκα), just as the cup is encircled by plants and the scene is inside either plant or cup or both. Entanglement characterises the narrative of both the woman and the cup on which she is figured.

ἔντοσθεν δὲ γυνά is also a compelling opener in terms of gendered spatial relations. Whether the woman is inside the cup or the foliage or both, there are societal and poetic expectations that she will be inside – inside the home, inside the domestic sphere, the epitome of the indoors. Emblematic of this association is Hesiod's tender-skinned maiden:

καὶ διὰ παρθενικῆς ἀπαλόχροος οὐ διάησιν,
ἥ τε δόμων ἔντοσθε φίλη παρὰ μητέρι μίμνει
οὔ πω ἔργ᾽ εἰδυῖα πολυχρύσου Ἀφροδίτης·
εὖ τε λοεσσαμένη τέρενα χρόα καὶ λίπ᾽ ἐλαίῳ
χρισαμένη μυχίη καταλέξεται ἔνδοθι οἴκου

[The wind] does not blow through the tender-skinned maiden
who stays inside the house next to her dear mother,
not yet knowing the works of much-golden Aphrodite.
Having washed her tender skin well and anointed it richly with oil
she lies down in the innermost chamber inside the house.
(Hesiod *Works and Days* 519–23[16])

---

[14] Hunter translates 'within [the frame of the plants]', noting that 'The oldest witness reads ἔκτοσθεν, which would remove the potential ambiguity of "inside", i.e. "inside the frame" or "inside the cup", but seems an unnecessary specification; it may have arisen precisely to remove the ambiguity' (Hunter 1999 *ad loc.*). Gow takes a different approach, commenting on ἔντοσθεν: 'sc. τοῦ κισσυβίου, though incidentally the scenes are also within the band of ivy-pattern which runs round its rim'.

[15] See Chapter 3 (pp. 115–17) for the spatial relationship between the fisherman and his rock.

[16] All Hesiod text comes from West 1966 and 1978 respectively. Translations are my own.

The anonymous maiden is young and innocent, washed and anointed – pure, chaste, perfect. She is inside the house (δόμων ἔντοσθε … ἔνδοθι οἴκου), in the innermost chamber (μυχίη), the protection of the house commensurate with her purity. One difference between the settings of the passages, however, is important for our reading of the entanglements of *Idyll* 1. The *Works and Days* passage is part of Hesiod's description of winter, specifically the effects of the winter wind Boreas. Hesiod depicts Boreas as affecting the land (*WD* 505–11), animals (512–18, 524–6) and people (518–23, 527–8), and animals and people alike have to protect themselves against it (animals, 529–35; people, 536–46). That man and beast are in it together is emphasised by thematic shifts from animals to people and back again; a simile at 533–5 which likens the beasts of the forest to a man with a stick; the common vocabulary used to describe them (τανύτριχα, 516; τρίχες, 517; τρίχες, 539); the explicit link between the two at 558; and the balancing of their rations at 559–60. The tender-skinned maiden, though part of this entangled narrative structure (she is paralleled with the sheep whose wool is too thick for the wind to penetrate, or the Boneless One in his house; she is contrasted with the old man bowled along by the gusts of wind), is explicitly separated out from the effects of the wind, and the realm of men. The wind does *not* blow through her (οὐ διάησιν), and she stays with her mother alone. By contrast, the woman of *Idyll* 1 is not separated out from the forces of nature. The schism between nature and culture, between materiality and discourse, dissolves, as figuration and artistry become movement and action – as foliage frames the female, and cup becomes character. Further, the woman defies our expectations about the 'woman inside'. Inside the cup, inside the plants – but not secluded inside a gendered domestic sphere. She is in the company of men. The setting is not specified – we don't learn anything of the group's surroundings. Has she gone out, or have they come in? Or was there no line to begin with?

The materiality of the scene is reinforced and foregrounded by τί θεῶν δαίδαλμα τέτυκται, created with godlike artistry (or: a statue of the gods – see further below, pp. 60–2): the woman (γυνά) is not introduced without contextualisation in terms of craft. As Hunter notes, there are three main intertextual points of reference here: the tapestries in *Idyll* 15 (to which I shall come later in this chapter); the 'standard language of ekphrasis'; and Pandora, 'the most famous "fashioned" woman of Greek story'.[17] I first consider the implications of the allusion to Pandora for a material-feminist reading of this passage. The myth of Pandora as told in Hesiod's *Theogony* and *Works and Days* is replete with ontological indeterminacy and blurred boundaries. If we consider Pandora within her material landscape in the poems, we see that she is nature, she is culture and, more than a combination of the two (what is

---

[17] Hunter 1999 *ad loc.*

nature anyway?), she is a meeting point for various human and nonhuman agencies. The ontological slippage in the Hesiodic accounts of Pandora points towards a more integrated view of material agency than studies have so far allowed.[18]

ζῶσε δὲ καὶ κόσμησε θεὰ γλαυκῶπις Ἀθήνη
ἀργυφέῃ ἐσθῆτι· κατὰ κρῆθεν δὲ καλύπτρην
δαιδαλέην χείρεσσι κατέσχεθε, θαῦμα ἰδέσθαι·
[ἀμφὶ δέ οἱ στεφάνους νεοθηλέας, ἄνθεα ποίης,
ἱμερτοὺς περίθηκε καρήατι Παλλὰς Ἀθήνη·]
ἀμφὶ δέ οἱ στεφάνην χρυσέην κεφαλῆφιν ἔθηκε,
τὴν αὐτὸς ποίησε περικλυτὸς Ἀμφιγυήεις
ἀσκήσας παλάμῃσι, χαριζόμενος Διὶ πατρί.
τῇ δ' ἔνι δαίδαλα πολλὰ τετεύχατο, θαῦμα ἰδέσθαι,
κνώδαλ᾽ ὅσ᾽ ἤπειρος δεινὰ τρέφει ἠδὲ θάλασσα·
τῶν ὅ γε πόλλ᾽ ἐνέθηκε, χάρις δ᾽ ἐπὶ πᾶσιν ἄητο,
θαυμάσια, ζωοῖσιν ἐοικότα φωνήεσσιν.

Grey-eyed goddess Athena dressed and adorned her
in a silver garment. Down from her head she held a
well-wrought veil with her hands, a wonder to behold.
[And around her head Pallas Athena put
lovely wreaths of fresh flowers.]
And around her head she put a wreath of gold
which the famed lame one made
with his hands, fashioning it for father Zeus.
In it were wrought many intricacies, a wonder to behold:
as many terrible creatures as the land and sea nourish.
Of these he incorporated many, and grace breathed all around them,
Wonders, like living, speaking creatures.
(Hesiod *Theogony* 573–84)

These are the adornments of the Woman in the *Theogony* version of the myth.[19] The Woman (nameless as she is in this version) has both a garland of flowers and a golden diadem. Jenny Strauss Clay writes that the combination, 'with its doubling of

---

[18] My argument here is expanded in Canevaro forthcoming a, in relation to discussions about Artificial Intelligence.

[19] This passage has been much discussed, particularly in terms of Hesiod's attitude to women, and I have weighed up Hesiod's narrative choices here and in the corresponding *Works and*

the natural and the artificial, of nature and culture, would seem the perfect emblem of the Woman/Wife herself and the marital institution she embodied'.[20] But what if we put one of the tenets of Material Feminism into practice, and resist the nature/culture dualism? The Woman embodies both nature and culture, a lively body yet emphatically a product of divine technology. Furthermore, in addition to garland and diadem, the *Theogony* Woman also has a veil. And it is in fact the three items, not just two, that blur into one another. All three are given by Athena (γλαυκῶπις Ἀθήνη, 573; παλλὰς Ἀθήνη, 577). Both flowers and gold are garlands (στεφάνους, 576; στεφάνην, 578). Both the veil and the decoration on the diadem are a wonder to behold (θαῦμα ἰδέσθαι, at the ends of lines 575 and 581). Both the veil and the decoration on the diadem are δαιδάλεος (καλύπτρην δαιδαλέην, 574–5; τῇ δ' ἔνι δαίδαλα πολλὰ τετεύχατο, 581), the clear link with our Theocritus passage. The presence of a third item muddies the posited dualism, and the interlinking of all three objects offers a much more integrated picture than the division between nature and culture will allow.

Pandora is made of earth and water (γαῖαν ὕδει φύρειν, *WD* 61). So too are we, according to the myths about Prometheus as creator of mankind.[21] The attributes she is given include speech, strength, skills, grace, a devious mind and a thievish heart – all very human characteristics. Amy Lather points to the problem here:

> Pandora's figuration in terms of the same substances and capacities that define humans raises a troubling question: exactly how human is Pandora? Conversely, are humans themselves examples of the kind of animatron embodied by Pandora: that is, a kind of 'black box' consisting of a physical body animated mysteriously from within?[22]

Is Pandora a person or a thing, a cyborg or a 'humanimal' – and what does that make us?[23] Our questions about Pandora's ontology create a disquieting feedback loop, leading us to question our own boundaries.

Days version in Canevaro 2015a. I do not wish to rehearse the full scholarly debate here, but rather offer a reading of the material narrative in this passage.

[20] Clay 2003: 120.

[21] The sources (Sappho, Aesop, Menander, Philemon, Aristophanes, Apollodorus, Callimachus, Aelian, Pausanias, Ovid, Horace, Propertius, Statius, Juvenal, Lucian, Hyginus, Oppian) are deftly collected and presented in Mayor 2018: 105–6.

[22] Lather 2021: 121.

[23] For the ideas of huma(n)chine and humanimal and their application to Pandora, see Canevaro forthcoming a and Chesi and Sclavi 2020.

In the *Theogony* passage, it is the diadem made by Hephaestus that takes centre stage in the description – and, more specifically, the terrible beasts of land and sea that are wrought on it. The figures are lifelike – even more so, it seems, than the (here unnamed) Woman herself. There is little attention given to her physical description in this version, and she stands mute before the gods. The creatures worked on the diadem, by contrast, are 'like living speaking beings' (ζωοῖσιν ἐοικότα φωνήεσσιν, 584) – they are 'like' the living (just as Pandora is 'like' a woman[24]), but with voice as an additional attribute. These creatures, a material representation of nonhumans, exhibit a vitality that seems to go beyond that of the created Woman. It is still tempered by being life*like*, keeping the ultimate agency with the gods – but the construction of the passage is such that the Woman is subordinated to her adornment, with nonhuman creatures in the emphatic position at the culmination of the description, highlighted as θαυμάσια, wonders. In a broader material reading, what becomes clear is that Pandora is one part of a constructed material entanglement, and she is not necessarily prioritised within it. Created in place of fire (ἀντὶ πυρός, 570); made from earth and wearing flowers; decorated by Athena just like her veil; made by Hephaestus just like her diadem; physically encircled by creatures of the land and the sea whose vitality eclipses her own.

This idea is supported by Brockliss's reading of Pandora in the *Works and Days*. With Brockliss we return to Pandora's creation from earth and water:

> Pandora's origins in earth and water undermine distinctions between her body and the natural environment. If listeners read the tale of Pandora as an indication of the origins of humanity in general ... such elements of the story suggest intersections between human bodies and their environments. On this reading earth and water do not merely surround us but also constitute us.[25]

This gives a material-ecocritical cast to the discussion, recognising in our material makeup an affinity between humans and the environment and dissolving the separated notion of 'nature'. Brockliss goes beyond the standard 'misogynistic' interpretations of, for example, Pandora's 'canine mind' (κύνεον νόον, *WD* 67), reading not a limited assimilation of *woman* and animal but rather a more generalising acknowledgement of the proximity between *human* and animal. He argues that the poem's

---

[24] One of the central phrases in discussions of Pandora's 'being' is παρθένῳ αἰδοίῃ ἴκελον, a *likeness* of a modest girl, which appears at both *Theogony* 572 and *Works and Days* 71. Similarly indeterminate is *WD* 63: παρθενικῆς καλὸν εἶδος ἐπήρατον, the fine lovely form of a maiden.

[25] Brockliss 2018: 10.

early audiences, familiar with the difficult environments of the poem, would have been sensitive to its dark-ecological implications. Rather than viewing the human/animal relations in a hierarchical, top-down manner, they might instead have seen Pandora as representing humanity in general, her 'canine mind' a suggestion of what *all* humans can be like. Brockliss argues that these receptive listeners might have interpreted Pandora's 'canine mind' as a pessimistic statement that equates human and animal psychology. And this is one of the key characteristics of Morton's dark-ecological aesthetic: dark-ecological art disrupts clear distinctions between the cognitive traits of humans and (other) animals. In sum, there is a pessimistic undertone to the assimilation of the first woman with the nonhuman, whether her vitality and agency is being eclipsed by material evocations of animal life, or her human psychology related to animal cognition. As Brockliss concludes, this is not 'a celebration of human and animal interconnectedness, but ... a challenge to the notion of human psychological exceptionalism and hence as a statement of an unfortunate fact about the world'.[26]

In tracing the Pandora episode between the *Theogony* and *Works and Days*, we are setting up an intertextual relationship between the two – something supported by, for instance, Jenny Strauss Clay's influential perspective on the poems as a 'diptych'.[27] In following the materiality of the episode, we are also utilising an intermedial approach, as set out in Chapter 1. To foreground some of the themes we have considered so far in this section, we might also venture into a transmedial exploration ('the appearance of a certain motif, aesthetic, or discourse across a variety of different media'[28]), following Pandora outside her texts. The key example of such an endeavour is Dora and Erwin Panofsky's 1956 book *Pandora's Box: The Changing Aspects of a Mythical Symbol*, which traces the myth's and specifically the jar's metamorphoses across time and across media (ending with an epilogue about 'Pandora on the stage'). As D. and E. Panofsky's study made eminently clear, and as we know from our own experiences, Pandora has indeed travelled in time, space and significance, moving between contexts and between media. The focus on the 'box' (that is, the evolution of the jar) is particularly important in terms of materiality, as it is this material catalyst, this material equivalent or correlative of Pandora herself, that has become synonymous with the story.[29]

---

[26] Brockliss 2018: 10.
[27] Clay 2003: 6.
[28] Rajewsky 2005: 46.
[29] See Canevaro forthcoming a for discussion of Pandora's jar in relation to Haraway's theory of the cyborg.

The 'dark-ecological' reading of the Pandora episode certainly looms large in the lines about the jar, as the human body intersects and overlaps with manmade material. Presumably an earthenware jar, the *pithos* is made from the same ingredients as Pandora; both contain evils (ills and diseases in the one case, lies and a thieving nature in the other); both jar and women are connected with livelihood, self-sufficiency and the threats posed to them.[30] There are many readings that give a particularly materialist inflection to this interpretation, likening Pandora's jar to the womb, her generative potential encapsulated in her agent object.[31] Once again, we can, with Brockliss, take this beyond the straightforward misogynistic reading of equating women with evils, and follow dark ecology in extrapolating a more overriding pessimism about the human condition:

> Jars are not only products of human manufacture but also in some sense expressions of human nature. Again, this assimilation of the human and the nonhuman would reflect an unfortunate fact about the human condition: the susceptibility of humans to hunger, and their need for food.[32]

Pandora and her jar are linked at the most fundamental level. The pessimistic interpretation of this is that the human body is hollow, hungry, needing to be filled. The Iron Age is epitomised by this material equivalence.

One contemporary example that showcases the pervasive and immersive nature of this story and its materiality is the 2014 piece *Root of Evil*, at Mosciano Sant'Angelo in Abruzzo, Italy, by street artist MP5 (Fig. 2.1).

---

[30] See Bevan 2018 for an historical/anthropological account of the role of the *pithos* in Mediterranean social complexity and landscape investment. Bevan draws on the story of Pandora's jar to think through the deeper consequences of container culture. 'For better or worse, Pandora's "hope" or "expectation" is this very forward-looking, speculative, acquisitive feature of container culture: the seed corn kept back or vintage unopened with all of their attendant best-laid plans or fears for the New Year. Indeed, at the heart of any kind of human response to long-term accumulation ... there is often an iconic artificial container, fashioned in impressive or even divine ways, but still full of human frailty and concentrated risk' (Bevan 2018: 13).

[31] See e.g. Zeitlin 1996: 64–5. Zeitlin notes in support of this argument that 'later medical and philosophical texts associate and even correlate the womb with a container or jar. Throughout the Hippocratic corpus and the works of later, more sophisticated anatomists, the woman's uterus is likened to an upside-down jar'.

[32] Brockliss 2018: 10.

Fig. 2.1 'Root of Evil', mural by street artist MP5, Mosciano Sant' Angelo, Abruzzo, Italy. Photo credit: MP5

This is a large-scale, black-and-white painting of Pandora on the side of a building. The artist puts Pandora in the public eye – and through the large scale and strategic placement, draws us as passers-by into her all-encompassing story. This is porosity in action. Her clothing flows over the pavement, allowing us to walk through her, with her. Here the jar-turned-box has merged with a window, as the word is reconnected with the world and the story integrates its material environs. That the container coalesces with a feature of a house neatly encapsulates many elements of the archaic iterations of the Pandora story: from *elpis*' 'unbreakable dwelling place', to the paradoxical domestic ramifications of the first woman's creation (the *kalon kakon*; the male dilemma). That Pandora is depicted on a house is similarly significant. She is aligned with the house, yet it is notable that she is portrayed on its *outside*, visible and prominent. Her agency is evident, as she is in control of the environs, enacting her agency through materiality. Yet the questions that have surrounded her agency since Hesiod's poetry persist. In the *Works and Days*, is the unleashing of evil Zeus' fault for sending the jar, Epimetheus' fault for receiving it, Pandora's fault for opening it, the gods' fault for creating Pandora (complete with cunning) or Prometheus' fault for stealing fire in the first place? And in Abruzzo, is it Pandora who opens the window – or an unseen and unknown occupant of the building? Is our role only to walk through Pandora's story – or is it to participate in it, become another of the myth's disputed agents, share in the blame? And by extension, what does it mean for someone to be in the house? Are we good or evil? Are we Hope? The figure of Hope poses a further question, this time about the durability of the story in this form. Street art is often noted for its immediacy, but also for its ephemerality. Will the painting weather, degrade, gradually disappear? The medium has a vibrancy to it, but like anything vital it is also at the mercy of time. In this contemporary piece we are given a window onto an intertextual, intermedial and transmedial story that has been transmitted through a transmuted object across millennia – and that continues to pose questions, through materiality and indeed *about* materiality.

But to return to *Idyll* 1. The basics of Theocritus' allusion are that τί θεῶν δαίδαλμα τέτυκται at *Idyll* 1.32 points us towards the foregrounded craftsmanship of ekphrasis and, in the creation of woman, refers us to Pandora. The two elements come together most notably in the ekphrastic description of the decorated diadem forged by Hephaestus and worn by the first Woman in Hesiod's *Theogony*. In his discussion of Achilles' shield, Bill Brown notes that such wonders of the artist's craft 'would seem to insist … on a kind of indeterminate ontology, in which the being of the object world cannot so readily be distinguished from the being of animals, say, or the being we call human being'.[33] Brown complains:

---

[33] Brown 2015: 2.

For all the centuries of commentary on the Shield, such a speculation has hardly been broached. The ontological ambiguity has been elided in behalf of rhetorical analysis, above all the analysis of ekphrasis, specified most clearly as '*the verbal representation of visual representation*.' Achilles' Shield has served as the archetypal instance of ekphrastic poetry. In that service animate matter has been fettered into immobility, fixed between the pictorial and the verbal, the image and the word.[34]

And further: 'The commanding role that the Shield has played in the history of modern ekphrastic criticism has all but denied it any role in the history of animate matter.' By avoiding here an explicit discussion of ekphrasis (what it is; what it does; the wealth of scholarship on it), I attempt to read these passages together in a different, exploratory way. What happens when, rather than immediately pigeonholing a rhetorical phenomenon, we allow the described elements their full vitality, and let them guide our reading? Both the shield and the cup present people. Those people may not be characters in the main narrative – but as the above discussion has shown, the woman on Thyrsis' cup is arguably just as animate as myth's first Woman: if not, in fact, even more so (she is not sidelined to her adornments, but rather is shown in control of her vignette). Brown asks: 'What if Homer's point is instead to undermine the opposition between the organic and inorganic, the vibrant and the inert?'[35] From a dualistic perspective we might expect the narrative of the woman in *Idyll* 1 to be bounded by the cup; confined and curtailed by it. But as we have seen, already this boundary is problematic. Where exactly is she, in relation to the cup, in relation to the foliage? Where is she, in terms of creation and generation? A daughter of Pandora because she is a woman, or a successor to her because she is a created object? Where is she in relation to her garments? The fine line between (wo)man and material is manifest in ἀσκητά, which Gow notes 'is used elsewhere of the garment (e.g. 24.140) or the wool (18.32n.), rather than the wearer' – she might not be subordinated to

---

[34] Though scholarship on ekphrasis has progressed substantially since its publication, Gow's commentary is emblematic of this reductive approach: 'T. is interpreting rather than describing, since a work of art can only suggest, not depict, successive action on the part of the figures.'

[35] Brown 2015: 3. He goes on to write: 'Or, rather: what if that point is strikingly beside the point, precisely because the poem does not acknowledge our more modern convictions about the difference between the animate and inanimate, subject and object, persons and things?' In Canevaro 2018b: 227 I discussed this statement, arguing: 'Though boundaries blur, networks of agency form, and particular objects such as the shield call certain dichotomies into question, it is not the case that Homer does not display an awareness of those dichotomies.' I might offer a similar conclusion in relation to Theocritus – but I want to let the monism play out for now.

her clothing, but in a way, she is assimilated to it. She is δαίδαλμα, whereas in the *Theogony* scene the *daidal-* words are used to describe the veil and diadem. Finally, where is she in her story? She has a man on each side, arguing over her, but she seems to control the scene, turning to each suitor, smiling at both but persuaded by neither. It is to her story that I now turn.

To understand the materiality of this scene, we need to take a step back and look again at the cup as object, its physical properties. We also need to consider the *non*-physicality of it as an object imagined for and by literature. First, why a cup, and what difference does it make to our reading that it is a cup? What difference does it make to our reading of this first scene in particular? This is potentially a tactile object, an object that is designed to be handled, to fit into a human hand.[36] It is therefore of a certain size, meaning that the scenes are depicted in miniature. Much like the shield of Achilles, we are to imagine a lot going on in a relatively small space. This crowding in of figures and agents on an object meant to be held has an urgency and immediacy to it, particularly in the very dynamic first scene. It is also an object meant to be raised to the lips, which adds a further level of potential sensory engagement and has implications for our position in the flirtation of the initial scene (the handler of the cup is somehow more than a spectator of this scene). The lack of boundaries and framing to the cup is connected with its shape, its roundedness. Again, like the shield, this roundedness complicates our reading of the object, as it becomes frameless and endless and urges the viewer to keep turning the object or to keep moving round it, twisting just like the tendrils. We can't see it from all sides at once. But of course, we can't actually see it at all. The poet can't *describe* it all at once. It is an entirely literary object, evoked solely through language. And there is a layering effect to the literary and the material here, as the men try to convince the woman with flyting words – words we cannot read or hear and which we can only 'see' through the poet's description. Yet the woman is unaffected by what is said – she is unconvinced by her two wooers. Despite the tactile object on which she is depicted, she remains untouched: the unattainable woman. This in its way perfectly encapsulates the literary object which is beyond our touch – and, more extensively, it is the perfect metaphor for the 'withdrawn' object, the unreachability of the object that is at the centre of Object-Oriented Ontology.

Hunter comments on the two men arguing their case: 'Other Theocritean lovers do not, however, "contest" before their rivals, cf. Idylls 3, 10, 11: such a stylised and

---

[36] I say 'potentially' because – see the discussion of *Idyll* 1.59–60 in Chapter 4 (p. 154) – the cup has not yet touched the goatherd's lips. See too the discussion of the silver-gilt Theocritus cup in Chapter 5 (pp. 195–201).

controlled display is possible only in the freezing grip of pictorial art.'[37] This is an interesting statement in the context of this chapter, as it foregrounds the materiality of the cup. Hunter has summarised the relationship between the shield of Achilles and the cup of Thyrsis, picking up on the legal *neikos* of the shield recast as a 'fruitless erotic quest', the diction marking the '"epic" origin of the scene' (ἔπος in the bucolic *Idylls* only here).[38] He draws in the bucolic *agon*, but ultimately attributes the scene to a reworking of Homer facilitated by the material presence of the cup. This could not happen, he suggests, with characters in the main narrative: it can only occur within a captured scene, a frozen moment made material. This is a way of tracing the passage's ekphrastic lineage and paying attention not only to the rhetorical device but also to the force exerted by its materiality. It makes a difference, Hunter suggests, that these characters are part of a cup, part of an artwork – they can do something that other characters could not. What is it that is attributed to these frozen characters? 'A stylised and controlled display'. Indeed, what is particularly striking about the vignette is how orderly it is. The woman with a man at each side, turning her smiling attention first to one, then the other. It is almost a dance. A dance whose rhythm slows at line 38, δηθὰ κυλοιδιόωντες ἐτώσια μοχθίζοντι, the spondaic rhythm mimetic of the men's failed wooing.[39] The men are part of the woman's story, which is part of the cup, which is part of the poem – and the distinctive use of the metre here draws the assemblage together, as form and content converge.

Line 38 navigates a delicate balance, with actions attributed to the carved characters (the men and their persuasive speeches), yet ultimately those actions prove fruitless in the face of abject materiality (the unresponsive statue). It plays with what is possible through ekphrastic description. Hunter writes of this line: 'They "labour in vain" because, as Σ observes, "who could persuade a statue?" As in 35, the "naïve" interplay between the narrative and the carving explores the principles of ecphrastic description.' But we might probe the scholiast's statement further. What is the scholiast actually suggesting? That the woman taunts the men with her lifelike appearance – all the while being an inanimate and unresponsive statue – but that the men are in a position to persuade? That they are animate though she is not? There is an ostensible slippage here between a vital and non-vital reading, with a

---

[37] Hunter 1999 *ad loc.*

[38] Payne (2001: 269) points out the ambiguity here, noting that 'νεικείουσ' ἐπέεσσι sounds like a familiar formula, but in Homer verb and noun are accompanied by an adjective that makes clear exactly how the speaker is addressing his interlocutor. Without qualification it is unclear whether the men are chiding, quarreling, or competing, just as the absence of pronouns means that we cannot tell whether their words are directed at each other or the woman.'

[39] Hunter 1999 *ad loc.*

gendered cast to it. The men are allowed the full degree of agency bestowed upon them by the ekphrastic description – but the woman is left in the middle ground between person and thing, and in that limbo loses her agency. The control of the scene is nevertheless hers – she blocks the suitors' advances – but through the limits imposed by materiality, rather than through human agency. This reading may stem purely from a reader-response position: the scholiast puts himself in the men's shoes. It might stem from the greater physical detail given of the men: they have 'fine heads of hair', and 'eyes dark-rimmed from love', while all we know of the woman's physical appearance is that she wears a cloak and headband, and that she smiles. But I would suggest that the portrayal of the woman is in fact the more complex. The men are described at one level – they have the motivator of love, and are worn out by it. The woman, on the other hand, is smiling at her suitors – but in her thoughts she is not convinced (τὰ δ' οὐ φρενὸς ἅπτεται αὐτᾶς). We might read this 'conflict' along the lines of the scholiast's argument: she cannot be persuaded in her thoughts, because as a statue she doesn't have any (Payne 2001: 269 conjectures that this line 'suggests a more than human unconcern' – like a statue, or like a god?). We might, on the other hand, see in her an agency that encompasses not only control but also movement, emotion, cognition. She is no more statue than are the men, and though the ekphrastic description plays with our expectations of agency, it does not close down a fully vital-materialist reading.

To bring this back more concretely to the text, let's return to the δαίδαλμα of line 32. Payne fleshes out the narrative here:

> Since this is the first extant occurrence of δαίδαλμα we may wonder what he means by it. The stem might lead one to suppose that the word is simply a metrical alternative to δαίδαλον. The scholia to verse 38 ἐτώσια μοχθίζοντι, 'they labor in vain' – appear to look to the suffix -ma, however, for they ask: τίς γὰρ ἂν ἄγαλμα πεῖσαι δυνήσεται; 'for how could anyone persuade a statue?' So δαίδαλμα presents us with a choice: is the woman 'a fabrication of the gods,' or is she, more concretely, 'a statue of the gods'?[40]

In this way, Payne offers another rationale behind the scholiast's question. He posits that the scholiast may have been influenced by ἀσκητὰ in the following line, but goes on to show that this fits just as well with the artfully wrought headband or indeed cup in general as it does with a statue. He concludes that 'the scholiast's question seems to mark a rather crude attempt to get a definite picture from the goatherd's indefinite words'. The poem leaves open interpretations that the scholiast closes down.

---

[40] Payne 2001: 265.

I noted above that in Theocritus' *Idyll* it is the woman who is δαίδαλμα, whereas in the *Theogony* passage the *daidal-* field is applied to the veil and diadem. Payne critiques Hunter's assertion that 'δαίδαλμα belongs to the standard language of ecphrasis', noting that in the passages he cites (*Iliad* 18.482 – the shield of Achilles; *Argonautica* 1.729 – the cloak of Jason; and *Europa* 43 – the basket of Europa),

> δαίδαλα is qualified by πολλά; it occurs at the beginning of the ecphrasis, and summarizes the images which will be described individually. In *Idyll* 1, by contrast, the word is used to mark out a single figure on the bowl. It separates the woman from her companions, and suggests that she is somehow more artificial than the other images around her.[41]

He then goes on to draw the parallel with Pandora, and notes the use of δαίδαλα πολλά at *Theogony* 581. However, as we noted earlier, there is also the internal parallel between the veil and diadem within the *Theogony* passage (καλύπτρην δαιδαλέην, 574–5; τῇ δ' ἔνι δαίδαλα πολλὰ τετεύχατο, 581). The duplication of *daidal-* words here complicates the picture, as it is in fact not the case that the *Theogony* passage has an all-encompassing ekphrastic gesture in δαίδαλα πολλά against which the individualism of *Idyll* 1 can be set, but rather that the *Theogony*, just like *Idyll* 1, picks out examples of the well wrought. And these *Theogony* examples, as we have seen, are the things that are foregrounded over and above the human. The woman in *Idyll* 1 is, then, 'separated' from her companions, picked out, highlighted – but is she necessarily the *more* artificial? The opposite argument might also be made: that, as our analysis of the diadem suggested, the better wrought the thing is, the more vitality it displays, whether or not it is anthropomorphic. The woman of *Idyll* 1 is like Pandora – some say she *is* Pandora (τινὲς τὴν Πανδώραν φασί, Schol.1.32) – but she is also like the diadem. She is created; she is wrought; she is artificial – but equally, she is animated, agentic, vital. As nature and culture blur, so do life and artifice, person and thing.

Payne writes: 'The goatherd is making a story out of a picture; he introduces time into the visual representation'.[42] He cites Heffernan, *Museum of Words*, who writes of a 'narrative response to pictorial stasis'[43] – cited too by Bill Brown in his analysis of the shield of Achilles. As Brown sees it, the shield has served to stage the distinction between the visual and the verbal, the spatial and the temporal, stasis and kinesis, pictures and stories. He notes that readers have retained an emphasis on narrative,

---

[41] Ibid. pp. 266–7.
[42] Ibid. p. 268.
[43] Heffernan 1993: 4–5.

and that in the process somehow the object as object has been elided. The story of the shield is told as 'the translation of image into story':[44] the visual element is an image (not an object), sometimes like a canvas.[45] He argues further:

> Even efforts to argue beyond such an understanding of ekphrasis by regarding the Shield as an 'imagetext' do not bring the represented object – as object – into focus: Homer's whole point seems to be to undermine the oppositions of movement and stasis, narrative action and descriptive scene, and the false identifications of medium with message. But what if Homer's whole point, undermining the opposition of movement and stasis, has nothing to do with literary modes (description and narration), and less to do with linguistic and pictorial media than with the medium of metal?[46]

And this proceeds to the question cited earlier: 'What if Homer's point is instead to undermine the opposition between the organic and inorganic, the vibrant and the inert?' Brown shifts our attention to other dualities: those which go beyond literary tropes and instead get to the root of our thinking about our place in the world. He suggests that we focus not on literary modes or rhetorical forms, but on 'what literature and the visual and plastic arts have been trying to teach us about our everyday object world'.[47] This approach 'repeatedly points to the uncanniness of the ordinary, the oscillations between the animate and inanimate, for instance, which Homer renders extraordinary'.[48] In the case of the shield, Brown brings out the ordinary lives embedded in this extraordinary object of war (a Marxist-inflected reading, the labour concealed by the commodity). He connects this with Latour's notions of assemblage and quasi-objects, his exposing of the human drama within the nonhuman – the agency distributed among multiple actants, with weaponry a particularly rich site of examples.

The scenes depicted on Achilles' shield, though motionless in their object state, tell tales of movement. This may surprise the modern reader: as Ruth Webb notes, 'description itself is popularly conceived as treating a particular class of

---

[44] Becker 1995: 21.
[45] Brown 2015: 3n9 notes: 'Elsewhere, with regard to the *Iliad*, the elision of the object qua object can be gleaned quickly from an uncertainty that approximates an uncertainty that concerns me here: "One is not sure whether the pictures on the shield are static or alive," Cedric Whitman writes, as though the shield were canvas. *Homer and the Homeric Tradition* (Cambridge, MA: Harvard University Press, 1958), 205.'
[46] Brown 2015: 3, quoting Mitchell 1994: 178.
[47] Brown 2015: 5.
[48] Ibid. p. 5.

referent: static objects or persons assimilated to static objects'.[49] But as Webb goes on to explain, 'the strict division between narration and description and the association of description with static, non-human or dehumanized referents are absent from the ancient accounts. Instead we find a marked continuity between ekphrasis and narration'. To reiterate Brown's claim, the shield 'enacts a drama of animate matter'. Weddings, festivals, dances, quarrels, battles, farming – the shield is a hive of frenetic activity. Simile embeds yet more movement in the description when the dancers are compared with a potter at his wheel. As Alex Purves notes, 'the scenes, although only representations, move through time and space as if they were animated by living creatures'.[50] Full of motion too is the context which frames the description, that of Hephaestus' bustling workshop with its golden attendants that already hint at the god's animating abilities. The importance of the creative context of a literary object is shown in Webb's 2018 article on Odysseus' bed, which she casts as an *ekphrasis tropou*: a detailed narrative of making rather than a description of an object. This discussion highlights the convergence of description and narrative in a rather different way, as people, things and story are triangulated not within the description of the object as object but in the presentation of its coming into being. It is of particular relevance to the current discussion that 'if the *matter* is identified very precisely, and some parts named, the overall *form* of the bed remains unclear, rendering the object itself difficult to conceive'.[51] The focus of the ekphrasis in *Odyssey* 23 (183–204) is not on the finished product but on the process, with the result that 'the bed is distinguished by the difficulty the reader has in conceiving of it as a finished object and by the need to fill in the gaps and to propose means of articulating the discrete elements mentioned by Odysseus'.[52]

Bill Brown bemoans the lack of interest from Homeric scholarship in the shield *as* shield – and he is right, given the detail in which its finished state is described. It is worth noting, however, that this does not pertain to all Homeric objects, even those most essential to the plotline. As Webb shows, in the case of Odysseus' bed, we would actually do well *not* to focus on the object as object – and, rather, we would be following Homer's cue were we to take more interest in both the material and the rhetorical process here. After all, 'Both audiences, internal and external, are called upon to imagine'[53] – for the external audience, in particular, there is no object pre-existing the description, but only the words of the poem. I raise this example mainly to set it

---

[49] Webb 2009: 8.
[50] Purves 2010: 46.
[51] Webb 2018: 71.
[52] Ibid. p. 72.
[53] Ibid. p. 67.

in contrast with the shield and, to an even greater extent, with the cup. The shield is part of Hephaestus' workshop, part of a process, with a big narrative investment in its teleology – and yet it is ultimately the finished product that is foregrounded, with its internal narrative charge.[54] The cup, at the other end of the spectrum, does retain its creative processes – but it quickly moves beyond these, and becomes much more a matter of its finished form, its scenes, its characters (though, to complicate this further, the final scene in particular is trained on process – see Chapter 4, pp. 146–55).

We need to go beyond the interpretation that 'the goatherd is making a story out of a picture'. This is not a picture. It is a thing. By this I mean that there is more to the scene than the pictorial: there is also the material. The ambiguous spatial relationship between scene and frame; the disputed placement of the scene on the cup; the properties of the material from which it is made; even the portable, tactile nature of the object itself – all of these factors need to be considered together, in one material narrative. They also need to be considered alongside their verbal representation, in a material-discursive narrative. In this material-ecocritical reading, the goatherd is not making a story out of a picture, a human agent imposing a narrative on an inanimate object, bestowing upon it a semblance of vitality. Instead, the goatherd, the cup, the woman are all actants: all are animate. Together, they participate in an assemblage that makes up the poem's descriptive and narrative elements, their agency overlapping, blurring ontological just as much as rhetorical dichotomies. It is arguably in such radical rethinking of entrenched dualisms, in rhetorical theory as in everyday thought, that we can open up new readings of classical texts – and, in the process, allow underprivileged actants (women and the nonhuman) more agency than anthropocentric readings permit. Theocritus is imagining the goatherd describing (/imagining) a decorated cup. But the cup exerts its own force, as the characters are so lifelike that they have an impact on the way in which they are described.

It is from the scenes and the characters, from the material object, that this book takes its structure. This first scene, of the woman at the centre of the male gaze yet looking those men over in turn, of a female body that is a represented actant,

---

[54] Squire (2013: 160–1) explores this temporal paradox, emphasising the coexistence of process and finished product in the description of the shield. He writes: 'our understanding of the Homeric shield oscillates between infinite process and finite result. If the passage is structured around continuous action (Hephaestus in the act of making the shield), our view of it is also premised on the idea that the shield comprises a finished product (we look upon an already accomplished object). There is a paradox here in that the completed object endlessly defers its own completion. True, we hear how Hephaestus "fashioned", "forged" and "made" the shield, a process unambiguously situated in the past. Look at the resulting scenes, however, and we find them projected into a sort of multitemporal limbo, one which encompasses past, present and future.'

lends itself to an analysis drawing on the approaches of the Material Feminisms. These approaches urge us to revisit the material/discursive dichotomy, breaking it down yet retaining both elements, without privileging either. In this section I have discussed key ekphrastic descriptions of women and/as objects, but have given attention to the force exerted by materiality as well as to the rhetorical device. In reading across a full material-discursive narrative, allowing both humans and nonhumans their agency and animacy, and exploring their entanglements and networks, we have taken a fresh look at some canonical passages and a new angle on much-rehearsed interpretive questions. Though we have been concerned with a full network of actants, we took our cue from one: the woman. It is to Theocritus' other women that I now turn, hoping to extend this material-discursive analysis further. This is a strand of this book's persistent paradigm of intertextuality through objects. In terms of its subject, it centres on the female; in terms of approach, it continues to draw on Material Feminism. The two are, of course, organically linked: but it is important to note that Material Feminism is not just 'about women'.

Idyll 2: Reading Bodies

Ἴυγξ, ἕλκε τὺ τῆνον ἐμὸν ποτὶ δῶμα τὸν ἄνδρα.

Magic wheel, draw that man to my house.

Repeated ten times, this is the refrain that structures the first half of Theocritus' second *Idyll*. The incantation speaks of and to the *iunx*: a bird and a mating cry, a love charm and an emotion. This section, too, takes its structure from the *iunx*, reading its story across the human and animal worlds, as animate creature and inanimate yet powerful object, as instigator of a bodily narrative of desire.

According to mythology, Iunx was the daughter of either Peitho or Echo. She used magic to seduce Zeus, either for Io or for herself. As punishment, Hera turned her into a bird – the *iunx*, or wryneck.[55] The bird was then used as part of a love charm: a spoked wheel with an *iunx* fastened to it (whether the whole bird or its entrails), spun to draw in a love object. This charm is given an aetion story (πρῶτον ἀνθρώποισι) by Pindar in *Pythian* 4, when he describes how Aphrodite bound the wryneck to a wheel and taught Jason how to use it:

---

[55] Callimachus fr. 685 Pf. Noted by the scholiast *ad* Theocritus 2.17. For detailed discussion of the *iunx* in its various manifestations, see Detienne 1972: 159–72 and Segal 1973. There are some versions of the myth that identify Pan as Iunx's mother – on Pan and the *syrinx*, see further Chapter 5 (pp. 186–95).

πότνια δ' ὀξυτάτων βελέων
ποικίλαν ἴυγγα τετράκναμον Οὐλυμπόθεν
ἐν ἀλύτῳ ζεύξαισα κύκλῳ
μαινάδ' ὄρνιν Κυπρογένεια φέρεν
πρῶτον ἀνθρώποισι λιτάς τ' ἐπαοιδὰς
ἐκδιδάσκησεν σοφὸν Αἰσονίδαν,
ὄφρα Μηδείας τοκέων ἀφέλοιτ' αἰδῶ, ποθεινὰ δ' Ἑλλὰς αὐτάν
ἐν φρασὶ καιομέναν δονέοι μάστιγι Πειθοῦς.

The Cyprian-born queen of sharpest arrows
bound the dappled wryneck to the four spokes
of the inescapable wheel
and brought from Olympus that bird of madness
for the first time for men, and she taught
the son of Aeson to be skillful in prayers and charms,
so that he might take away Medea's respect
for her parents, and so that desire for Hellas might set
her mind afire and drive her with the whip[56] of Persuasion.
(Pindar *Pythian* 4.213–19[57])

The first thing to note, particularly relevant to our mapping of a material landscape that can be read into and outside of ancient poetry, is that aetia by and large give explanations about the origins of institutions and practices that exist in the time of the author. The story is cast into mythical time, but the aetiological formulation suggests that it is intended to underpin a current practice, a contemporary object. Though this practice may seem alien to us, such may not have been its effect on Pindar's audience.[58] As Christopher Faraone argues, 'it would seem that Pindar uses this myth about Aphrodite and the *iunx* spell in part to explain why men in his own day use *iunx* spells to drive women from their homes'.[59] And yet, in his article

---

[56] On the *mastix* of Peitho, see Johnston 1995: 190–1. She argues that the *mastix* in this context is the cord that works the *iunx*, putting Peitho in control of the *iunx*. This has ramifications for our consideration of 'persuasive analogy' – persuasion is, according to poetry and mythology, already linked with this tool of magic.

[57] For discussion of Pindar's *iunx*, see Johnson 1995; for an interpretation coloured by New Materialism and focusing on *poikilia* (the ποικίλαν ἴυγγα here), see Lather 2021: 155–6.

[58] As a parallel for this, see Petrovic and Petrovic 2022: a detailed reading of Hesiod's *Works and Days* lines 724–60 which shows how the seemingly opaque and obscure ritual precepts given there fit with evidence we have of Greek ritual norms.

[59] Faraone 1999: 58.

'Desperate Simaetha' Michael Lambert shows that the equation between literary representation and ritual practice is not as easy as we might think. He questions the real-world mapping of the ritual practices described in Theocritus *Idyll* 2, pulling apart the parallels from the magical papyri drawn by Gow and noting in conclusion: 'Noticeable is Gow's inability to find parallels in the papyri for the use of the ἴυγξ, the wheel which forms the crux of Simaetha's magic ritual and which has a distinguished literary and artistic pedigree.'[60] Is Pindar's, then, an aetion that points us to the real world, only to send us back again empty handed?[61] This would create a feedback loop, centring on the object. The story revolves around the *iunx* – which is simultaneously generated by the story. The aetiological colouring of the passage directs us to a time, a place, a reality – but in its potential misdirection, it may well send us circling back to the poem.

The *iunx* is a 'bird of madness' (μαινάδ' ὄρνιν). *Iunx* can also refer to the aphrodisiac cry or scent of mating animals,[62] and shifting from the animal to the human sphere, we see it used figuratively to mean 'desire' or 'longing'.[63] The semantic field encompasses the 'madness' of animal desire, and transfers this to human interactions and human emotions. The *iunx* might take away Medea's *aidos* and inflame her. It is assumed that the actual bird had disappeared from the wheel by Theocritus' day. But even if the body of a bird is not affixed to Simaetha's charm, the name and purpose persist – as do the combustive connotations, and a reference to the mythological aetion. Theocritus' Simaetha uses fire metaphors to describe her emotions,[64] and we might observe that the correlation between woman and fire in fact stretches back even beyond Pindar, to Hesiod, in whose *Works and Days* Pandora is given in exchange for fire (*WD* 57); in midsummer the heat which scorches men's heads only makes women more lustful (*WD* 586); and a bad wife burns her man without a brand (*WD* 705). As for the aetion, we might note with Segal that Simaetha's first reference

---

[60] Lambert 2002: 79.
[61] Johnston (1995: 180) notes that 'the Pindaric passage stands almost alone in describing an *iynx*-bird as being yoked to a wheel. Other than this passage, I know of only three, late descriptions of the magical wheel that mention a bird being attached (Σ P. 4.381a, Σ Theocr. 2.17 and Suda s.v. *iynx*), all of which possibly drew on the famous Pindaric passage itself. I know of no artistic representation of the wheel that shows a bird attached … we need not suppose that the bird was ever attached to the wheel outside of Pindar's imagination.'
[62] Segal 1973: 35. See Aelian *Nat. An.* 15.19.
[63] Pindar *Nemean* 4.35, Aeschylus *Persians* 989, Aristophanes *Lysistrata* 110.
[64] Segal 1973: 36. He adds the note: 'The figurative use of fire in the *Idyll* occurs in lines 29, 40, 82, 131, 133–4; and actual fire occurs in lines 18–26 and 28. Cf. also 85 and 141, where heat is involved'.

to the *iunx* in line 17 is immediately preceded by an allusion to Medea in line 16.[65] Not only does the fire imagery unify a narrative of female desire, but the charm creates a community of sorceresses across mythological and literary time.[66] Simaetha explicitly draws on that inherited power, asking Hecate:

φάρμακα ταῦτ' ἔρδοισα χερείονα μήτε τι Κίρκας
μήτε τι Μηδείας μήτε ξανθᾶς Περιμήδας.

make these drugs no less powerful than those of Circe
or Medea or fair-haired Perimede.
(*Idyll* 2.15–16)

In the Pindar passage, the *iunx* is to be used by Jason as protagonist, on Medea as love object. Simaetha inherits this network but ostensibly recalibrates it, comparing the power of her *pharmaka* and other magical accoutrements with those of Medea. This is of course justified by other intertexts, other objects: Medea's intervention in book 4 of Apollonius' *Argonautica* and her treatment of Glauke's dress in Euripides' play are the obvious points of reference. And yet, to what extent is this renegotiation of the aetiological network actually successful? In the end, what we take from *Idyll* 2 is that the spell doesn't work. Simaetha doesn't manage to take control, to draw Delphis in.[67] Simaetha tries to subvert the Pindaric aetion, putting Medea, and herself too, in the position of power over a male love object – but ultimately, she is proven powerless. Indeed, the origin story did not bode well in the first place, targeted as it is at the ill-fated love of Jason and Medea. Whichever side of the network Simaetha fell on, it was never going to end well.[68]

To this list of unstable love affairs, Segal adds that of Circe and Odysseus.[69] Segal notes that 'in evoking these figures [Circe, Medea, Perimede] just when she

---

[65] As Segal explores, the network linked by the *iunx* is pervaded by 'unhappy, unstable unions': the mating call suggests 'the insistent, repetitive circularity of unsatisfied desire'; its figurative uses stand 'in contexts of sudden, violent love which offers no continuity' (Segal 1973: 36).

[66] We might find a parallel to this in the tapestries of *Idyll* 15, which bring together Theocritean and Homeric women through materiality – see Chapter 2 (pp. 81–90).

[67] Segal 1973: 35.

[68] As Segal concludes, the *iunx* appears 'as a symbol of unstable, illegitimate, non-durable love' (ibid. p. 41).

[69] There are further connections with Odysseus in this *Idyll*. In an article of 1984, Segal shows that Theocritus combines a literary echo of Sappho (fr. 31) with one of Homer: 'The description of Delphis ἐπὶ χθονὸς ὄμματα πάξας in 112 ("fixing fast his eyes on

sets in motion the magic that is supposed to win back her own beloved, Simaetha is unknowingly confirming her own position among unhappy lovers, victims or agents of seduction and inconstancy'.[70] Rather than focusing on the instability and inconstancy, however, I would turn our attention to the concrete, the material: the physical objects that draw these women together. Simaetha and Medea are linked through Pindar and the *iunx*, and through Euripides and *pharmaka*. Circe does not obviously participate in the *iunx* connection, but through Homer she is known for her drugs – and drugs that, in turn, have a functional connection with the love charm of Pindar's Aphrodite. According to Pindar, the *iunx* is to take away Medea's respect for her parents, her sense of shame and proper behaviour. This lowering of inhibitions is what will allow Medea to leave her home and follow Jason. Similarly, Homer's 'Circe of many drugs' (Κίρκης πολυφαρμάκου, *Od.* 10.276: an epithet used also of Medea in Apollonius' *Argonautica*) uses baneful drugs, φάρμακα λύγρα, to make men forget their fatherland (ἵνα πάγχυ λαθοίατο πατρίδος αἴης, *Od.* 10.236). In taking away her guests' memory, Circe subverts the mechanism of *xenia*, which relies on a reciprocal relationship (remembering past kindnesses in future interactions), and she subverts one of the key roles of women in Homer: that of *preserving* memory.[71] By making her guests forget, she severs their ties to their homeland and their past, altering their emotional entanglements and consequently their motivations and intentions, just as the Pindaric *iunx* is to affect Medea. Helen uses *pharmaka* for a similar purpose in *Odyssey* 4.219–30: her drug banishes pain, allays anger and makes one forget all evils – to such an extent that the victim would not react to the death of a loved one. Again, emotional ties are broken, the desire for homecoming dulled.

But what of Simaetha? She wants her *pharmaka* to control emotion, just like Homer's Circe and Helen (and Pindar's Jason). She wants to bring Delphis to her, just as Circe wants to entrap Odysseus – but as with the Medea connection, ultimately this parallel points towards failure, as Odysseus does eventually leave Circe. And to maintain our material focus, we might note the importance of *pharmaka* on both sides in this Homeric episode. Hermes gives Odysseus a 'good drug' (φάρμακον ἐσθλόν, *Od.* 10.287) to counteract Circe's baneful drugs, and it is by fighting *pharmaka* with *pharmaka* that Odysseus will regain his freedom.

---

the ground") recalls Homer's wily speaker and cunning persuader [Odysseus] as he is described admiringly by the Trojan Antenor in the Teichoskopia (*Iliad* 3.216–19)' (203); 'to the reader familiar with Homer the gesture ... connotes the deceptive appearances and the premeditation and skill of Odyssean craft' (204).

[70] Segal 1973: 37.
[71] See Canevaro 2018b: 172–81.

I would like to focus in even further now, moving from the mythological to the material, and return to our core object: the *iunx*.[72] Whether or not there was ever a real object that had a bird affixed to a wheel, the proximity of object to bird is important to note. As Sarah Iles Johnston puts it, 'it is difficult to be certain whether an author is referring to the bird or to the wheel'[73] – there is a conflation, an overlap, between these different types of material agent. The particular quality of the wryneck from which the love charm gets its name is its ability to turn its long neck at uncanny angles, writhing its head in a serpentine way.[74] The turning wheel is thus augmented by its passenger (an augmentation retained or generated *in absentia*, through the name): as Tavenner puts it, 'Add … the bird which rotates its head as though pulling something toward itself, and you have still another cumulative power'.[75] Even without the actual bird present, the name transmits that idea of turning – turning someone's head, turning someone's heart. It is an object that takes its power from a complex combination of its mythological aetia, its supposed (grisly) construction, and its intricate fit of form to purpose. As Gow *ad* 17–63 points out, in this section of *Idyll* 2 'the magic acts are almost all of the "sympathetic" kind in which the object to be affected is represented by a symbol' – so Simaetha melts wax to melt Delphis' heart (28–9), or turns the rhombus to make Delphis turn to and fro at her door (30–1).[76] But from the perspective of material agency we can see that there is more to this than symbolism and representation – and, moreover, that what is going on here is central to a material-ecocritical reading of Theocritus.

To cast magical acts of this 'sympathetic' sort as symbolic seems to me to underestimate their believed efficacy, their purported power.[77] We might instead use

---

[72] Studies of this object tend to focus on its rhetorical function – see e.g. Johnston 1995 and the argument that 'Pindar places an *iynx* in Jason's hands as part of an extensive exploration of the effects of voice – human and divine – that he pursues throughout the ode, an exploration that can be understood as one of the earliest manifestations of the fifth century's deep concern with the power of speech to effect change' (178).

[73] Johnston 1995: 183.

[74] Johnston (1995: 182) argues that the salient quality is rather the *iunx*'s voice.

[75] Tavenner 1933: 117.

[76] Tavenner (1933) argues that the *iunx* and rhombus are one and the same object, but his view is not unanimously upheld. What is clear is the spinning movement of both, and their purpose of turning the love object's head.

[77] Useful summary in Faraone 1999: 42n4: 'The usual terms for describing a magical action of this sort ("sympathetic" or "homeopathic") are problematic. Tambiah (1973) 199–229 … distinguishes instead between the operation of "empirical analogies" (used in modern scientific discourse to *predict* future actions) and "persuasive analogies" (used in rituals by traditional societies to *encourage* future action). Such rituals … reveal a profound belief in the extraordinary power of language.'

terminology more keyed into material agency, such as 'persuasive analogy': the idea that rituals encourage future actions. Faraone argues that rituals operating through persuasive analogy 'reveal a profound belief in the extraordinary power of language', but I would add that persuasive analogy also suggests an equally profound belief in the power of *materiality*. It is not just the incantation that channels the power, but also the objects being acted upon, the nonhuman things that are standing in for their human counterparts, prefacing human affect with that of their own. In magical practices that operate on the basis of persuasive analogy, then, there is a powerful alignment made between thing and person, a perceived proximity between them that supposedly allows the transference of an action or affect from one to the other. In the case of the *iunx* in particular, a complex network of correlations matches the animal to the human world, through the exercising of power and control. Simaetha uses a magical wheel whose type once subdued its ornithic namesake, with the intention of overpowering her love object.

This nexus of power and control is inevitably tied up with the question of gender. Joan Burton introduces *Idyll* 2, along with 14 and 15, as one of *Theocritus' Urban Mimes*: a subcategory of Theocritus' poetry that needs to be treated separately from the pastoral poems specifically in terms of gender. She writes:

> The factor of gender complicates any attempt to equalize social responses toward the fictive characters of Theocritus's pastoral and urban poems. Theocritus's pastoral poems explore the function of song and friendship by focusing on the male experience, with women entering the poems mostly as the 'other,' who can reject or threaten a male's sense of autonomy and integrity, and thus paradoxically reinforce male friendships and solidarity. All of Theocritus's urban mimes, on the other hand, represent women in more central and powerful roles, and two are presented through female characters and represent the subjective experiences of women.[78]

The pairing of *Idylls* 2 and 15 in this chapter is driven partly by generic criteria, in terms of the operation of gender dynamics. Burton interprets Simaetha's magic, utilisation of alternative channels of agency and pointed subversion of Delphis' patriarchal (sympotic, gymnastic) context as having a disquieting effect on the male reader. By showing how Simaetha's ritual disrupts Delphis' world, Theocritus evokes male fears about female agency through magic: fears that through witchcraft women might seek to control and redefine men, and sexual discourse.[79] The agentic and transgressive figure of the witch is a preoccupation throughout literary

---

[78] Burton 1995: 7.
[79] Ibid. p. 66.

history.⁸⁰ These male fears and the alternative channels of female agency that evoke them emerge as a persistent thread, and it is certainly feasible to discern them in *Idyll* 2. However, Lambert (2002) makes a rather different argument that casts an entirely different light on the figure of the witch, the character of Simaetha and the gendered power dynamics in this poem. He believes that Theocritus' second *Idyll* is not, as many scholars would have it, an example of the demonising of women as witches, an attestation of female involvement in erotic magic and their power in the ritual sphere – but, rather, 'a comic parody of a magic ritual in which the love-sick practitioner perpetrates ritual mayhem for the entertainment of Theocritus' audience, in which real magic was the domain of men, not women (as the papyri overwhelmingly testify)'.⁸¹ To return to the mapping of literary representation onto the real world, Lambert argues: 'The search for precise parallels in the magical papyri is indeed doomed; there aren't any.'⁸² According to this reading, Simaetha gets it all wrong, and makes a fool of herself in the process. All the instabilities and uncertainties noted by Segal come to the fore and take on a tone of comic irony – or, if we read the pessimistic tone through its material expressions, dark ecology.

It is interesting to note, however, that gender is not the only factor at play here. In fact, we might profitably use an intersectional lens to consider the place of Simaetha in this *Idyll*. Gender, ethnicity and class – all are mobilised in *Idyll* 2, to set this single character at a disadvantage, or at least at odds with the man she desires. Simaetha is a woman. She is also of a different ethnicity than Delphis, referring to him as 'the Myndian' (ὁ Μύνδιος) at 96. As Burton puts it, 'the emphasis on the social gap between Simaetha, whose non-elite friends include a Thracian nurse and a flute girl's mother, and Delphis, a member of the upper-class gymnastic and sympotic set, brings the issue of class difference to the center of *Idyll 2*'s poetic project'.⁸³ Simaetha seems disconnected from family or advantageous socio-political ties: yet another peg she is taken down. In this vein, it should be noted that *Idyll* 2 is presented as a monologue, not a dialogue. As Burton writes,

> By not giving Simaetha a friend with whom to talk, the poet also can emphasize a negative side of the Hellenistic world's mobility: the loneliness and powerlessness that can come (especially to women) from the absence of kinship ties within a community.⁸⁴

---

[80] On the witch in Homeric epic and Pre-Raphaelite art, see Canevaro 2015b.
[81] Lambert 2002: 71.
[82] Ibid. p. 80.
[83] Burton 1995: 19.
[84] Ibid. p. 40.

But to whom is the monologue addressed? To what extent is Simaetha really lonely and powerless? Simaetha does not talk to herself, but in the first instance to her attendant Thestylis, and then to the Moon – to nature, to a celestial *body*. Burton notes of the gendered power dynamics here: 'Delphis, the privileged male colonizer, an elite Greek foreigner from Myndus, assumes erotic privilege in a patriarchal system, and Simaetha, the subordinated female, finds recourse in an alternative realm of magic, nature, earth.'[85] We come back to the idea of alternative channels of agency – which we must continue to weigh up and evaluate. Simaetha is subordinated by gender and class (and differentiated by race), but she carves out her own kind of agency – an agency enacted not only through material magic, but also through bodies in nature.[86] We have gone back and forth on the question of whether or not Simaetha's magic is in fact potent, successful – and we could do the same with her connection to nature. Below I discuss Simaetha's physical symptoms of desire, showing that in her decline she is set at odds with her environs. And her invocation to the moon inevitably falls into the same disputed category as her material magic, her refrain of the *iunx*, as it is a call for help that ultimately falls flat. It is indicative that there is an alignment between Simaetha's 'audience' and the object of her desire: when Delphis and Eudamippus come from the gym, their chests gleam more than the moon (στήθεα δὲ στίλβοντα πολὺ πλέον ἢ τὺ, Σελάνα, 79). Perhaps, then, we are to suppose that Simaetha's connection with the moon is just as ill fated as that with Delphis. And yet, it is surely relevant that by the end of the poem Delphis has dulled in Simaetha's eyes, while Selene is 'of the shining throne' (Σελαναία λιπαρόθρονε, 165). It turns out that the allegiance between woman and Lady Moon – between Simaetha and her environs, broadly conceived and personified – outlasts a faded infatuation.[87]

A narrative of the madness and, ultimately, futility of desire is written across the body of a bird, a crafted object, a network of human participants (willing or not) and a variety of nonhuman agents. I would like, now, to continue to read this same narrative across the female body, through the 'symptoms' exhibited by Simaetha, and to extend the discussion to the male correlate, the effects projected upon Delphis through persuasive analogy. This method of reading the body is propagated by the Material Feminisms, as introduced earlier in the chapter (pp. 44–8). Stacy Alaimo makes the interesting observation that 'while desire, especially sexual desire, can be

---

[85] Ibid. p. 43.

[86] See Canevaro 2018b on the secret channels and alternative forms of commerce adopted by Homer's supposedly commodified women.

[87] As Burton (1995: 68–9) puts it, 'by having Simaetha strip Delphis of his adjective and give it to the Moon, her ally in magic, Theocritus also shows Simaetha deconstructing her image of Delphis and returning from her obsession with his world to reclaim her own life … The night is over, and the moon has played her role as confidant in Simaetha's ritual therapy.'

readily celebrated as a form of material agency, when one's own body baffles, annoys, disappoints, or falls ill, such actions are rarely valued'.[88] This she then connects up with the burgeoning field of disability studies, as a field that seeks to redress this balance. *Idyll* 2 is particularly important in this regard, as it bridges the gap between the two perspectives: the focus on desire, and that on bodily failure.[89] Simaetha's corporeal story may be one of sexual desire, but it is also one of illness and failure – and the conclusion of both Delphis and Simaetha's material narrative is, ultimately, bafflement. We might bring the *iunx* back in here. It is a love charm, an object meant to create desire. In its mythological aetion it comes from a story of desire. Yet in its initial conception it is not just an object but also a body, blurring any divide between animal and thing. And, more importantly, it is a body that has been subdued, repressed, pinned down and captured. As a love charm it has a sympathetic potency in terms of control – but it is worth noting that this is also a broken body, one that has experienced failure.

Alaimo notes that 'the celebratory tone of most feminist writing about the body signals the failure to fully confront the "experience of the negative body"'.[90] From a materialist perspective, 'the agency of the body demands an acceptance of unpredictability and not-quite-knowing'.[91] Alaimo argues that there is also an ethical dimension to this, which brings together a reading of the body with consideration of materiality in a broader frame:

> If one cannot presume to master one's own body, which has 'its' own forces, many of which can never fully be comprehended, even with the help of medical knowledge and technologies, one cannot presume to master the rest of the world, which is forever intra-acting in inconceivably complex ways.[92]

It is from this integrated standpoint that I consider the symptomology of *Idyll* 2. By way of introduction, I turn to a 2022 article by Giulia Sissa about intentional objects and erotic materialism. In her discussion of desire, Sissa resists the crude binary logic of 'objectification' – that is, a human viewed as an object by another human – instead exploring the dialectic of desire as embodied, but targeted at another person's

---

[88] Alaimo 2008: 249.
[89] This has something in common with my approach to stone in Chapter 3: we both desire stone's companionship and fear its agency. Both lines can be connected to Heidegger's broken hammer (see Heidegger's 1971 essay 'The Thing'): a tool with which we enact a collaborative agency, yet which really only makes itself evident when it falters.
[90] Alaimo 2008: 249.
[91] Ibid. p. 250.
[92] Ibid. p. 250.

desire rather than at the possession of a reified body. She argues that 'desire does not dehumanize the person. On the contrary: via idealization, desire hyperpersonalizes a body.'[93] Just as our materiality, our concreteness, our proximity to and overlap with objects need not endanger our humanity, so our being desired is not necessarily debasing. To make this point, Sissa differentiates between object/thing and object of[94] – but we have seen that the agency of objects can make this point in and of itself. This takes us back to the crucial details of the new-materialist balancing act discussed in Chapter 1 (pp. 11–23): the process of elevating the nonhuman rather than degrading the human, in levelling the ontology between them. It very much resonates with the argument put forward by Wallace about Pope's *The Rape of the Lock* (see above, pp. 47–8), in which the simple equation between inert matter and passive woman is problematised through the New Materialisms. And it connects with Bennett's suggestion that anthropomorphism may reveal isomorphism (see further Chapter 4, pp. 155–69). What if we see matter as vital? How does this affect our reading of 'objectification'? We might use the new-materialist perspective in reevaluating the idea of objectification, considering what happens to this notion when we reassess the agency of the object, treating it not as subordinate but as ontologically (if not grammatically) parallel to the subject.[95] In this section I pick up some of these ideas, considering Simaetha and Delphis in terms of desire, embodiment and agency.

We can take an important starting point from Sissa's article, noting that objectification and scopophilia are not perpetrated exclusively by men in ancient poetry and directed at women – but, on the contrary, that they work both ways, crossing the gender divide in both directions. Sissa uses the *Homeric Hymn to Aphrodite* as an opening example: Aphrodite seeing and desiring Anchises, Anchises seeing and desiring Aphrodite in return. And one of her central examples is Odysseus' beautified body being the object of Nausicaa's 'gaze that is admirative, discriminating, intent and optative'.[96] It is not only women who are objectified. Sissa writes more broadly of bodies as 'intentional object[s]'; of 'the matter of the visible, and its vitality'[97] (again resonating with Wallace's arguments about the importance of vitalism in our consideration of the mechanisms of objectification). These observations are relevant to Theocritus' second *Idyll*, given that here we certainly have the female desiring gaze: as Burton points out, 'by having Simaetha emphasize her role as spectator (rather than spectacle), the poet unsettles patriarchal assumptions about

---

[93] Sissa 2022: 51.
[94] Ibid. p. 47.
[95] See further Canevaro 2018b.
[96] Sissa 2022: 23.
[97] Ibid. p. 47.

the relations of men and women in a public space'.⁹⁸ Further, we have a woman, Simaetha, who is approaching the man Delphis as – or, indeed transforming him into – a series of objects. Yet the magical element in this *Idyll* takes us beyond Sissa's argument, to a truly materialist setting. Simaetha's desire is active, reactive, proactive – transformative. Desire is embodied, bodies become intentional objects and persuasive analogies set up a causal relationship that is materially manifest. At some points in the poem, we have a material substitution: an object acting as a constitutive symbol of a human agent.⁹⁹ For instance, at line 156 Simaetha recalls how Delphis would leave his Dorian oil flask with her after his visits: a promise to return, materially constituted. This is a pervasive form of symbology seen often in poetry, from Homeric epic to South Slavic song and beyond.¹⁰⁰ In this way, the body is given a material correlate, which stands in for the man in his absence, acting as placeholder and tangible reminder. But *Idyll* 2 goes beyond such standard modes of material symbology. Simaetha's attempts to affect Delphis operate from a distance – 'the wretch has not come near me for twelve days' (ὅς μοι δωδεκαταῖος ἀφ' ᾧ τάλας οὐδὲ ποθίκει, 4) – yet they are all about alignment. Barley grains scattered, to scatter the bones of Delphis; a lizard crushed, to grind Delphis' bones. Laurel burnt up, to consume Delphis' flesh. Wax melted, to melt Delphis' heart. There is also an element of synecdoche and substitution, part for the whole: the fringe of Delphis' cloak set on fire in lieu of him. It is through material objects that Delphis' distant body is invoked; he is materialised and embodied in his absence through these material instantiations of his person. In enumerating this list of magical acts, ingredients and objects, Theocritus manages to have us read across the body of someone who is not actually present. Persuasive analogy is a particularly effective term, as not only do we imagine the victim being 'persuaded' by the acts (that is, the acts having their desired and anticipated effects on the target's body), but we are also persuaded of the

---

⁹⁸ Burton 1995: 44.
⁹⁹ Here and elsewhere I use a term from Colin Renfrew and Material Engagement Theory, as it takes us beyond models of symbolism and what objects stand in for, to what objects can do. Renfrew (2005: 89–90) writes of constitutive symbols: 'where the material *thing* which does indeed work as a symbol, that is to say has a symbolic role, is not representing something else but is itself active. We might call it a *constitutive symbol* … Some material symbols, then, are constitutive in their material reality. They are not disembodied verbal concepts, or not initially. They have an indissoluble reality of substance: they are substantive. The symbol (in its real, actual substance) actually precedes the concept. Or, if that is almost claiming too much, they are self-referential. The symbol cannot exist without the substance, and the material reality of the substance precedes the symbolic role which is ascribed to it when it comes to embody such an institutional fact.' See also Renfrew 2012.
¹⁰⁰ See Canevaro 2019c.

ontological analogies between human and nonhuman: the proximity between the two that can facilitate this sort of substitution.

A different material and corporeal narrative is told by the figure of Simaetha, our protagonist: the present, immanent, narrative persona of *Idyll* 2. First, she is in antithesis to, or out of alignment with, her natural surroundings:

ἠνίδε σιγῇ μὲν πόντος, σιγῶντι δ' ἀῆται·
ἁ δ' ἐμὰ οὐ σιγῇ στέρνων ἔντοσθεν ἀνία,

See, the sea is silent, and the winds are silent;
but the pain in my breast is not silent.
(*Idyll* 2.38–9)

While the sea and winds are calm, her emotions are in turmoil. The affective relationship we see elsewhere in the *Idylls* between human and nonhuman nature is distorted here, disrupted, as a way of emphasising Simaetha's instability. So overwrought is she that she cannot be grounded in her environs, and dark ecology looms large here as the disconnect between woman and nature bodes ill. Next, Simaetha describes herself as 'all ablaze' (πᾶσα καταίθομαι, 40), this between her burning the bran (to set Delphis afire) and melting the wax (to melt Delphis' heart). There is a slippage between Delphis' projected bodily narrative and Simaetha's, as the persuasive analogy is shown to be based in Simaetha's lived experience. Simaetha wants to make Delphis feel as she does – to transfer her embodied emotions to him through material media.[101] And there is a link between the two, as fire comes up again when Simaetha recounts her first glimpse of Delphis ('my wretched heart was seized with fire', ὥς μοι πυρὶ θυμὸς ἰάφθη | δειλαίας, 82–3):[102] it is an emotional state that originated in the one viewing the other, and one which Simaetha tries to perpetuate across both parties. The burning instigated by this desirous gaze reduces Simaetha to illness: a fever (καπυρὰ νόσος) that rages for ten days.

Simaetha's bodily narrative is an evident one, as her internal symptoms are supplemented by external manifestations: her beauty melts (τὸ δὲ κάλλος ἐτάκετο, 83);

---

[101] There are other examples of parallelism between Simaetha's symptoms and the effects she intends to have on Delphis: she wants him to waste away from love for her, as her beauty is wasting (τάκοιθ' ὑπ' ἔρωτος, 29; τὸ δὲ κάλλος ἐτάκετο, 83), and to come to her house like a man driven mad, as she was driven mad when she saw him (καὶ ἐς τόδε δῶμα περάσαι | μαινομένῳ ἴκελος, 50–1; χὡς ἴδον, ὡς ἐμάνην, 82).

[102] πυρί is given by the papyri, περί by the manuscripts. Gow *ad loc.* rightly argues that 'πυρί seems preferable to περί since love is constantly referred to as a fire … and the compound περιάπτω is not otherwise known'.

her skin becomes pale as fustic (μευ χρὼς μὲν ὁμοῖος ἐγίνετο πολλάκι θάψῳ, 88); her hair falls out (ἔρρευν δ' ἐκ κεφαλᾶς πᾶσαι τρίχες, 89). There are wider material inflections to some of these symptoms, which go beyond the corporeal. That her beauty 'melts' connects up with the set of heat and fire references just discussed. The verb τήκω can be used metaphorically, of wasting away or pining – but it has a material correlate, referring to the melting down of metal, or the melting away of snow. Similarly, the skin pale as fustic gestures to the material world, fustic being a shrub from the island of Thapsos that is used for yellow dye. Through this simile, the colour of the body is elucidated via nature, as it is utilised by human craft. The skin approximates a crafted object, the process of desire being as transformative as that of dying cloth. In the aftermath of these symptoms, Simaetha is reduced to skin and bones (αὐτὰ δὲ λοιπά | ὀστί' ἔτ' ἦς καὶ δέρμα, 89–90). Her personhood has been worn away, her signs of self eroded, until she is nothing but the bare material components of a human being. This is all part of Simaetha's desiring from a distance: a voyeuristic moment that exemplifies the double gender dynamics presented by Sissa (the woman views and desires the man). Symptoms multiply and shift again when the gaze becomes a meeting.

Again, the description of Simaetha's embodied emotions when Delphis arrives at her house is grounded in materiality: a series of similes and metaphors that anchor the emotions not only in the body, but also in its environs. The material narrative created is one that stretches across body and material nature, by virtue of figurative language. It is in this way that word, world and woman are powerfully enmeshed, all responding to each other. First, she turns colder than snow (πᾶσα μὲν ἐψύχθην χιόνος πλέον, 106),[103] and the sweat on her forehead is like damp dew (ἐκ δὲ μετώπω | ἱδρώς μευ κοχύδεσκεν ἴσον νοτίαισιν ἐέρσαις, 106–7). Her embodied emotions connect with features of environment and climate. Next her silence and stiffness transform her first into a whimpering child, then into a doll or a puppet (δαγῦδι, 110). We might posit here an alignment, a 'meeting in the middle', of Simaetha and Delphis: she approximates a 'doll', not necessarily the plaything of an innocent child but perhaps a wax effigy used in ritual, and she 'melted the wax' to melt Delphis' heart. Both are given nonhuman proxies, blurring ontological divides through figurative language as much as through persuasive analogy. This resonates with the idea of 'trans-corporeality', as developed by Stacy Alaimo. She defines this concept: 'the time-space where human corporeality, in all its material fleshiness, is inseparable from "nature" or "environment"'.[104] Simaetha's corpore-

---

[103] For a similar symptom, see e.g. Daphnis at *Idyll* 7.76 ('he melted like snow', εὖτε χιὼν ὥς τις κατετάκετο).
[104] Alaimo 2008: 238.

ality embraces and incorporates the natural environment as well as other 'kinds' of humanity and manmade materiality. In being alert to this, our reading can share in the ethical and political implications posited for trans-corporeality:

> Imagining human corporeality as trans-corporeality, in which the human is always intermeshed with the more-than-human world, underlines the extent to which the corporeal substance of the human is ultimately inseparable from 'the environment.' It makes it difficult to pose nature as a mere background for the exploits of the human, since 'nature' is always as close as one's own skin.[105]

This is the first Theocritean instance in which I apply this theory – but as we progress through the corpus, it becomes evident that the model might persist more and more. The fisherman and his rugged rock (a focus of Chapter 3, pp. 113–40), for instance – where does the one end and the other begin? Is there really a difference between the two?

In focusing on Simaetha's symptoms, and the effects she strives to inflict on Delphis, we have fragmented the body, reading across its narrative chapter by chapter. Let us conclude our reading by zooming back out to the body as a (porous and permeable) whole. Burton makes an observation that is crucial to our considerations:

> He [Delphis] described Philinus as χαρίεις ('graceful,' 115) and himself as ἐλαφρός καὶ καλός ('agile and fair,' 124–25). In both cases the epithets apply to the whole person. But the epithet he uses to describe Simaetha (καλόν, 'lovely,' 126) is applied to only one body part (στόμα, 'mouth,' 126), treated solely as an object of his personal, sexual pleasure: εὖδόν τ', εἴ κε μόνον τὸ καλὸν στόμα τεῦς ἐφίλασα ('I would have slept, if I only had kissed your lovely mouth'; 126).[106]

Delphis's attitude to Simaetha is one of fragmentation too – but rather than being a slow, detailed appreciation of her narrative (as I have attempted here), it is a degrading deconstruction that contrasts pointedly with his own integrated and intact embodiment. However, I would note that this fragmentation can be read in more than one direction. Simaetha fragments Delphis' body, as we have seen, casting spells to target his bones, his flesh. But she also uses formulations that emphasise her entirety, her wholeness. It is her *whole* body that becomes cold as snow; her fine skin all around (καλὸν χρόα πάντοθεν, 110) that becomes stiff like

[105] Ibid. p. 238.
[106] Burton 1995: 45.

a doll. Yet ultimately, she too sees herself as fragmented, as she describes her own symptomology, piece by wasted piece.

Idyll 15: Women's Work

This chapter on Theocritean women inevitably builds to a crescendo with *Idyll* 15 – another of Theocritus' 'urban mimes', often used as evidence for the lives of Hellenistic women, the patronage of Arsinoe, the festival of Adonis and Hellenistic religious and cultic life more generally. It is mined by cultural historians as much as by literary critics, and it is a poem that just seems to keep on giving – a fact attested by the wealth of scholarship it has generated. My aim is not to delve into all these topics, nor to rehearse all the manifold debates generated by this one rich *Idyll*. Within the confines of this section, it would be too much even to claim that I can do justice to all the gender arguments drawn from *Idyll* 15. I intend, rather, to take my cue from the preceding sections and, now that we are on firmer ground with respect to Material Feminism and its tenets and pay-offs, to launch straight into the materiality of the poem.

This *Idyll* was mentioned earlier in the chapter (p. 50) as an evident intertextual reference point for the ekphrastic description of the woman on the cup in *Idyll* 1. Unsurprisingly, ekphrasis will once again be at the centre of our discussion here, and all the more so if we frame this intertextual reference as an intermedial one: a connection perpetrated through and by objects within the text. So a focal point will be the ekphrastic description of the tapestries in the poem. However, from the perspective of materiality, it is crucial to begin from the poem's scene-setting: the proliferation of material objects that give the *Idyll* its situatedness, the marked domestic thrust in its first part. It is from these foregrounded material environs that the agency and viewpoint of the female characters emerge, as character and object are entangled in a single material-semiotic narrative. This is a specifically gendered narrative: a female story that the men misunderstand and that creates a gendered intermediality linking Theocritus' women with their Homeric counterparts and indeed their real-world correlates.

Burton surveys scholarship on *Idyll* 15's tapestry ekphrasis prior to her 1995 book, finding that 'many scholars have expressed the belief that the poem mocks the aesthetic taste of the fictive women (who "express naive wonder at the lifelikeness of the tapestries")'.[107] Over the course of her third chapter she questions this assumption of mockery, and indeed since then the scholarship has rather levelled out.[108] Within its

---

[107] Burton 1995: 94.
[108] For a more recent appraisal of the women in *Idyll* 15, see Skinner 2001.

aesthetic, social and cultural frames, the debate comes down to a core question: that of reality. And it is this central theme that has ramifications from a materialist standpoint. In this section I will consider the question of reality in conjunction with the material-ecocritical ties between word and world introduced in Chapter 1, while also providing a lead-in to the imagined landscapes of Chapter 3 (pp. 91–113). Further, we can also use *Idyll* 15 to push forward with our from-below, Marxist-inflected readings, offering a material-feminist analysis that reveals the labour behind the object.

The two female protagonists of this *Idyll*, Gorgo and Praxinoa, are situated within a proliferation of objects right from the poem's outset. They are set specifically in a female domestic idiom, which men do not understand – a gender imbalance that is made clear when their husbands get it wrong:

Πραχινόα
ἁπῷς μὰν τῆνός γα πρόαν – λέγομες δὲ πρόαν θην
'πάππα, νίτρον καὶ φῦκος ἀπὸ σκανᾶς ἀγοράσδειν' –
ἵκτο φέρων ἅλας ἅμμιν, ἀνὴρ τρισκαιδεκάπαχυς.

Γοργώ
χώμὸς ταὐτᾷ ἔχει· φθόρος ἀργυρίω Διοκλείδας·
ἑπταδράχμως κυνάδας, γραιᾶν ἀποτίλματα πηρᾶν,
πέντε πόκως ἔλαβ᾽ ἐχθές, ἅπαν ῥύπον, ἔργον ἐπ᾽ ἔργῳ.

Praxinoa
Yet that papa the other day – just the other day I said to him
'Papa, go and get some soda and red dye from the stall' –
and he brought me back salt, the great lummox of a man.

Gorgo
Mine's that way too. Money is nothing to Diocleidas.
Yesterday for seven drachmas he bought five fleeces that were like dogs' hair,
pluckings off old skin bags, nothing but dirt, work upon work.

(*Idyll* 15.15–20)

The men don't understand material worth or commodification; they don't grasp the material makeup of things. When put in charge of objects, all they do is add to the women's workload: ἔργον ἐπ᾽ ἔργῳ. This gender dynamic is brought into even starker relief by its Hesiodic parallel, ἔργον ἐπ᾽ ἔργῳ ἐργάζεσθαι at *Works and Days* line 382. In that passage, which precedes the agricultural calendar, Hesiod is instructing his audience to work hard and build up profit, wealth and stores.

It follows hot on the heels of his infamous advice not to let a woman with a tarted-up arse deceive your mind with wheedling words while she rifles around in your granary (he who trusts a woman, trusts cheaters).[109] It is particularly clear in this part of the poem that the advice is for a *male* audience, and a male audience suspicious of and out of sync with women who might deceive, cajole and cheat them.[110] It is striking, then, that Theocritus should use the formulation ἔργον ἐπ' ἔργῳ of women whose men don't understand their work. Importantly, the mismatch between the male and female experience is still there, but Theocritus has reversed the polarity. Whereas the *Works and Days* foregrounds men's labour and the threats to it (including women), through Theocritus' response to this Hesiodic phrase *Idyll* 15 refocuses our attention on female labour.

At the poem's outset, then, we are given an insight into a female world, characterised by ubiquitous objects and by a propensity to work, *erga*. Already we see the female labour behind the finished products: a labour that is marked by a gender disparity in practice and in understanding. Similarly, at line 35 Gorgo asks Praxinoa how much her dress cost, and Praxinoa replies that 'it cost more than two minae of good money, and I put my soul into the work' – again commodification and labour go hand in hand, with both quantitative (two minae) and qualitative (ἔργοις) aspects involved. Further, these passages about the women's shopping and weaving are interspersed with Praxinoa's commands to her slave woman Eunoa: commands which also centre on objects (27–33: pick up the spinning; bring water; hand over the soap; bring the key to the clothes chest; 39–40: bring a wrap and sun hat). A hierarchy is set up between the women and the slave, cast in material terms – but work is established as a constant across the divide. This begins, then, as a strikingly situated poem, a poem that evokes a world of women and of objects, a world in which 'attentiveness to things' necessitates an attentiveness also to the hands behind the handiwork.

When Gorgo and Praxinoa venture out into the street, the cacophony of Alexandrian life is conveyed through an entangled narrative of women and slaves walking, horses rearing, crowds processing like ants ('they're like ants, countless and innumerable', μύρμακες ἀνάριθμοι καὶ ἄμετροι, 45), pushing and shoving like pigs (ὠθεῦνθ' ὥσπερ ὕες, 73)[111] and the contrast with baby (and dog) at home – and

---

[109] *Works and Days* 373–5.

[110] For more on the clash of the sexes in the *Works and Days*, see Canevaro 2013.

[111] The comparisons between humans and animals here resonate with passages of Hesiod's *Works and Days*, in which humans are assimilated or approximated to animals. In 504–63 the cold north wind Boreas blows through the winter landscape, affecting humans and beasts alike and bringing them into alignment (a simile at 533–5 likens the beasts of the forest to a man with a stick). This continues into the Days section, where the spider spins

the concern for material things persists, in Praxinoa's frantic worry for her cloak (69–71). The lines create a vivid image of an urban landscape, rapidly moving and full of vitality. It is within this context – after the establishing of a female domestic labour, and against the backdrop of such energetic environs – that we are to consider the ekphrastic description of the palace's tapestries: the first thing seen by the women as they progress inside. Gorgo notices first of all their quality: that they are fine and elegant (λεπτὰ καὶ ὡς χαρίεντα, 79). Gow and others have marked this as a specific intertextual allusion, referencing *Odyssey* 10.222–3:[112]

ἱστὸν ἐποιχομένης μέγαν ἄμβροτον, οἷα θεάων
λεπτά τε καὶ χαρίεντα καὶ ἀγλαὰ ἔργα πέλονται.

She was plying a great immortal web, such as the
works of goddesses are: fine and elegant and splendid.

This is the way in which Circe is introduced in the *Odyssey*. Gow notes: 'T. is thinking of *Od*.10.222 (Circe) ... but the two adj., which refer respectively to the texture and the design of the stuff, are applied to garments at *Il*.22.511, *Od*.5.231, 10.554 also.' Similarly, Burton identifies the primary allusion, and the other comparanda as secondary, on (above all) contextual grounds: 'Through Gorgo's use of this exclamation as she enters through doors to the palace grounds, Theocritus recalls Homer's representation of the moment Odysseus's men stood in Circe's gateway and saw Circe's woven materials hanging before them.'[113] Whereas Gow's statement is sweeping and unsupported, Burton provides an appendix with full argumentation that includes poetic and linguistic as well as contextual points, and I am fully convinced by her argument.[114] And yet, with all of the other factors at play, what ultimately fades into

---

its web and a woman works at the loom; the 'knowing one' is the ant, gathering its heap; and good days are prescribed for the birth of girls and boys, the castration of goats, the fencing of sheep pens, all mixed in together.

[112] Burton (1995: 102) discusses this allusion, focusing on its 'possible role in characterizing Gorgo's subjectivity'; she then elaborates in her Appendix 2, with a fuller discussion of the passages in tandem.

[113] Burton 1995: 102.

[114] Burton 1995: 174 provides full argumentation: 'At both *Od*.10.223 and *Id*.15.79, the adjectives λεπτά and χαρίεντα are plural in number, stand first in their lines, refer to woven materials, and are qualified by a genitive plural of θεός in close proximity. Further, in *Idyll* 15's passage, the qualifying clause θεῶν περονάματα φασεῖς (*Id*.15.79) directly follows the adjectives, and in *Odyssey* 10's passage the words οἷα θεάων directly precede the adjectives. Similarities of circumstance reinforce the linkage between *Od*.10.223 and *Id*.15.79 in several ways. First, when Odysseus's men enter the doorway of Circe's house, they see Circe

the background in this intertextual analysis is the material aspect of the allusion. Bill Brown noted of scholarship on the shield of Achilles ekphrasis that such discussions 'do not bring the represented object – as object – into focus',[115] and I would argue that a similar trajectory holds true here. The hierarchy of allusion created by these scholars is centred on the rhetorical function of ekphrasis and on other poetic features, rather than on the materials themselves. From the perspective of materiality and intermediality, by contrast, it would be more rewarding to consider all of these allusions as being in force simultaneously and equally, the two material adjectives evoking an array of Homeric objects.[116] In this way, rather than a straight line between Gorgo and Circe, there is a more expansive female network set up that also includes Andromache (vowing to burn Hector's clothes at *Il.* 22.511) and Calypso (wearing a 'fine and elegant' garment at *Od.* 5.231). This gives a different slant to Burton's core question about subjectivity: 'Is the allusion meant to be perceived as intended by the character in the poem or only by the poet creating the character? Is Gorgo meant to be perceived as herself alluding to the Circe passage?'[117] According to the argument of a more restrictive or specific allusion, Gorgo would be paralleling her experience of entering the palace and viewing the tapestries with the experience of Odysseus' men when they arrive at the house of Circe. By contrast, with a more open allusive network, we would have Gorgo drawing a connection between the material qualities of the tapestries and those of various important Homeric textiles. There is a subtle shift between an experiential and a materialist reading, not just on our part but also on that of Gorgo (and Theocritus).

> and the woven materials she is working on her loom. So too when the Syracusan women enter through doors to the palace grounds, they see woven materials hanging before them (78). Second, brutish crowds jostle both Odysseus's men and the Syracusan women on their way to these respective realms. Around Circe's house, Odysseus's men encounter animals under Circe's spell (*Od.*10.212–19). As the Syracusan women approach the palace grounds, they encounter a crowd Praxinoa describes as shoving like swine: ὄχλος ἀλαθέως. ὠθεῦνθ' ὥσπερ ὕες (*Id.*15.72–3). Odysseus's men are subsequently transformed into swine (*Od.*10.239–40). Circe changes men into animals literally; Praxinoa, metaphorically. Third, Odysseus's men and the Syracusan women are both entering realms different from their normal worlds, realms that are magical and seductive in their allure.'

[115] Brown 2015: 3.
[116] Burton (1995: 176) notes that Gow 'is the last of generations of critics to recognize the allusion as a specific one. Some contemporary scholars dismiss the fashion for citation of parallels that was a hallmark of edition-making in the nineteenth century, and with it they dismiss some important observations.' My argument is not that we should dismiss specific parallels, but quite the contrary: that giving weight to the full range of comparanda can give us a more materialist reading.
[117] Burton 1995: 102.

Many interpretations of this scene emphasise its Hellenistic aesthetics: the contemporary literary relevance of the particular adjectives (the Callimachean praising of 'fine' poetry). My aim here is to direct us back to the material narrative rather than the meta-narrative: to physicality, to the sensorial, the tactile. Gorgo's first reaction is to the material quality of the tapestries, and our first intermedial reaction should naturally follow in the same vein. The result of this is a renewed recognition of the objects as objects, and, moreover, their importance, their *agency*, within their narratives. If Gorgo is drawing connections with Circe's weaving, Calypso's clothes, the garments that Andromache marks as transient, ephemeral, perishable (just like human life), then she is drawing on objects that have their own strong material meanings. We can tell a story through wider contextual considerations – but we can tell an equally compelling story (and one that, crucially, is more strongly anchored to female communication and agency) through the material-semiotic alone.

Gorgo then says that the tapestries are fit for gods: θεῶν περονάματα φασεῖς (79). The formulation with the genitive θεῶν here echoes that of the woman on the cup in *Idyll* 1 (discussed on pp. 57–65), who is described as τί θεῶν δαίδαλμα τέτυκται (1.32). In that *Idyll* there was some ambiguity and therefore debate about the interpretation of this line: is the woman on the cup wrought by the gods, or a statue of the gods? How is her material narrative to be read? Here again the genitive could have various senses. Textiles fit for the gods, perhaps – or textiles made by the gods? It is clear that the tapestries and their makers are both being praised here, but whether they are human hands making godly textiles or godlike hands making textiles is not entirely transparent. In the ambiguity there is a merging of the material objects and the agents of their creation, with either or both being ascribed divine attributes. In terms of materiality, there is a further interesting link with line 21 that entirely changes our perspective on the description:

ἀλλ᾽ ἴθι, τὠμπέχονον καὶ τὰν περονατρίδα λάζευ.

But go and get your shawl and robe.

(*Idyll* 15.21)

περονάματα at 79 recalls περονατρίδα at 21, connecting the imagined divine materiality with the domestic material landscape we have already encountered in the first part of the poem. There is a layering of material functions here: at 21 περονατρίδα clearly refers to a garment, to be fetched and worn by Praxinoa;[118] at 79 Gow

---

[118] There is also the cognate ἐμπερόναμα at 34, also of Praxinoa's garment.

comments: 'The rectangular pieces of tapestry are so splendid that they would serve gods for ἱμάτια. There is no implication that they are in fact being worn'. The περονατρίς is some kind of buckled or brooched garment, fastened by a περόνη.[119] As there is no implication that the tapestries are being worn at 79, there is then an extended usage here – an imagining of what the tapestries *could* be used for, given their splendour. And the extended imaginative connotation loops back round to the women's familiar domestic environs and, moreover, an extended bodily narrative (the tapestries are imagined as being put on the body). It is of further interest that Gorgo associates the tapestries with this garment in particular. Etymologically connected as it is with its mechanism of attachment, the περονατρίς is a garment whose composition is connected as much with its non-woven as its woven elements. One thing we might say about this is that it further complicates the correlation between comparanda: not only are the tapestries assimilated to garments, but woven objects are layered with garments that are both textile and fastening. Another step we might take is the following: if we assume that the pin or brooch was made of metal, this then potentially looks ahead to the metal evoked by the tapestries themselves: Adonis' silver chair at 84. In short, from a materialist standpoint, there is a lot we can make of Gorgo's comment, which was ostensibly a throwaway remark. There is the intermedial element, *Idyll* 15 recalling *Idyll* 1; there is the ambiguity of the material narrative here, in terms of the human, the divine, the material and the distribution of agency among the various parties; there is the detail of the actual material objects evoked, their composition, use, situatedness and equivalence. And there are further interpretations: Burton suggests that 'by using rare cognate words to describe both gowns fit for gods … and Praxinoa's more humble clothing … Theocritus can associate lower and higher classes, cross social boundaries, and mix genres'.[120] I offer this as an indicative example of the material details to be uncovered in even the most innocuous-seeming lines of this *Idyll*.

Praxinoa's thoughts go immediately to the crafts(wo)manship behind the tapestries:

πότνι᾽ ᾽Αθαναία, ποῖαί σφ᾽ ἐπόνασαν ἔριθοι,
ποῖοι ζωογράφοι τἀκριβέα γράμματ᾽ ἔγραψαν.

---

[119] Cleland et al. (2007: 145) give as a definition of περόνη 'Tongue of a BUCKLE or BROOCH, and these items themselves. *Odyssey* 19.226; Sophocles, *Women of Trachis* 925; Herodotus, 5.87', and of περονήμα, περονήτρις 'A garment PINNED on the shoulder with a buckle or BROOCH. Theocritus, 15.79, 15.21; *Greek Anthology* 7.413.'
[120] Burton 1995: 105.

Lady Athena, what skilled workers they must have been to make them,
what artists that drew the lines so precisely.

(*Idyll* 15.80–1)

Before we launch into the ekphrastic description, we learn about the materiality of the tapestries: their quality, their creation, the (hypothesised) labour behind them. This is crucial in our reading, as it connects the viewers with what is being viewed: there is a connection set up between Praxinoa and Gorgo, as women attuned to materiality and creation, and the women not quite hidden behind the tapestries. Though they are set at a distance in terms of aesthetic admiration, the female protagonists are simultaneously enmeshed in the objects they are contemplating. This is important when considering the role of the women here, or rather Theocritus' attitude towards them. The viewing of the tapestries (the narrative frame for the ekphrasis) does not exist in a vacuum, but is part of the labour-centric and entangled urban landscape established in the first part of the poem. While Gorgo and Praxinoa's husbands do not understand the value of money or the work necessitated by materials, the women themselves can read the material narrative of a created product back to the hands that created it.

This brings us to the crucial lines of the ekphrasis, in terms of reality and indeed materiality:

ὡς ἔτυμ' ἐστάκαντι καὶ ὡς ἔτυμ' ἐνδινεῦντι,
ἔμψυχ', οὐκ ἐνυφαντά. σοφόν τι χρῆμ' ἄνθρωπος.

The figures look real when they stand and real when they move,
alive, not woven. How clever humans are!

(*Idyll* 15.82–3)

In her assessment, Praxinoa attributes vitality to the figures in the tapestry, and this vitality is not dependent on apparent movement. Even when they are standing still, she says, they seem 'true', and they appear alive, not woven. This declaration then culminates in an exclamation about human skill.[121] There is an exploration here of vital materialism – but it is explicitly and self-consciously set within the remit of human artifice. Material things can be imbued with vitality – but by human will,

---

[121] I have followed Hopkinson here in translating ἄνθρωπος as the gender-nonspecific 'human' – Gow translates 'What a clever thing is man!' but though 'man' is arguably generic, its potential specificity does risk eliding the female creators responsible for the tapestry.

not through independent material agency. The emphasis on human creation forges a link with the woman on Thyrsis' cup in *Idyll* 1, discussed at p. 62 in terms of the *daidal-* lexical field. It contrasts, however, with the introduction of the cup itself, which, as we noted in Chapter 1, lacks the standard ekphrastic markers and therefore takes us deeper into a vital materialism from the outset.

We might here return to our refrain from Bill Brown and aim yet again to 'bring the represented object – as object – into focus'. To reiterate, as Brown notes of the shield of Achilles,

> Homer's whole point seems to be to undermine the oppositions of movement and stasis, narrative action and descriptive scene, and the false identifications of medium with message. But what if Homer's whole point, undermining the opposition of movement and stasis, has nothing to do with literary modes (description and narration), and less to do with linguistic and pictorial media than with the medium of metal.[122]

We certainly see the opposition of movement and stasis collapsing here, as the figures look real both when they stand still and when they move. There is also a folding in of medium and message, as the woven figures are paradoxically 'alive, not woven'. To follow Brown's thought through, we might resist the standard interpretation of ekphrastic description by focusing not on the literary mode (the representational aspect), but rather on the materiality: not, here, 'the medium of metal', but rather the medium of the woven object. I would emphasise the importance of focalisation in this passage (as Burton emphasises subjectivity in this *Idyll*): crucially, it is the two women who read the tapestry's material-semiotic narrative. We see this sort of gender-specific interpretive act in Homeric epic, with Homeric women being particularly attuned to woven objects, able to track their dispersion and interpret their codes (we might think of Arete recognising Odysseus' gifted garments as created within her own household, for example).[123] In Homer we also see the kind of 'misreading' of which Praxinoa and Gorgo's husbands are accused – take, for instance, Odysseus' alter-ego Aethon being ignorant of the provenance of Odysseus' much-admired clothes in book 19.[124] Especially against the bustling backdrop of the first part of the *Idyll*, we can see this ekphrastic introduction as indicative of a particularly female labour-oriented perspective on materiality.

---

[122] Brown 2015: 3.
[123] See further Canevaro 2018b: 55–107.
[124] See further ibid. pp. 104–7. On misreading works of art, see Burton 1995: 96.

Many discussions of this ekphrasis focus on the Adonis figure described at 84–6, noting the immersion of Praxinoa in the ritual context and the congruity of the description with that context.[125] What interests me here, however, is the congruity of the initial lines of the ekphrasis with the female lived experience as depicted in the first part of the poem. The attunement to materiality that stems from a proliferation of objects in the domestic sphere, the female code and conversation that centres on things, the gender-specific understanding of materiality, particularly in its creative and created aspect. Burton notes that 'By admiring the life in the tapestries, by imaginatively and sympathetically experiencing Adonis's coming to life in the tapestries, the viewer recreates for that brief moment the magic of the resurrection of Adonis'[126] – but it is to be noted that the admiration of lively figures comes before the description of Adonis, and that the two are separated by the exclamation about human ingenuity. The female viewer's reflection on material vitality and on the creative mechanism behind the material product actually precedes the depiction of the divine, and so has, I would argue, an initial level that operates independently of (or at least in parallel with) the religious contextual interpretation. This is not just about the magic of the festival, but also about the intrinsic magic of the material.

---

[125] Burton 1995: 98: 'Praxinoa's description concentrates on those aspects of the work of art integral to the festival of Adonis: his incipient manhood, the love he inspires, and the transition between the realms of Aphrodite and of Persephone that the festival reenacts. Praxinoa "reads" the work of art in its context: the sensual pleasure of viewing Adonis's representation contributes to the religious experience that viewing him inspires.'

[126] Ibid. p. 101.

3   The Fisherman and the Rock

Idylls 7 and 21: Imagined Landscapes

τοῖς δὲ μετὰ γριπεύς τε γέρων πέτρα τε τέτυκται
λεπράς, ἐφ' ᾇ σπεύδων μέγα δίκτυον ἐς βόλον ἕλκει
ὁ πρέσβυς, κάμνοντι τὸ καρτερὸν ἀνδρὶ ἐοικώς.
φαίης κεν γυίων νιν ὅσον σθένος ἐλλοπιεύειν,
ὧδέ οἱ ᾠδήκαντι κατ' αὐχένα πάντοθεν ἶνες
καὶ πολιῷ περ ἐόντι· τὸ δὲ σθένος ἄξιον ἄβας.

Near them are fashioned an old fisherman and a rugged rock,
on which the old man hurries to drag his great net for a cast.
He is the very image of effort.
You would say that he was fishing with all the strength of his limbs,
so much do the sinews stand out all over his neck,
although he is grey-haired. His strength is worthy of youth.
                                        (Theocritus *Idyll* 1.39–44)

This is the second scene on the cup: an old fisherman hard at work, dragging his catch onto his rugged rock. The transition from the previous scene to this one is made through the idea of toil: the erstwhile wooers labouring in vain (ἐτώσια μοχθίζοντι, 38), the fisherman the very image of effort. There is some kind of relationship set up between the types of labour – the one about words and emotion, the other more physical – though whether they are paralleled or set in antithesis to one another is not immediately clear. An idyllic intertext that might elucidate the connection is *Idyll* 7, and a recurrence of the phrase ἐτώσια μοχθίζοντι. I begin this section with a discussion of this passage from *Idyll* 7, as it takes us back to the Hesiodic roots of *oiko*-criticism noted in Chapter 1 and brings together song and materiality in concrete fashion, before we move on to consider the broader theme of sung worlds or imagined landscapes.

ὥς μοι καὶ τέκτων μέγ᾽ ἀπέχθεται ὅστις ἐρευνῇ
ἶσον ὄρευς κορυφᾷ τελέσαι δόμον Ὠρομέδοντος,
καὶ Μοισᾶν ὄρνιχες ὅσοι ποτὶ Χῖον ἀοιδόν
ἀντία κοκκύζοντες ἐτώσια μοχθίζοντι.

I very much dislike the builder who strives to
build a house as high as mount Oromedon,
and those birds of the Muses who, crowing,
labour in vain against the Chian singer.
(*Idyll* 7.45–8)

Simichidas, the narrator of *Idyll* 7, is on his way from the city to a harvest festival at his friends' country estate. On the road he meets the goatherd Lycidas, whose reputation as a singer is known to the narrator – and they start up an exchange of songs.[1] The bucolic context is very similar to that of *Idyll* 1, making for a natural comparandum, and indeed it recaps many of the themes of the bucolic *Idylls*. This passage is Lycidas' preface to his song, in which he sets out his rhapsodic preferences. Like our passage from *Idyll* 1, here it is not the primary characters who are 'labouring in vain', but other inset characters (the two wooers competing on the cup; those who 'crow'). There is a closer connection in *Idyll* 7 between the labour and the song, however, as here the wasted work is not that of a lover but that of a singer; and a particular kind of singer: one who tries, hubristically we are to understand, to compete with Homer. It has often been noted that this recalls a Callimachean aesthetic of epic versus slender poetry: Lycidas is about to offer a 'little song' (τὸ μελύδριον, 51) which he worked hard on (ἐξεπόνασα). Also noted is the Hesiodic resonance of this scene – it is this that I would like to take up, but framing it specifically in terms of materiality.

---

[1] Payne (2007: 129) argues that this is not a song *contest* as such, as the performances complement but do not respond directly to one another. Both songs are cast as pre-existing creations rather than spontaneous performances, so they don't have the exact correspondences we might expect from an agonistic exchange.

First, the τέκτων of *Idyll* 7 line 45 unavoidably recalls *Works and Days* lines 25–6:

καὶ κεραμεὺς κεραμεῖ κοτέει καὶ τέκτονι τέκτων,
καὶ πτωχὸς πτωχῷ φθονέει καὶ ἀοιδὸς ἀοιδῷ.

Potter vies with potter and builder, builder;
beggar envies beggar and singer, singer.

The connection between builder and singer is clearly (we might say proverbially) established in these Hesiodic lines, and the theme of competition introduced. *Idyll* 7 follows the pattern: the τέκτων precedes the ἀοιδός, the materially grounded occupation setting up the singer's more intangible product. In *Idyll* 7 the parallel pairs – the builder and the singer – create a materially inflected metaphorical connection between the house as tall as a mountain, and the song on a Homeric scale. Building blocks of a song, of a house; a mountainous, insurmountable epic – the two ambitions are brought into alignment. And the metaphorical language persists within the occupations, as the poets are referred to as the 'birds of the Muses' (Μοισᾶν ὄρνιχες) – preliminarily neutral (winged words), until they are said to utter a discordant 'crow' (κοκκύζοντες). Singer becomes animal, words are reduced to dissonant noise. The pessimistic tone of these lines fits the dark-ecological reading applied by William Brockliss to the *Works and Days*. The Strife passage, of which *WD* lines 25–6 form a part, is cited by Brockliss as a Hesiodic example of dark ecology, as 'the description of the two Strifes is not only consistent with Morton's emphasis on the interweaving of the human and nonhuman, but also carries negative connotations in keeping with the tone of his dark ecological aesthetic'.[2] In the Hesiod passage, envy crosses over between positive and negative; in Theocritus, the striving of the builder has become something to be scorned, the assimilation of manmade and natural environs something to be held under suspicion.

Second, these lines from *Idyll* 7 are preceded by a Hesiodic scene of poetic initiation – transposed to a bucolic mode.

'τάν τοι', ἔφα, 'κορύναν δωρύττομαι, οὕνεκεν ἐσσί
πᾶν ἐπ᾽ ἀλαθείᾳ πεπλασμένον ἐκ Διὸς ἔρνος.'

'I present you', he said, 'with this stick, because you are
a sapling all moulded for truth by Zeus.'
                                                                (*Idyll* 7.43–4)

---

[2] Brockliss 2018: 6.

The Muses in line 47, the mountain in line 46 – both follow on from this gift of a stick, associated with truth and with Zeus. The nexus of ideas repeats, reconfigures and reinvents that in the scene of Hesiod's inspiration from his *Theogony*. It is the material aspect that interests me here. First, it is not a *skeptron* that is given, ubiquitous though this object is in both Homeric and Hesiodic poetry. It is something more rough, more rural: κορύνη, a word meaning stick or staff, but also used to refer to knobby buds or shoots in plants,[3] giving an idea of its rustic makeup. This evocation of the natural environs also translates across to the human characters, as there is an alignment between man and material when Lycidas describes Simichidas as a sapling, a shoot (ἔρνος). Nature and culture meld together as the stick initiates the exchange of song, in which a shoot formed by Zeus participates. Just as Zeus in his capacity as god of weather moulds the shape of trees as they grow, so he moulds Simichidas 'for truth' (ἐπ' ἀλαθείᾳ). The reference to truth is another ineluctable Hesiodic allusion, recalling that most memorable and confounding of passages:

ἴδμεν ψεύδεα πολλὰ λέγειν ἐτύμοισιν ὁμοῖα
ἴδμεν δ' εὖτ' ἐθέλωμεν ἀληθέα γηρύσασθαι.

We know how to speak many falsehoods that sound like truths,
and we know, when we wish, how to speak true things.
(Hesiod *Theogony* 27–8)

Πεπλασμένον in *Idyll* 7.44 means 'fashioned', 'educated' – but it also means 'made up', 'invented', 'not true'.[4] The Muses' paradox is played out in this ambiguous craft metaphor. Hunter also draws attention to the crookedness of the staff (ῥοικὰν κορύναν, 18–19), crookedness being the main threat to justice in Hesiod's poetry. As Hunter writes, 'Simichidas is thus as shifting and illusory as poetry itself'. To bring together these alignments, then, man is equated with natural environs, material with song and song with man. Again we see in operation a central nexus that interests us in this book– and it is particularly relevant to material '*oiko*-criticism' that this is triangulated through Hesiod. The allusions to Hesiod's initiation persist throughout the *Idyll*, making it a running theme. At 91–3 Simichidas tells how the Nymphs taught him his songs while he tended his herd in the hills:

[3] Thphr. *HP* 3.5.1.
[4] Hunter 1999 *ad loc.*

> 'Λυκίδα φίλε, πολλὰ μὲν ἄλλα
> Νύμφαι κἠμὲ δίδαξαν ἀν' ὤρεα βουκολέοντα
> ἐσθλά, τά που καὶ Ζηνὸς ἐπὶ θρόνον ἄγαγε φάμα·

> Lycidas my friend, the Nymphs taught me
> very many good songs as I tended my herds in the mountains,
> songs whose fame may even have reached the throne of Zeus.

This is a replica of the *Theogony* scene, with the Nymphs standing in for the Muses. Interestingly, Hopkinson in his Loeb translation elides the distinction, translating as 'the Muses have taught me', perhaps assuming a slippage or overlap with line 95 (ἐπεὶ φίλος ἔπλεο Μοίσαις: 'since you are a friend to the Muses'). As Gow notes on line 91, 'it would be going too far to say that T. means the Muses, but the relationship of Muse and Nymph is close and not precisely definable'. I wonder, however, if the reference to the nymphs enhances the poem/poet's connection to the land,[5] as the nymphs are the more notorious for inhabiting that ambiguous space between mortal and immortal, between character and personification, between the inhabited and the natural world.[6] Then at 128–9 Lycidas finally hands over the promised staff, now explicitly a mark of *xenia* from the Muses (ἐκ Μοισᾶν ξεινήιον), and now a λαγωβόλον, a shepherd's staff or a stick for chasing hares – still a specifically rustic, contextualised object.

In terms of reality and imagination, it is important to consider the potential autobiographical reading of this *Idyll*: something that will also provide a contrast with the probably non-Theocritean *Idyll* 21, to which I move next. I have so far referred to the characters as Lycidas and Simichidas – but it remains to be noted that Simichidas is not named until line 21, and indeed we are in *his* first-person

---

[5] Similarly, at 7.148–57 Simichidas questions the nymphs, and Hunter *ad loc.* comments that he '"bucolizes" the epic practice of questioning the Muses'.

[6] In Greek thought, nymphs are treated as divinities, but lesser ones who are so close to mortals that they can be encountered by them without disguise or epiphany; they are given a name that can shift between the immortal and mortal realms, meaning both 'female water or landscape deity' and 'bride'; and indeed their (im)mortality was debated among ancient authors: for example, Pausanias claims 'the poets say that the nymphs live for a great number of years, but are not altogether exempt from death' (τὰς νύμφας δὲ εἶναι πολὺν μέν τινα ἀριθμὸν βιούσας ἐτῶν, οὐ μέντοι παράπαν γε ἀπηλλαγμένας θανάτου, ποιητῶν ἐστιν ἐς αὐτὰς λόγος, Paus. 10.31.10). Larson (2001: 30) draws our attention to e.g. Hes. fr. 304, in which the nymphs 'outlive ten phoenixes': as she explains, 'Relative to humans, nymphs were immortal, but relative to the Olympian gods, they were not.' For a full discussion of nymphs, see Larson 2001 and Pache 2011.

narration. Is there a correlation between Simichidas and Theocritus himself? This has been suggested since antiquity. Bowie argues that 'Simichidas both is and is not Theocritus',[7] and Hunter adds 'similarly, the setting of the poem both is and is not Cos'.[8] There are contextual markers, such as Simichidas and Lycidas discussing real Hellenistic poets, and a reference to song reaching the throne of Zeus thought to signify the court of Ptolemy Philadelphus, patron of the island.[9] Notable, too, is the narrative stance in this poem: it is set in the past (unlike the present-tense narration of other Theocritean bucolics), an account of something that 'happened'. Both autobiography and geography are as slippery as the poetry itself, and there is a paradoxical impression of familiarity yet elusiveness that maps across person, place and poem. This parallels Hesiodic poetry and readings of it: the eternal question of autobiography still looms large in Hesiodic studies, primarily because Hesiod provokes such discussion by littering his poems with potentially autobiographical details. He makes his persona immanent, present, knowable – but, as with the studied delay between the fable he tells and the moral with which he solves it, he maintains enough distance, ambiguity and illusion that we are faced not with facts but with still more questions.

The most sustained discussion of autobiography and fiction in this *Idyll* is given by Mark Payne in Chapter 4 of his book *Theocritus and the Invention of Fiction*. He summarises: 'Reality effects coexist with elements of manifest fiction, so that it is impossible to understand the poem as straight-forward autobiographical narration.'[10] Payne traces the trajectory of Simichidas into his reflection on the rustic symposium at the end of the *Idyll*, and argues that Lycidas has inspired Simichidas with 'the same desire to project a world of bucolic characters to which he can aspire in his imagination that animates his own psychic life'.[11] In this reading, the bucolic fiction (that is, Lycidas) is given authority over the 'real-life' Simichidas, and

---

[7] Bowie 1985: 68. Gow is rather more unequivocal in his interpretation: 'the identity between Simichidas and T. is complete' (Gow 1950: 128). He cites some explanations from the scholia for the name – for instance, that Simichidas is a patronymic (though, as Gow points out, the tradition of the *vitae* has it that Theocritus' father was not Simichus or Simichidas but Praxagoras) – but ultimately concludes that 'the significance of the name Simichidas escapes us'.

[8] Hunter 1999: 146. For Ὠρομέδοντος (7.46) there is the variant εὐρυμέδοντος, keeping the landscape identification open. Scholars (from the scholia on) have looked for an Oromedon peak in the mountain range on the south coast of Cos. The proper name versus the more general descriptor encapsulates the tension between a specific and a general reading.

[9] Payne 2007: 117; for the Ptolemaic interpretation, see Gow 1950 *ad* 7.93.

[10] Payne 2007: 116.

[11] Ibid. p. 117.

influences his biographical development. Payne concludes: 'What in the other poems is represented as an autonomous fictional world appears in this poem as a model for behavior in a world that is a mimetic image of historical reality.'[12] This is particularly relevant for the current discussion, as it gestures towards degrees of entanglement. Payne suggests that, while the other bucolic *Idylls* have some distance between the real and represented worlds, in *Idyll* 7 there is greater integration, as the real world is supposed mimetically to emulate the fiction.

Hunter relates the ambiguous autobiography of *Idyll* 7 to the very question of the genre of bucolic poetry, arguing that Lycidas' disconcertingly fixed smile throughout the poem 'marks the irony at the heart of the "bucolic" tradition – "true" knowledge of the countryside is not in fact important for the production of "bucolic song"'.[13] Just as Simichidas need not be Theocritus, or 'Hesiod' need not be Hesiod, so the landscape need not be *the* landscape. Much twentieth- and early twenty-first-century Hesiodic scholarship focused on the issue of autobiography: who was Hesiod, who was Perses, who was their father? The scholarly trajectory has moved away from this, however, and is now more concerned with what we can know about the poem, regardless of whether or not we can know a 'real' Hesiod. There has been a sidelining of the autobiographical questions in favour of a literary criticism that embraces the importance of the 'reality effect', regardless of reality *per se*. Similarly, in the case of Theocritus, this *Idyll*, with its subtle explorations of truth and fiction, lies and veracity, autobiography and storytelling, helps us to differentiate real from imagined landscapes. The fallacy of autobiographical reconstruction applies to Theocritus and his landscapes as much as to Hesiod: even when poets choose to include factually accurate autobiography in their work, they do so because it makes poetic sense, so the presumed mapping of Simichidas onto Theocritus can never fully explain Simichidas' presence in the poem, or the unfolding of the poem more generally. An appeal to (supposed) biographical reality cannot, in other words, provide a substitute for convincing literary interpretation. Whether or not these things are real, there is always literary intervention involved, and so even if we should want to ask these questions about the real world, we can never ask *just* these questions.

The questions are complicated further by whatever it is we might mean by imagined landscapes, versus reality. I make such a distinction throughout this chapter, primarily for ease of analysis: as a way to differentiate between different levels of inset story. But as a theoretical and indeed philosophical standpoint, it is neither a given, nor uncontested. In their 2012 book *Imagining Landscapes: Past, Present and Future*, Monica Janowski and Tim Ingold explore different approaches

---

[12] Ibid. p. 118.
[13] Hunter 1999: 150.

to imagination, beginning with Belgian surrealist artist René Magritte and historian Simon Schama,[14] both of whom contend that all seeing is imagining. 'To perceive a landscape is therefore to imagine it':[15] this renders the distinction between real and imagined landscapes somewhat arbitrary, or at least far more complex than it seems. Schama argues that it is our shaping perception that converts the raw material of the land into what we might call a landscape: a vista, a design, a beauty. This view has its opponents: Ingold cites psychologist of perception James Gibson (1979), who argues that the shape of the land is already there, awaiting discovery, and that perception and imagination are poles apart. This is expressly an ecological approach. With characteristic insight, Ingold weaves a way between these two views, proposing an approach that is, I think, much more conducive to a material-ecocritical analysis:

> Our aim in this volume is to find a way beyond these alternatives: a way that would reunite perception and imagination while yet acknowledging the human condition, *contra* both Magritte and Schama, to be that of a being whose knowledge of the world, far from being shaped by the operations of mind upon the deliverances of the senses, grows from the very soil of an existential involvement *in* the sensible world. To achieve this aim, we will need to reconsider the significance of the imagination: to think of it not just as a capacity to construct images, or as the power of mental representation, but more fundamentally as a way of living creatively in a world that is itself crescent, always in formation. To imagine, we suggest, is not so much to conjure up images of a reality 'out there', whether virtual or actual, true or false, as to participate from within, through perception and action, in the very becoming of things.[16]

This summary raises a whole host of possibilities interesting for our purposes here. It moves away from Schama's division between the interior and exterior, the mind and the world, towards a much more entangled perspective. It dislodges the anthropocentric focus engendered by statements like Schama's 'landscape is the work of the mind',[17] instead foregrounding the collaborative interactions between mind/body and land. It takes us from an epistemological to an ontological stance: our knowledge does not operate in splendid isolation, but through involvement in the world. It connects with the tenets of the current sensory turn, seeing the senses not as a top-down

---

[14] See Schama 1995.
[15] Ingold 2012: 2.
[16] Ibid. p. 3.
[17] Schama 1995: 6.

tool of 'shaping perception' but rather as an emergent property working in tandem with the world to be sensed. It casts imagination not just as representation, but as participation: as something not projected onto the world, but devised in conjunction with it (recalling Barad's ideas of intra-action). All of these possibilities resonate with the material-ecocritical approach espoused in this study and can help set the place of the current section in that overall framework.

Before moving on from *Idyll* 7, I would like to pick out one passage in particular that establishes the multilayered landscape I have been discussing. Lycidas sings of the parallel and striking ordeals of 'the goatherd' and Comatas:[18]

ἀσεῖ δ' ὥς ποκ' ἔδεκτο τὸν αἰπόλον εὐρέα λάρναξ
ζωὸν ἐόντα κακαῖσιν ἀτασθαλίαισιν ἄνακτος,
ὥς τέ νιν αἱ σιμαὶ λειμωνόθε φέρβον ἰοῖσαι
κέδρον ἐς ἁδεῖαν μαλακοῖς ἄνθεσσι μέλισσαι,
οὕνεκά οἱ γλυκὺ Μοῖσα κατὰ στόματος χέε νέκταρ.
ὦ μακαριστὲ Κομᾶτα, τὺ θην τάδε τερπνὰ πεπόνθεις·
καὶ τὺ κατεκλάσθης ἐς λάρνακα, καὶ τὺ μελισσᾶν
κηρία φερβόμενος ἔτος ὥριον ἐξεπόνασας.

And he shall sing how once a wide chest received the goatherd
alive by the evil impieties of the king,
and how the blunt-nosed bees came from the meadows
to the fragrant chest of cedar and fed him on tender flowers
because the Muse had poured sweet nectar on his lips.
Blessed Comatas, these pleasures were your fate:
you too were shut in a chest, and you too were fed on honeycomb
and you laboured hard in the springtime of the year.
(*Idyll* 7.78–85)

As Goldhill puts it, 'The chest is part of a veritable Chinese box effect of songs within songs, frame upon frame, as each song's content becomes the frame for the next song.'[19] Layering, framing and containment become driving forces in this poem. The motif of the container is a particularly compelling one for a materialist

---

[18] This parallelism is dependent on interpreting καὶ τὺ at line 84 as marking out Comatas as a different character to the goatherd. Another reading sees Comatas and the goatherd as one and the same, and the comparison instead with Daphnis. Hunter *ad loc*. argues that the verbal parallelisms between the parts of this passage support the former interpretation.

[19] Goldhill 1990: 235.

analysis. Containers by their very nature have great potential: vessels ready and waiting to be opened, used, filled with meaning. Storage containers are objects in and of themselves, and yet they simultaneously point towards something else. They have a compelling possibility, and poets ancient and modern make good use of it.[20] In an article of 2017, Hunter Dukes examines Samuel Beckett's 'animated' containers from a new-materialist perspective, using Alfred Gell's take on the idea of the homunculus. Gell argues that 'there is a certain cognitive naturalness of the idea of the mind or soul or spirit as a homunculus; that is, like a person but contained within a person',[21] and he sees creating material homunculi as a way of animating the object world. Dukes takes up this idea, exploring Beckett's vessels as lively sites of subjectivity that blur the boundary between human and nonhuman. To take this to the more general level, Lakoff and Johnson offer a consideration of 'the container metaphor' in language:[22] it is a cognitive metaphor we can see feeding into literature. The cognitive is another level on which we might consider a particular set of intermedial examples. There is the direct intertextual relationship between instantiations of an object type. There is also the parallel material plane to which the instantiations might connect and across which they might travel. And there is the cognitive level: the fact that we think in patterns and tropes that include 'the container metaphor'. We are provided with a further plane that sees materiality embedded in our very thought processes, our way of seeing the world also to an abstract degree, formulating it in figurative language.

To come back to the containers of *Idyll* 7. As Dukes writes, neatly summarising Gell's argument, 'the "homunculus-effect" can be achieved wherever there is concentricity and containment'.[23] That is, wherever we can see a material representation of interiority (something inside something else), we make connections with our own embodiment. This passage from *Idyll* 7 is especially compelling, as the generalising and abstract coincide with the specific: notions of containment, interiority and embodiment are actually conveyed through a story of a man inside a chest. In this story, the contents of the container are well and truly animated, the homunculus effect rendered literal. What is also interesting about this passage from the perspective of material agency and entanglement is that the human contents are overpowered by the container itself. The goatherd is contained, imprisoned,

---

[20] This is something I have discussed at length in Canevaro forthcoming b in relation to Homer, and for instance Joshua Billings in a 2018 chapter offers an examination of Orestes' urn in Sophocles' *Electra* that casts it as a kind of actor, bearing a great burden of meaning, emotion and affect.
[21] Gell 1998: 131.
[22] Lakoff and Johnson 1980: 29.
[23] Dukes 2017: 78.

entombed within the chest.²⁴ It is only through more nonhuman agency that he can survive, as the bees sustain him. There is, however, crossover between the imprisoning and the sustaining agents: the bees are said to come 'to the fragrant cedarwood chest', an evocation of the alluring sensory affect of the chest, which contributes to its prisoner's survival. This is an entangled image: the man in the chest, sustained by the bees that are attracted to both chest (fragrant) and man (nectar on his lips) – and song (the meaning of this symbolic sweetness).

In their introduction to a 2018 *History and Anthropology* journal forum issue, Andrew Shryock and Daniel Lord Smail set out a theoretical framework for a 'deep history' of the container. They see containers as an 'engine of history' and 'time machines', suspending time or slowing decay as 'anti-entropy machines'. Indeed, the survival of the goatherd depends on this suspension of time, as he is 'preserved' in the chest. Shryock and Smail note that containers are by no means a human invention, but occur in the natural world – membranes, hives and dens, for example – and that when early humans used shells or gourds as containers, they were repurposing them for uses that closely resembled their natural functions: 'Rarely has a clear culture/nature divide been essential to the way humans think about and make their containers.'²⁵ That the authors include hives in their list of natural containers is of course particularly pertinent to our passage. In *Idyll* 7 the bees cross between the natural and human worlds, the line blurred by the container that is manmade but from natural organic materials and that the bees seem to treat like a hive.

Fantuzzi and Hunter allude to the entanglements in this passage. They comment:

> There are some exceptional cases in which [Theocritus] suspends the selective 'realism' with which he habitually presents his characters, and allows the world of nature and the world of human activity and suffering to flow into each other. The exceptions are Daphnis (7.72–7 and 1.64–145) and the 'divine' Comatas of 7.78–85.²⁶

I hope by this point to have shifted our perceptions on this: to have shown that such a 'flow' between humans and nonhuman nature is not restricted to these cases, and that Daphnis and Comatas are not entirely exceptional in this regard. And yet it cannot be disputed that the blurred boundary is emphasised with these characters as nature crowds in. The emphasis extends also to the representation of the environs

---

²⁴ Hunter 1999 *ad loc.* notes that the use of cedar for coffins is relevant here (citing Eur. *Tr.* 1141 and *Alc.* 365).
²⁵ Shryock and Smail 2018: 1.
²⁶ Fantuzzi and Hunter 2004: 149.

in *Idyll* 7: as Fantuzzi and Hunter write, 'In only one case do we find an extensive description of a *locus amoenus* which culminates in a radically idealised, and therefore unrealistic, representation of the sympathetic participation of the world of nature; the passage comes at the end of *Idyll* 7'.[27]

> πολλαὶ δ' ἄμμιν ὕπερθε κατὰ κρατὸς δονέοντο
> αἴγειροι πτελέαι τε· τὸ δ' ἐγγύθεν ἱερὸν ὕδωρ
> Νυμφᾶν ἐξ ἄντροιο κατειβόμενον κελάρυζε.
> τοὶ δὲ ποτὶ σκιαραῖς ὀροδαμνίσιν αἰθαλίωνες
> τέττιγες λαλαγεῦντες ἔχον πόνον· ἁ δ' ὀλολυγών
> τηλόθεν ἐν πυκιναῖς βάτων τρύζεσκεν ἀκάνθαις·
> ἄειδον κόρυδοι καὶ ἀκανθίδες, ἔστενε τρυγών,
> πωτῶντο ξουθαὶ περὶ πίδακας ἀμφὶ μέλισσαι.
> πάντ' ὦσδεν θέρεος μάλα πίονος, ὦσδε δ' ὀπώρας.
> ὄχναι μὲν πὰρ ποσσί, παρὰ πλευραῖσι δὲ μᾶλα
> δαψιλέως ἁμῖν ἐκυλίνδετο, τοὶ δ' ἐκέχυντο
> ὄρπακες βραβίλοισι καταβρίθοντες ἔραζε·

> Many poplars and elms whispered above our heads,
> and nearby the sacred water
> from the cave of the Nymphs trickled babbling.
> On the shady branches the dusky cicadas
> worked hard at their chirping, and far off in the
> dense thorns the tree frog kept murmuring.
> Larks and finches sang, the turtle-dove was moaning,
> and humming bees were flying around the spring.
> Everywhere there was the smell of the rich harvest, the smell of the
>   fruit-gathering.
> Pears at our feet and apples by our sides
> were rolling plentifully, and the branches bent down to the ground
> weighed down with sloes.
>   (*Idyll* 7.135–46)

The description is multisensory (moving from sound to smell to taste), but centres on the aural: the sounds of trees, streams, cicadas, frogs, birds and bees. Lycidas and Simichidas have performed their songs, and now it is nature's turn.[28] This is more

---

[27] Ibid. p. 146.
[28] On the voices or music of the nonhuman and nature, see LeVen 2021.

than a closing frame: it is suggestive and indeed programmatic in terms of material agency. This *Idyll* is thought to model the initiation of the bucolic genre, Simichidas standing in for Theocritus; it is worth noting, therefore, that this pastoral poetry also comes with and through nonhuman voices. Fantuzzi and Hunter continue:

> In this single case, a primitivistic idealisation suggestive of the Golden Age, in which the fruit automatically dropped off the trees for the men, is achieved in the ritualised atmosphere of a rural harvest festival. The idealising imagination grows from rural reality – there is indeed a superabundance of fruit in the season of the harvest – and from the logic of religious thought.

Though the *Idyll* is ultimately 'unrealistic', it is grounded in real-world activities – and, by extension, in the real-world interactions between humans and nature.

This passage is overtly artificial. It 'dramatises the ironic fracture at the heart of the "literature of nature", in the 'imposition of (urban) art upon (rural) nature, a process from which "nature" cannot emerge unchanged'.[29] Yet the impetus of Material Ecocriticism would prompt us to consider the feedback loop, the other side of the story. For a rural *locus amoenus* we might look back to Hesiod's description of the Golden Age in his *Works and Days*:

καρπὸν δ' ἔφερε ζείδωρος ἄρουρα
αὐτομάτη πολλόν τε καὶ ἄφθονον·

The grain-giving field bore fruit
of its own accord, much and plentiful.
  (Hesiod *Works and Days* 117–18)

This is Hesiod's description of an idyllic state, free from care: yet it is one he formulates from a farmer's point of view. Similarly, in the pre-Pandora world 'you would easily have worked enough in one day to have sufficient stores for a year of idleness',[30] and the Race of Heroes on the Isles of the Blessed get three crops a year.[31] This is the *farmer*'s idea of heaven. It is an artificial idyll that nevertheless is inseparable from reality, in which the interdependence between humans and the land is not jettisoned but modified. Art may be imposed on nature – but nature looms so

---

[29] Hunter 1999 *ad loc.*
[30] *Works and Days* 43–4: ῥηιδίως γάρ κεν καὶ ἐπ' ἤματι ἐργάσσαιο | ὥστέ σε κεῖς ἐνιαυτὸν ἔχειν καὶ ἀεργὸν ἐόντα·
[31] *Works and Days* 170–3.

large in our material makeup and our literary imagination that it exerts its own force in return.

Idyll 7 concludes with these lines:

Νύμφαι Κασταλίδες Παρνάσιον αἶπος ἔχοισαι,
ἆρά γέ πᾳ τοιόνδε Φόλω κατὰ λάινον ἄντρον
κρατῆρ᾽ Ἡρακλῆι γέρων ἐστάσατο Χίρων;
ἆρά γέ πᾳ τῆνον τὸν ποιμένα τὸν ποτ᾽ Ἀνάπῳ,
τὸν κρατερὸν Πολύφαμον, ὃς ὤρεσι νᾶας ἔβαλλε,
τοῖον νέκταρ ἔπεισε κατ᾽ αὐλία ποσσὶ χορεῦσαι,
οἷον δὴ τόκα πῶμα διεκρανάσατε, Νύμφαι,
βωμῷ πὰρ Δάματρος ἁλωίδος; ἇς ἐπὶ σωρῷ
αὖτις ἐγὼ πάξαιμι μέγα πτύον, ἃ δὲ γελάσσαι
δράγματα καὶ μάκωνας ἐν ἀμφοτέραισιν ἔχοισα.

Nymphs of Castalia who dwell on Mount Parnassus,
was it a bowl like this that old Chiron served to Heracles
in Pholus' rocky cave?
Was it nectar like this that set the shepherd by the Anapus
dancing among his sheepfolds, the mighty Polyphemus,
who pelted ships with mountains?
This was the kind of drink you Nymphs then mixed for us
by the altar of Demeter of the threshing floor. On her heap
may I plant again the great winnowing shovel, while she smiles
on us with sheaves and poppies in both hands.

(*Idyll* 7.148–57)

Here we have more than an exaggerated *locus amoenus*. We have a window onto a way of being-in-the-world, an entanglement that is not only grounded in real-world interactions between human and nature but mythologically exemplified – that has a precedent, albeit in mythical time. The emphatically pastoral elements of this poem transport the reader not to an unrealistic enlivened landscape but to a 'beforetime' (as Mark Payne puts it), when boundaries were *even more* blurred. The festival is 'a gateway to the ancient spirit of the wild',[32] as 'interpellation by idyllic, surrounding

---

[32] Payne 2019: 154. Payne's chapter, his contribution to the 2019 book *Antiquities Beyond Humanism*, spans Schiller, Hölderlin and Hellenistic poetry. He notes: 'Schiller points to the Hellenistic period as a moment in the history of poetics in which the apprehension of a loss of naturalness in human sociality impels its poets to adopt the roles of "nature's

nature in *Idyll* 7 is what affords imaginative access to the shared life of primordial humanity with beings as a whole'.[33] Mythology therefore acts as a catalyst for pastoral poetry, just as Simichidas models its initiation.

From the prompt of the fisherman in *Idyll* 1, and the direction of our discussion of *Idyll* 7, we move now to *Idyll* 21 and the strong connection it presents between fishermen and their environs. Through a seaweed bed, a plaited hut and a leafy wall, the fishermen are anchored in the environment. This is the poet's imagined landscape – and through a fisherman's dream, we are transported to a secondary imagined world embedded in the first. With this *Idyll* we can take up the cue from *Idyll* 7, continuing to reflect on the imagined worlds of Theocritean poetry, how they map onto or diverge from the real world and what we can learn from those narrative gaps or convergences. It is worth noting at the outset that the Theocritean attribution of this *Idyll* is generally discredited, on metrical, linguistic and stylistic grounds:[34] nevertheless, I include it in my discussion because of those blurred and moveable boundaries of the Theocritean corpus discussed in Chapter 1 (pp. 23–37).

The moral of the story introduces the *Idyll*, and with it we are back in a context of toil, as poverty is said to be the teacher of work: μόχθοιο διδάσκαλος (2). The fishermen's occupation is cast as a particularly material one: a job defined by its equipment, its paraphernalia, its clutter and its close ties with the land- (and sea-) scape.

Ἰχθύος ἀγρευτῆρες ὁμῶς δύο κεῖντο γέροντες
στρωσάμενοι βρύον αὖον ὑπὸ πλεκταῖς καλύβαισι,
κεκλιμένοι τοίχῳ τῷ φυλλίνῳ· ἐγγύθι δ᾽ αὐτοῖν
κεῖτο τὰ ταῖν χειροῖν ἀθλήματα, τοὶ καλαθίσκοι,
τοὶ κάλαμοι, τἄγκιστρα, τὰ φυκιόεντα δέλητα,
ὁρμιαὶ κύρτοι τε καὶ ἐκ σχοίνων λαβύρινθοι,
μήρινθοι κῶπαί τε γέρων τ᾽ ἐπ᾽ ἐρείσμασι λέμβος·
νέρθεν τᾶς κεφαλᾶς φορμὸς βραχύς, εἵματα, πῖλοι.

---

witnesses and avengers" for their contemporaries' (p. 141) – yet another reason to focus the current material-ecocritical study on Theocritus.

[33] Payne 2019: 154.

[34] For an overview, see Gow 1950: 369. Gow finds the metrical and linguistic (vocabulary) grounds unconvincing but considers the argument from quality of language weightier: he calls *Idyll* 21 'bald and undistinguished' (see Chapter 3 pp. 113–40 for Gow's similar assessment of *Idyll* 23). Gow is particularly struck by the lack of allusion to earlier poetry in this *Idyll*, in particular that of Homer, and by its moralising tendency.

> Two old fishermen were lying down together
> on a bed of dried seaweed strewn in their plaited hut,
> and they were lying against the leafy wall. Near them
> lay the tools of their labouring hands: baskets,
> rods, hooks, seaweed-covered bait,
> lines and weels and traps made from rushes,
> cords and oars and an old boat on props.
> A little mat for their heads, clothes, caps.
>
> (*Idyll* 21.6–13)

The two fishermen sleep on a makeshift bed of seaweed in a hut of plaited branches still with their leaves. It is an image of entanglement: joined together by their work and their poverty, the fishermen are a united pair (ὅμως δύο); the hut is created through a process that is the very epitome of entanglement (πλεκταῖς καλύβαισι);[35] they recline against the leafy wall (κεκλιμένοι τοίχῳ τῷ φυλλίνῳ), their bodies connecting with all parts of their nature/culture surroundings (raw yet constructed). The entanglement continues into the list of their possessions, which are near them (ἐγγύθι δ' αὐτοῖν: a phrase that intrudes into its line, making sure the word order replicates the objects' proximity to their possessors). The list progresses from tools of fishing, through to materials for the body, which comes into view in τᾶς κεφαλᾶς.[36] The catalogue gives an impression of proliferation, with human (ταῖν χειροῖν, τᾶς κεφαλᾶς) and nonhuman parts intertwined. This gives a similar impression, albeit in miniature, to the final Days section of Hesiod's *Works and Days*, which has been treated by Brockliss 2018 under the aesthetic of dark ecology. Brockliss writes of the Days:

> It is very unlikely that ancient listeners (any more than their modern counterparts) would have remembered how each particular human, animal, plant, or human product mentioned in the section relates to each particular day. Rather, they would have taken away the impression of a mélange of bodies and objects ... all of which follow in quick succession. Audiences would have sensed an assimilation of these different kinds of living and nonliving things to one another ... But the passage also gives the impression of a numberless profusion, an effect similar to that of

---

[35] On plaiting see discussion in the first section of Chapter 4 (pp. 146–55).
[36] There is a textual variant in the final line, πύσοι for πῖλοι. πῖλοι gives the more attractive reading, providing an intermedial mapping onto Hesiod's sage advice at *WD* 545–6: κεφαλῆφι δ' ὕπερθεν | πῖλον ἔχειν ἀσκητόν, ἵν' οὔατα μὴ καταδεύῃ ('wear a well-fitting cap on your head so that your ears don't get wet').

Morton's 'hyperobjects.' Listeners would have witnessed the general presence of these humans, animals, plants, and objects in the environments of the days section more readily than their individual instantiations.[37]

This is to pick up on Morton's idea of the hyperobject: a material encountered not so much through 'individual instantiations' but as an overarching presence.[38] Radioactive waste is Morton's prime example: a substance that permeates not only what we might think of as the external environment, but also our own bodies through toxicity.[39] The individual components of this list, then, like Hesiod's individual days, may not be as important, or at least may not be as striking to the reader, as the overall material saturation in these lines. It is a busy, entangled scene, with a pervasive materiality to it.

The objects in the catalogue are introduced as τὰ ταῖν χειροῖν ἀθλήματα. According to Gow, this phrase might indicate 'the implements of their toilsome trade', or 'the implements they have laboriously fashioned' – either way, there is a strong connection between the people and their objects. I have translated the phrase as 'the tools of their labouring hands', in order to bring out ταῖν χειροῖν that is elided in Gow's formulations. The hands are crucial in this material-ecocritical reading, and not to be overlooked. Later in this chapter (pp. 140–5) I will pick up on the hands as the porous and permeable boundary between the human and nonhuman, and in Chapter 4 (pp. 155–69) I will draw our attention to the hands of Theugenis in *Idyll* 28, in terms of women's *erga*. Here I highlight the elided hands, to point out just how smoothly human hands can disappear from notice when they are operating in tandem with material objects.[40] In *Idyll* 21 we have a phrase that sets up a collaboration of agents – the hands and the tools – and that (presumably because of its unusual formulation with ἀθλήματα) becomes a hybrid in translation.

One of the items listed is the λαβύρινθοι, on which Gow comments: 'the word is not elsewhere used of fishing apparatus but plainly denotes some form of trap like

---

[37] Brockliss 2018: 25.
[38] See Morton 2013: 130–5. On the hyperobject in classical thought, see Porter 2019.
[39] Toxicity and pollution are much discussed in Material Ecocriticism: see, for example, the chapters in Iovino and Oppermann 2014 by Dana Phillips ('Excremental ecocriticism and the global sanitation crisis'), Stacy Alaimo ('Oceanic origins, plastic activism, and new materialism at sea') and Cheryll Glotfelty ('Corporeal fieldwork and risky art: Peter Gion and the making of nuclear landscapes').
[40] See Canevaro 2018b: 129–42 for this phenomenon in the *Odyssey*, where effective rowing constitutes a hybridity between person and oar in which the hands disappear – hands that only come back into view when the hybrid agent is separated, the collaboration disrupted.

the κύρτος, the exit from which is hard to find.' With the plaiting and the multiple kinds of trap, this passage recalls the final scene on the cup of *Idyll* 1, the boy plaiting his grasshopper trap. It also gives a cumulative image of enmeshment, the list drawing us into the fisherman's material world, from which we struggle to find our way out. This impression of proximity and entanglement, of human and nonhuman hinging together and operating in close quarters, is enhanced in lines 17–18, when we get a clearer idea of the topography of the camp:

οὐδεὶς δ' ἐν μέσσῳ γείτων πέλεν, ἁ δὲ παρ' αὐτᾷ
θλιβομέναν καλύβᾳ τραφερὰν προσέναχε θάλασσα.

No neighbour was near, and right up to their hut
the sea confined and lapped against the land.

The sea and the land become one and the same, with the hut not so much a boundary as a continuation. As a temporary structure it seems not like a fixed point but as fluid and fluctuating as its surroundings.

These are the environs created, imagined, by the poet: a representation of human/nonhuman entanglement – of fishermen embodying their craft, of material clutter, of land and sea conjoined, of sea lapping against human habitation. But this *Idyll* goes further, taking us into a twice-represented landscape – through the fisherman's dream. We are propelled into the imagination of a character, prompting us to reflect on the process of representation, and the role of materiality and environs within it. First, the dream itself is added to the entangled narrative thus far, as it is equated with the fisherman's catch:

ὡς καὶ τὰν ἄγραν, τὠνείρατα πάντα μερίζευ.

Just as with your catch, share out all your dreams.
       (*Idyll* 21.31)

And the human and animal worlds intertwine when the dreamer offers a simile:

καὶ γὰρ ἐν ὕπνοις
πᾶσα κύων ἄρτον μαντεύεται, ἰχθύα κἠγών.

For just as all sleeping
dogs dream of bread, so I dream of fish.
      (*Idyll* 21.44–5)

This is a peculiar line, as we wouldn't suppose that dogs do dream of bread.[41] Many alternatives for ἄρτον have been suggested, including ἄγραν, repeating the catch at 31 – but as that line makes clear, fish can also be classed as ἄγραν, and so this suggestion blurs the divide between the two parts of line 45. The result of this absurdity is that in the intertwining of human and animal, there is a slippage between the two, with either the animal approximating the human (dreaming of bread) or the two meeting in the middle (in the parallel 'catch'). This evokes the posthumanist idea of the humanimal, an image of hybridity and porosity on the same spectrum as the huma(n)chine, or Donna Haraway's cyborg. The question 'do dogs dream of bread?' then, is not all that different from the haunting question 'do androids dream of electric sheep?'

The entangled environs are reiterated in the framing of the dream, as Asphalion is asked by his companion:

τί γὰρ ποιεῖν ἂν ἔχοι τις
κείμενος ἐν φύλλοις ποτὶ κύματι μηδὲ καθεύδων;

For what is a man to do,
lying in the leaves by the waves, if he can't sleep?
(*Idyll* 21.34–5)

---

[41] The practical is, I would argue, different from the poetic. Dogs in antiquity did eat bread. As Adrienne Mayor writes in her article 'Ancient Puppy Chow' for the *Wonder and Marvels* online magazine, hunting dogs would have bread as part of their diet: 'Ordinary pups get barley bread softened with cow's milk or whey. But more valuable puppies eat their bread soaked in sheep or goat milk. You might add a little blood from the animal you expect your puppy to hunt. At dinner with your family, you scoop soft chunks of bread from the center of a loaf to wipe grease from your fingers – and toss them to your dog, supplemented with bones and other table scraps, perhaps even a basin of meat broth. After a sacrifice or banquet, you make a special treat: a lump of ox liver dredged in barley meal and roasted in the coals.' Available at <https://www.wondersandmarvels.com/2012/02/ancient-puppy-chow-dog-food-in-classical-greece.html> (last accessed 17 November 2022). And that's the point – the treat is not the bread, but the meat. Surely this is what dogs dream about? In any case, it is not dogs who are characterised as bread-eaters in ancient poetry. In Homer, the formula 'those who eat bread' (σῖτον ἔδοντες) acts as an epithet of humans, differentiated from the immortals (*Il.* 5.341, *Od.* 8.222, 9.89, 10.101, 16.110). A related epithet (σιτόφαγος) is used of men at *Od.* 9.191, to show what Polyphemus is *not*. At Hesiod *WD* 146–7 the fact that the bronze race do not eat bread (οὐδέ τι σῖτον ἤσθιον) marks them out as something different from us Iron Age humans.

The first-degree landscape doesn't leave much space to manoeuvre physically, and poverty doesn't provide much opportunity for change – so the story casts us into a second-degree landscape through the medium of the fisherman's dream.

In the dream's opening image, Asphalion sees himself sitting on a rock, watching for fish and dangling his baited rod. This takes us back to *Idyll* 1 and the old fisherman and his rock – though, as I argue in at pp. 115–17, the positioning of human and nonhuman agents in that scene is rather more striking. We are then given a detailed and dramatic description of the fishing: a plump fish is hooked, the rod strains and bends, Asphalion slackens then tightens the line. Man and tools are in it together, both straining and striving, struggling and teetering on the brink of failure:

τὼ χέρε τεινόμενος, περικλώμενος, εὗρον ἀγῶνα
πῶς ἀνέλω μέγαν ἰχθὺν ἀφαυροτέροισι σιδάροις·

Stretching out my hands, bending around, I found that I had a struggle
to catch the great fish with my feeble tools.

(*Idyll* 21.48–9)

In περικλώμενος the body is contorting just like the rod, the hand stretching (τεινόμενος) just like the fishing line. The placing of τὼ χέρε at the beginning of line 48 and σιδάροις at the end of 49 encapsulates this passage as a collaboration of man and material, another expression of that hand/object hybridity discussed above. Indeed materiality takes centre stage as σιδάροις, literally 'iron' but used to refer metonymically to various objects made of iron, sets up a material contrast with the fish – which turns out to be made of gold (χρύσεον ἰχθύν, παντᾷ τοι χρυσῷ πεπυκασμένον, 52–3). Fearing the gods' wrath, the fisherman releases his catch, taking care that the gold doesn't snag on his fishhook (μή ποκα τῷ στόματος τἀγκίστρια χρυσὸν ἔχοιεν, 57). It is from a potentially hubristic act that the fisherman retreats – and this is materially manifest in the need to keep separate the 'iron' and the gold.

In his dream, the fisherman vows never again to 'set foot' on the sea (πόδα θεῖναι, 59) but instead to stay on land and rule over his gold (τῷ χρυσῷ βασιλεύσειν). Upon waking, he is troubled: he knows this is to undermine his very existence, rejecting his trade for wealth that he does not possess. His companion reassures him: the vision was nothing but lies (ἴσα δ᾽ ἦν ψεύδεσιν ὄψις, 64); he needs to resist the allure of the elusive gold and instead focus on 'a fish of flesh' (τὸν σάρκινον ἰχθύν, 66). We come back to the delicate balance between truth and lies explored in

Idyll 7 alongside its Hesiodic intertext. In *Idyll* 7 Simichidas is shaped for truth, but the presence of the Muses and the crookedness of the staff suggest that this truth might not be the whole story. In *Idyll* 21 the dream rings true enough to frighten Asphalion – and he needs his companion to interpret, to uncover the falsehoods and set him back on the right path. Storytelling is the common denominator in the two passages (and, indeed, in the Hesiodic lines quoted above): Lycidas and Simichidas are to exchange their songs; Asphalion is telling the tale of his dream. And both are driven by materiality: the staff initiating or ratifying Simichidas' song, Asphalion's predicament centring on the antitheses between iron and gold, gold and flesh.

As the companion dismisses the dream as 'lies', the embedded imagined world dissipates, and Asphalion is brought back to a context of toil and poverty, of fish and flesh. As a reader of the poem, it is a somewhat unsettling experience to see a world created in words punctured, deflated in one cast. With Asphalion we come back down to reality with a thump – yet is it his reality, or our own? How many story worlds have been ruptured? The moralising conclusion to the *Idyll*, which picks up the introduction, keeps us with the programme even as it ultimately seals off the poem as a self-contained entity. The fishermen have sorted out their interpretive problem, and they know who and where they are. But how fixed is that world? We might consider this in terms of its material landscape, and its durability. If we look back at the makeshift hut, the waves encroaching upon the land, we are met with hints of instability. Further, though the fishermen work with their natural world, there is a dissonance with their environs, as Asphalion begins to question the seasons. He calls those people 'liars' (ψεύδοντ', ὦ φίλε, πάντες, 22), who claim that the summer nights are short (he has already had countless dreams this night): the *topos* of falsehood resurfaces, seasonal sureties cast as fickle as dreamscapes. 'Do you blame the summer?' asks his companion (μέμφῃ τὸ καλὸν θέρος, 26) – Asphalion is casting aspersions on his environment, placing blame on seasonality. This is a compelling frame for the dream narrative, as it prefaces the embedded imagined landscape with doubts about the fishermen's own world. Asphalion begins to question everything – and leads the poem's readers to do the same. In *Idyll* 21 the landscape is as 'shifting and illusory' as is Simichidas in *Idyll* 7 – and it is the superimposition of one imagined environment onto another that creates that shimmering, hazy effect.

In *Idyll* 7, Lycidas challenges Simichidas, asking where he is hurrying to in the middle of the day, setting up the opportunity for song. He notes the effect of Simichidas' haste on the land:

ὥς τοι ποσὶ νισσομένοιο
πᾶσα λίθος πταίοισα ποτ' ἀρβυλίδεσσιν ἀείδει.

> How all the stones are falling over
> your feet as you go along, as they sing against your boots.[42]
> (*Idyll* 7.25–6)

Earlier in this section I discussed the Hesiod-inspired parallelism between builder and singer, used by Theocritus to establish a materially inflected metaphorical connection between the occupations. We might argue that this parallelism is prefaced here: the stone standing in for building blocks, the singing introduced by the verb. But from the perspective of material agency, there is more going on here. The λίθος is the subject of the sentence, and the human body part and its covering (feet, boots) are put in the dative. Something is happening *to* the human character, by virtue of the nonhuman subject. First, the stone stumbles against the feet (πταίοισα), rather than the other way round. Hunter observes: 'Lykidas' reversal both marks Simichidas' intrusion into an alien world where stones, but not Simichidas, belong and reveals his own peculiarly "bucolic" vision'.[43] Yet we can go further than this. The stubbing of one's toe against a stone has long been used as one of the quintessential examples of the meeting point between human and nonhuman agents: the moment in which the material world exerts its physical force and makes us take notice.[44] The stone on which we stub our toe is moving into the foreground. And here we can see the new-materialist balancing act at work: do we stub our toe on a stone, or does the stone stub our toe?[45] Where does the agency lie: with one of the two parties, with both independently, or reciprocally and collaboratively, precisely at the meeting point between them? This is a great example of human and nonhuman worlds converging – and the concomitant muddying of the ontological waters. In the case of *Idyll* 7, we do indeed have a reversal of expectation – it is the stones

---

[42] Gow *ad loc.* notes material parallels: ἀείδει used of a bowstring at *Od.* 21.411, of a tree in the wind at Mosch. fr. 1.8, and in a passage from Pepys' *Diary*, in which the poor man says he 'will make the stones fly til they sing before me'.

[43] Hunter 1999 *ad loc.*

[44] It is like Heidegger's infamous broken hammer (see the Heidegger 1971 essay 'The Thing'): we only begin to notice the hammer when it doesn't fulfil its role, when it 'acts out', when it draws our attention to it; we only notice the pane of glass in the window when it's dirty. Strictly speaking, the broken hammer belongs to the analysis of tool-being, of made objects, so it is not quite the same as the stone in nature, but the parallels are there.

[45] My eldest son would have a clear answer to this. Whenever he bumps into an inanimate object, it's the inanimate object that gets the blame and bears the brunt of the seven-year-old's fury!

that stumble against the feet. This is pulling out one of the interpretive options raised by the toe-stubbing scenario: the stones as active agent.

But to what extent is this really an 'alien world'? Might we not say that Theocritus is drawing out one possibility that exists in our own world – indeed, the possibility to which we instinctively and emotionally leap when we curse the stone that stubbed our toe? Lycidas continues. Not only do the stones stumble – they also sing. The force of the dative ἀρβυλίδεσσιν might be translated in many ways: the stones sing *against* your boots; in response to your boots; at the instigation of your boots; or simply *to* or *for* your boots. Within this range of translations is a spectrum of material agency: some interpretations put the onus on the boots' primacy, others suggest more of a mutual encounter. But what is clear is that the stones are given voice here – and, specifically, the voice of a *singer* (ἀείδει). We often see stand-ins for or replicas of the poet within poetry, whether a rhapsodic character or perhaps (as we have seen) a bird – here the stand-in is a material object from the landscape that in a moment of encounter, of entanglement, with a human agent takes on agentic force and a song of its own. I conclude the current section with these lines, as they bring us down to the nitty gritty of a material-ecocritical reading – and lead us into the next section, with a more sustained focus on stone and on potential readings of lithic agency in Theocritus' *Idylls*.

Idyll 23: Vital Stone

τοῖς δὲ μετὰ γριπεύς τε γέρων πέτρα τε τέτυκται
λεπράς, ἐφ' ᾇ σπεύδων μέγα δίκτυον ἐς βόλον ἕλκει
ὁ πρέσβυς

Near them are fashioned an old fisherman and a rugged rock,
on which the old man hurries to drag his great net for a cast.
(*Idyll* 1.39–41)

The old fisherman is part of his environment. He is both working with the sea and worn down by it (ἀλιτρύτοιο γέροντος, 45). Man and rock are fashioned together, and are working together to cast the net. In the previous section we followed the fisherman into the entangled environs of *Idylls* 7 and 21, considering the connections between the people and their objects, and the degrees of remove involved in imagined landscapes. But it remains to ask: why is it with a rock that the fisherman's agency merges? Jeffrey Jerome Cohen's book *Stone: An Ecology of the Inhuman* is a masterful treatment of the relationships people carve out with their stony environs – environs that are more durably embedded in deep time than are ephemeral humans.

Presenting lithic agencies seen in medieval writings and architectures, Cohen tells the stories of stone in the world around us and the language we use to describe it. Examples from our medieval past map a trajectory to the deep past – and in this section I suggest that classical examples might achieve something similar. In the previous section we drew a connection between this fisherman and his counterparts in other *Idylls* – here we can go further, and trace a connection between the fisherman and his rock, to other human/lithic entanglements in the *Idylls* and on to the wider span of geological time.

Geological considerations do not, I believe, necessitate knowledge of geology as a discipline, or even as a defined concept. In his book *Mountains of the Mind: A History of a Fascination*, Robert Macfarlane explores human perspectives on and interactions with mountains, and their stoniness, offering a historicising account that has strong diachronic elements and that offers a watershed for our fascination with mountainous landscapes. In his initial chapters, Macfarlane emphasises the importance of the emergence of geological thought and study in shaping the human relationship with geological phenomena. For instance, he writes: 'Looked at in the context of the bigger geological picture, rock is as vulnerable to change as any other substance. Above all, geology makes explicit challenges to our understanding of time.'[46] In this chapter I look at Theocritean stone 'in the context of the bigger geological picture' and consider the ideas of 'deep time' – but, unlike Macfarlane, I do not make such considerations contingent on geology as a science. Cohen's book shows that explorations of lithic agency and human entanglements with stony environs can stretch back to the Middle Ages – and in this section I show that ancient poetry can support analogous arguments. From readings of ancient literature it becomes clear that such 'explicit challenges' can be traced back much further than the seventeenth century (the focus of Macfarlane's initial diachronic discussion) – that, though geology indisputably shaped our relationship to stone, it by no means initiated it. I make this point to set Theocritus in his historical and conceptual context. As often, there is a 'nothing new under the sun' element here: Macfarlane's identification of the *protoi heuretai* of geological thought is of course accurate at the level of historicity, but as with many historicising readings, I would sound a note of caution and rather be inclined to expand our analysis outwards conceptually, and backwards chronologically. Just because the ancients didn't know about the earth's composition, the

---

[46] Macfarlane 2003: 43.

behaviour of tectonic plates or the movement of mountains,[47] that doesn't mean that the 'fascination' wasn't already there.[48]

In Chapter 1 (pp. 32–4) I introduced the methodology of intertextuality through objects, or intermediality: a more material phenomenon than its formal counterpart, and one which engages not only across texts but also at the real-world level operating in parallel. As I argued, even objects created by, within and for the purposes of a text have a parallel material life, mapping onto the real world at least to some extent. As such, they exist outside the confines of one text, and so can move between texts. But what happens when we look beyond discrete objects and expand the definition of 'object' to encompass an entire material category, and one as ubiquitous as stone?[49] The literary instances multiply – and the real-world anchor is amplified, too. We find ourselves surrounded by a stone circle. Will such analysis become unwieldy? A net of comparisons thrown too wide? Or will it, rather, show us some traits of our lithic enmeshment that individual instances don't quite convey? As Stacy Alaimo argues, 'material ecocriticisms are better served by focusing on intra-active systems and entanglements rather than the contemplation of isolated objects'. By broadening the scope of our intertextual study, we resist the isolation of the object and indeed the text, leaving ourselves open to broader considerations and, crucially for the study of stone, an extended chronology.

The first line of our passage presents us with two fashioned elements: the fisherman and the rock. The spatial relationship between them is not immediately evident, not spelled out until the second line (ἐφ' ᾇ).[50] In that first line, then, we meet two characters, two actants, initially presented as equals through τε … τε. Indeed, Gow points out that the verb τέτυκται 'is presumably singular rather than

---

[47] On representations of mountains from antiquity to modernity, see Hollis and König 2021, and for a cultural and literary history of mountains in classical antiquity, see König 2022. In this chapter I have used Macfarlane's work on mountains as a starting point, but my interest lies not in this feature of the landscape, but more generally in the material of which it is composed.

[48] In fact, James Taylor in his 2020 doctoral dissertation argues that the ancients *were* aware of the incremental progress made by geological processes.

[49] For discrete objects and specific instances of their occurrence in and across poetry, see the *iunx*, *pharmaka* or 'fine and lovely' garments in Chapter 2 (and see further Canevaro forthcoming b on jars in the Homeric and Hesiodic corpora).

[50] Equally unclear is the spatial relation between this scene and the previous one described. As Gow notes *ad loc.*, in Theocritus μετά with dative is used 'rather vaguely to mean *with* or *besides*'. On the spatial arrangement of scenes on the cup, see further Chapter 1 (pp. 12–15).

plural, and man and rock are thought of as forming a single scene'. This departs from the Homeric model:

ὡς ὅτε τις φὼς
πέτρῃ ἔπι προβλῆτι καθήμενος ἱερὸν ἰχθὺν
ἐκ πόντοιο θύραζε λίνῳ καὶ ἤνοπι χαλκῷ.

as when some man
sitting on a jutting rock with line and gleaming bronze
drags a holy fish from the sea.[51]

(*Iliad* 16.406–8)

This is a simile in which one of Patroclus' moves in battle (he stabs Thestor with a spear to the side of the jaw and through the teeth, hooking and dragging him with the spear over the side of his chariot) is compared with a man hooking a fish. The landscape is very different – from Homer's heroic bronze, Theocritus moves to rough environs; Homer's fisherman sits, while Theocritus' is emphasised in his movement and exertion. And this latter shift also changes the interaction between man and rock. In the Homeric example man and rock are juxtaposed (φὼς | πέτρῃ), but they are simultaneously separated by the line end, and it is only the man who is in the nominative. The postpositive ἔπι has its syntactical effect, and conceptually it separates out man and material. The dative rock becomes part of the fisherman's toolkit, along with the line and hook (further datives: λίνῳ καὶ ἤνοπι χαλκῷ). Further, Homer's fishing man is left undescribed – he is 'some man' (τις φὼς), none in particular, and lacking an attached adjective he has no distinguishing features. In this Homeric passage, the comparative impetus is between simile and main narrative – there is no suggestion that we should compare man with rock. We might also refer back to Theocritus' *Idyll* 21.41–3, part of the dreamscape discussed in

---

[51] θύραζε here, literally 'outdoors', is classed by Janko 1994 *ad loc.* as 'a dead metaphor'. In our material-ecocritical analysis, where we have seen and will see again the material inflections of metaphors, it might be worth revisiting this conclusion. In the context of our discussion at pp. 105–10 of the thin line between land, sea and fishermen, this idea of the sea's 'doors' takes on a particular resonance, as a term connoting human habitation is used of the seascape. Further, it is important for our analysis, as it marks a boundary: the fish is brought out of its usual environs into another realm, and this transition is marked by anthropocentric terminology. The door might symbolise death, the fish meeting its doom: again it is interesting for our purposes that this is couched in materiality, the fish going like a human to the door, the door reifying the notion of the line between life and death.

the first section of this chapter: there the fisherman Asphalion sees himself sitting on a rock, ἐν πέτρᾳ – there is a clearer identity to the fisherman here, as he is one of the *Idyll*'s main characters, but his positioning parallels the Homeric situation, the preposition and dative marking out the relationship between the human and nonhuman, and, again, the rock aligning with the rod as part of the fisherman's accoutrements.

This changes in the lines from *Idyll* 1, in which the fisherman is aligned with the rock because they resemble one another. Both are rugged: a description as much aesthetic and haptic (rough, hard skin resembling the unyielding rock face) as it is characterising (hardy, resilient). There is a persistent assonance in these opening lines that draws together πέτρα and πρέσβυς through repeated πρ and ρπ sounds. Man and rock resemble each other also in terms of age. The fisherman is an old man (γριπεύς … γέρων; ὁ πρέσβυς), he is grey-haired (πολιῷ, 44) – the emphasis serves to throw into relief his strength, which is more worthy of a youth (τὸ δὲ σθένος ἄξιον ἄβας, 44), but it also connects him with the steadfast rock. The juxtaposition γέρων πέτρα is compellingly apt, the adjective as conceptually applicable to the rock, with its strength unchanging, as to the fisherman – if not more so. As Cohen's book brings into focus, the lifespan of stone radically eclipses our own.[52] He writes:

> The world is not for us. Stones declare this truth better than texts, because the narratives we fashion tend to be convinced of our centrality. Having abided on earth several thousand or several billion years longer – having provided the foundational materials of this planet, and having endured its recurrent cataclysms – rock narrates a rather different story.[53]

The fisherman is equated with the rock to emphasise his age – and yet that claim to durability is superseded by the lithic lifespan, almost inconceivable to the fleeting human. 'Stones declare this truth better than texts' – but if we disassociate ourselves from assumptions of our own centrality, we can begin to detect hints of this truth within the poem. Human ephemerality is suggested in the merging of the old man and the youth in the one figure, and further in σπεύδων: the fisherman, simultaneously old and young, human temporality folded, must hurry to accomplish his task. We return to Hesiod's *Works and Days*,

---

[52] Similarly, Macfarlane (2003: 43) argues that an understanding of lithic chronology gives us a necessary perspective from which to view our own ephemerality. He writes: 'to acknowledge that the hard rock of a mountain is vulnerable to the attrition of time is of necessity to reflect on the appalling transience of the human body'.

[53] Cohen 2015: 63.

in which the Iron Age man must live day to day. This is a theme that Hermann Fränkel identifies in Homer, Archilochus, Simonides, Pindar and Theognis,[54] and which Andre Lardinois in a persuasive article traces throughout the *Works and Days*,[55] showing how this human ephemerality persists as an overarching concern uniting the Works and the Days sections of the poem. Hesiod's Good Strife makes us hurry to complete seasonal tasks at the right time,[56] and this sense of urgency resonates through the concluding part of the poem, in which the chronological span tightens from seasons and months to days and even parts of days. In the working landscape, whether that of farming or fishing, men are racing against time. The old fisherman may have lived a long life, but his days are always too short.

In his chapter 'Geophilia', Cohen too, through Emmanuel Lévinas, arrives at archaic poetry. He quotes Lévinas:

> When in the *Iliad* the resistance to an attack by an enemy phalanx is compared to the resistance of a rock to the waves that assail it, it is not necessarily a matter of extending to the rock, through anthropomorphism, a human behavior, but of interpreting human resistance petromorphically.[57]

This in its turn picks up on Bruno Snell's *Discovery of the Mind*, in which he wrote that we cannot say that the rock is interpreted anthropomorphically 'unless we add that our understanding of the rock is anthropomorphic for the same reason that we are able to look at ourselves petromorphically'.[58]

Cohen points out that 'the problem for petromorphism, though, is that rocks do not compose Greek epics'.[59] Stone is mute, stone is wordless. And without human shaping, human interpretation, stone is passionless. Cohen continues:

---

[54] Fränkel 1946.
[55] Lardinois 1998.
[56] σπεύδει, *WD* 22; σπεύδοντ', 24.
[57] Lévinas's essay 'Meaning and Sense' (Peperzak et al. 1996: 37).
[58] Snell 1953: 201. Snell posited a disintegrated view of man in Homer and cast Homeric man as a 'prehuman', an aggregate of separate parts and unaware of what it means to be an 'individual'. This is picked up by Purves (2015: 77–8) in her article about the blurred line between Ajax and his armour. Snell's model has its problems, in that it is evolutionary and therefore primitivising, but it can help us think through the agencies, both human and nonhuman, at play in archaic epic.
[59] Cohen 2015: 51.

'Stone hearted' and 'stone cold' are as much a part of our vocabulary as various expressions for stony silence. Stones are poetically imagined as crying out in protest or weeping in response to beautiful song precisely because that is what they never do.

But then, in characteristic fashion, he turns these assumptions around:

> What if our lexicon for stone is impoverished? What if stone, so often thought uncommunicative in the density of its materiality, can also be affect-laden, garrulous, animated? ... Stone's reticence is tied intimately to its stillness. Yet within its native duration stone is forever on the move.[60]

As he deftly puts it earlier in the book, 'Stone's movements are its aberrations. Or so it might seem to us, we whose lives are so short.'[61] In wending our way through Cohen's argument, we are alerted to a vast array of issues and questions surrounding human/nonhuman interactions, the liveliness of stone, deep time – and, crucially to this study, the parameters and indeed *deficiencies* of the language we use to describe the lithic. I begin by unpacking these questions, before testing them out on Theocritean stone. Lithic language might be impoverished – but what about literature? If rocks don't compose Greek poetry, what can Greek poetry tell us about rocks, and our creative responses to them?

First, Cohen presents us with a distinction between anthropomorphism and petromorphism: the one, an ostensibly anthropocentric equation; the other, a new-materialist disanthropocentric move that displaces the human subject and sets stone centre stage. There is a middle ground, which I explore in more detail in Chapter 4 (pp. 155–69) – particularly through Jane Bennett's view that 'anthropomorphism can reveal isomorphism'.[62] For the purposes of this chapter, it suffices to appreciate the specific shift Lévinas proposes. Rocks do not take on our attributes – we take on theirs. To repeat Cohen's dictum: the world is not for us. Human agency is not paramount, not discrete, not unreflective of its environment. It is ecologically entangled, and as such, 'morphisms' do not always work outwards from the human.

Second, through the stark statement that 'rocks do not compose Greek epics', we are led to conflate words with meaning. If a stone cannot speak or write, it cannot enact its agency in literature. And yet, as Cohen urges us to consider in his

---

[60] Ibid. pp. 51–2.
[61] Ibid. pp. 29–30.
[62] Bennett 2010: 99.

Edinburgh Excursus, a part of his book that for me hits particularly close to home, 'It [i.e. stone] speaks, when we stop insisting that communication requires words rather than participation in meaning's generation'.[63] Stone may not speak – but it participates in the production of acts of language, of literature. It participates as a topic (consider the medieval lapidaries that constitute one of Cohen's key case studies), as a medium (just ask an epigraphist), even as a character (Niobe, Galatea, Anaxarete – the list goes on) – but more subtly and more extensively than that, it participates as part of the entangled landscape within which the acts of language are formed. On the *Iliad*'s phalanx like a rock, Snell writes 'Man must listen to an echo of himself before he may hear or know of himself.'[64] He argues that objectification, which is part of humans' understanding of their own subjectivity, is still in progress in the Homeric poems. What men and rocks share is still being worked out, and a line is not drawn between them. As Payne 2014 suggests, 'Such similes are not merely a glimpse into kinds of human life that the martial content of the primary narrative excludes. They reveal, as a deep psychic stratum, the fundamental work of objectification that makes a human narrative possible'.[65] In this sense, rocks *can* compose Greek epics.

Third, Cohen raises the question of whether stone is inherently passionless, or rather 'affect-laden'. When poets present stone as participating in emotive states, whether as catalysts or, in Cohen's examples, effusive protagonists, is this indeed a poetic trope of reversal, of artistic licence permitting the impossible – or is it a way of amplifying something inherent in our engagement with our lithic environs? Is it just possible enough?

In order to consider all of these questions (petromorphism, lithic communication, affect and more), I turn to *Idyll* 23: a poem which takes us from hearts of stone to murderous statues. I discussed this *Idyll* in Chapter 1 (pp. 23–37) in terms of its position in the Theocritean corpus: its debated authorship and associated aesthetic critique. I shall return to its aesthetic qualities (and the aspersions cast on them) but focus first on its persistent petric character. In this *Idyll*, sometimes appearing under the title Ἐραστής ('The Lover'), stone brings together unrequited love, rejection, death and vengeance – and through the transition of wooer to corpse at the kicking away of a stone on the one hand, and the diving of a statue on the other, it dissolves the boundary between animate and inanimate. In Neil Hopkinson's introduction to the poem in the Loeb edition, he summarises: 'Hardness is the organizing theme'. But is that all there is to the prevalence of stone in this poem? I would argue, rather,

---

[63] Cohen 2015: 192.
[64] Snell 1953: 201.
[65] Payne 2014: 3.

that *Idyll* 23 explores stone in its manifold materialities. It is about hardness, coldness, silence – but it is simultaneously about passion, affect and vitality. It is also about time. Death and mortality; animacy and vitality – these are tropes that are anchored chronologically. Furthermore, the structure of the poem has something very neat and finite about it, with its parallel deaths and poetic justice. And yet, the focus on the material facilitates not only an intertextual move like that I have made from *Idyll* 1, but also, because of its specific stoniness, a shift towards a version of deep time. It is not deep time in a strictly geological sense – but rather a geological gesture towards the persistence of the human condition, an exploration of love drawn from time immemorial.

At the beginning of the *Idyll*, we find a man falling in love with a cruel youth who does not know Eros, who spurns the protagonist's advances and is unyielding (ἀτειρής, 6). This is already a strikingly material manifestation of the rejection.[66] In most of its Homeric occurrences, ἀτειρής is used to describe bronze.[67] At *Iliad* 3.60 it is equated with metal even in figurative language: 'always your heart is like an unyielding axe' (αἰεί τοι κραδίη πέλεκυς ὥς ἐστιν ἀτειρής). There are a number of instances in which it is transferred to human description, and in three out of these five cases it is used to describe voice (ἀτειρέα φωνήν).[68] What is interesting about these three examples, however, is that they are all descriptions of gods disguised as mortals: Poseidon like Chalchas (*Il.* 13.45); Athena like Phoenix (17.555); Athena like Deiphobus (22.227). The lack of parallels in relation to actual mortals may in fact suggest that the gods did not get it quite right.[69] Homeric mortals, even heroes, do not have an unyielding voice – and they are rarely unyielding in any sense. ἀτειρής is primarily a

---

[66] τείρω means to rub, to rub away; ἀτειρής is something that cannot be rubbed away, something indestructible. Though the verb is usually used metaphorically, materiality is embedded in the metaphor and in the uses of the adjective we can see that the tangible material aspect is not far away.

[67] *Il.* 5.292, 7.247, 14.25, 18.474, 19.233, 20.108; *Od.* 13.368. Lather (2021: 80) notes how the 'epithet used for bronze, ἀτειρής, "unyielding", characterises Diomedes' spearhead precisely when it penetrates flesh and slices off Pandarus' tongue' (*Il.* 5.292). She continues: 'these characterisations of bronze emphasise the disparity between metal and skin by highlighting the former's invulnerability and the latter's penetrability'.

[68] The exceptions are *Od.* 11.270, 'strength always unyielding' (μένος αἰὲν ἀτειρής), and *Il.* 15.697, 'unharmed and unyielding' (ἀκμῆτας καὶ ἀτειρέας – a description of both Achaeans and Trojans as they face each other at the ships). Another formulation for bronze voice in Homer is χαλκεόφωνος at *Il.* 5.785.

[69] We might also note that in these instances the gods adopt φωνή rather than αὐδή, the latter more usually associated with their disguise (and paired with δέμας as in these three cases). On the distinction between human and divine voice, see Clay 1974.

material trait, and the poet of *Idyll* 23 transfers this to the unresponsive target of the protagonist's affections.[70]

The unyielding material-man is then separated back out into the unwelcoming doors (στυγνοῖσι μελάθροις, 17) which shut out – and shut down – the ardent admirer. In lieu of access to his love, he kisses the doorpost (κύσε τὰν φλιάν, 18). The theme of the locked-out lover is familiar from, for instance, *Idyll* 3, in which the goatherd narrator pleads for Amaryllis to invite him into her cave, and more generally it is a pathetic twist on the epithalamium, a song performed outside the bedroom door of newly weds.[71] The narrator's desperation drives him to find a material stand-in for the cruel youth – after all, an inanimate door post is hardly less inviting than the boy. This is the first of the poem's lifeless kisses: the second is that envisaged by the narrator after his death: 'though I be dead, grace me with your lips' (κἂν νεκρῷ χάρισαι τεὰ χείλεα, 41). χείλεα, meaning 'lips', can also be used metaphorically of the 'edge' or 'rim' of things such as a cup or a bowl (*Od.* 4.616), a basket (*Od.* 4.132) or, famously, a jar at *Works and Days* 97.[72] We might argue that the material and the metaphorical work together in Hesiod's Pandora passage, given how closely the woman and her jar are aligned: the material narrative spans body and object. As all the evils are released into the world, Hope remains under the lip of the jar. This is a material manifestation of the paradox Pandora's own sexuality poses: the burden on resources versus the promise of procreation. Perhaps, then, we could read the inanimate into our Theocritus passage too, making the kiss given by the living to the dead even more ontologically complicated. Further, the lips as the edge or the rim looks back to the kissing of the doorpost, gesturing to liminality and transgression.[73]

---

[70] A usage interesting for our purposes is that at Apollonius' *Argonautica* 2.375, in which the wretched Chalybes have a harsh and unyielding land (τρηχείην ... ἀτειρέα γαῖαν), and they mine and work iron. This time it is the earth that is unyielding, a hostile landscape that generates hardship – and shapes the Chalybes' activities, driving them to metalwork.

[71] In *Idyll* 18 Theocritus imagines the epithalamium performed for the wedding of Helen and Menelaus.

[72] Also e.g. a ditch (*Il.* 12.52), the ocean or a river (Herodotus 2.70).

[73] The connection between lips and doors is reinforced by the etymology of χείλεα as traced by LSJ: 'Perh. from Root ΧΑ-, χάος, χειά, Lat. *hi-o*; strictly therefore, *that which opens*' (though Beekes 2010 *sub voce* states that there is no convincing etymology). The possible connection with χάος points again to transgression – though this is a bigger rabbit hole than we can explore here.

The protagonist then calls out to the youth:

ἄγριε παῖ καὶ στυγνέ, κακᾶς ἀνάθρεμμα λεαίνας,
λάινε παῖ καὶ ἔρωτος ἀνάξιε

Cruel and hateful boy, reared by a savage lioness,
boy of stone, unworthy of love.
(*Idyll* 23.19–20)

This again recalls *Idyll* 3, where at lines 15–16 Eros is described as having been suckled by a lioness (ἦ ῥα λεαίνας | μαζὸν ἐθήλαζεν), and at 18 Amaryllis is described as τὸ πᾶν λίθος, 'all stone'. On this description in *Idyll* 3 Hopkinson comments that it is 'unexpected in this context of praise', while Hunter takes the opposite stance, judging this 'appropriate both to Amaryllis' existence in a cave and to her "stony" heart'.[74] The goatherd might be trying to charm Amaryllis – but he is hurt by her recalcitrance, and is not above the odd snide remark. We might unpack both elements of Hunter's assessment. First, the observation that cave-like qualities are transferred to the cave's occupant: a wonderful example of the petromorphism introduced earlier. The description is a poetic device mapping lithic traits onto the human – but more than that, it is transformative, a mischievous suggestion that should Amaryllis stay in her cave much longer, she might become one with it. There are enough mythical examples of women transformed to stone to facilitate our mental leap.

The second element is Amaryllis' 'stony heart', and here we come back also to *Idyll* 23. While in *Idyll* 3 it is Eros who is raised by a lioness and Amaryllis who is stony, in the unyielding youth of *Idyll* 23 the cruelty of love and the stoniness of the woman combine. There is a juxtaposition of the wild and the detached, the lion and the stone (λεαίνας λάινε). In lines 7–9 we hear that the youth doesn't exhibit any of the outward signs of love: no smile, no bright glance, no blush, no word of encouragement; yet far from being aloof, he is rather 'like a beast in the woods glaring at hunters' (οἷα δὲ θὴρ ὑλαῖος ὑποπτεύῃσι κυναγώς, 10). But what does it actually mean to be stony? Hunter refers to Amaryllis' stony heart, and Hopkinson translates λάινε παῖ (23.20) as 'stony-hearted boy'. Yet there is no explicit mention of the *thumos* or any such qualifier. Are we too heavily swayed by our own vocabulary, in which, as Cohen notes, 'stone hearted' is firmly lodged? The reader is easily influenced by Homeric examples such as *Od.* 23.103: 'your heart is always harder than stone' (σοὶ δ' αἰεὶ κραδίη στερεωτέρη ἐστὶ λίθοιο). In this particular example, the stony heart is indeed a cruel one (ἀπηνέα θυμὸν, *Od.* 23.97), as Telemachus

---

[74] Hunter 1999 *ad loc.*

berates Penelope for turning away from Odysseus. But the same adjective recurs at *Od.* 19.494, when Eurycleia will hold as firm as stone or iron (ἔξω δ' ὡς ὅτε τις στερεὴ λίθος ἠὲ σίδηρος) – and in this instance it is Eurycleia's resolve and loyalty that are being described. In his novel *Penelope's Web*, Christopher Rush mitigates between the two when he presents Penelope as 'a statue of fidelity, carved out of patience'. The dual significance – cruelty and loyalty – might go some way towards explaining the use of this description in *Idyll* 3's ostensible context of praise. Further, it is clear from just these few examples that it is not necessarily, or not necessarily *only*, the heart that is stony. We might make this supposition in the context of a love poem – but, on the other hand, we need not do so. By leaving the lithic orientation open, we retain the more interesting readings: the cruel youth as complex in his wild detachment; 'stony' implying both cruelty (λάινε παῖ equating to ἄγριε παῖ, in the same position in the previous line) and resolve (he will not be swayed); the stone encompassing more than his heart – and beyond *Idyll* 23, Amaryllis merging with her cave; Homeric women as statue-like. Hunter commenting on *Idyll* 3 raises a provocative anthropomorphic question: 'Has the goatherd fallen in love with a stone statue of a nymph?'

The narrator calls out to the youth, telling him that he has come bearing a 'last gift' (δῶρά … λοίσθια, 20–1) – his noose. Death stands in place of life, despair in place of love, in this perversion of the motif of hanging a garland at a lover's door. The lithic seems to lurk at the edge of thought, recalled by λοίσθια (beginning line 21 as λάινε began line 20), and by τὸ λᾶθος (24), the oblivion that will be the universal remedy for lovers' suffering – until noose and stone meet:

Ὣδ' εἰπὼν λίθον εἷλεν ἐρεισάμενος δ' ἐπὶ τοίχῳ
ἄχρι μέσων ὀδῶν, φοβερὸν λίθον, ἅπτετ' ἀπ' αὐτῶ
τὰν λεπτὰν σχοινῖδα, βρόχον δ' ἐπίαλλε τραχήλῳ,
τὰν ἕδραν δ' ἐκύλισεν ὑπὲκ ποδός, ἠδ' ἐκρεμάσθη
νεκρός.

Speaking thus he took a stone and placed it on the
threshold, a fearsome stone, and fastened the thin rope
above the door, put the noose around his neck,
kicked away the support from under his feet, and hung there
a corpse.

(*Idyll* 23.49–53)

In his Loeb edition, Hopkinson notes that 'the text is irrecoverably corrupt'. He also notes of his approximate translation: 'this must have been something like the sense', and my translation largely follows his – with one significant difference. Despite the text as he presents it to us, more or less identical with that by Gow given here, Hopkinson offers no translation of φοβερὸν λίθον – he simply misses it out. Given his focus on hardness in his introduction to the poem, we cannot claim that Hopkinson has neglected to notice the importance of stone in *Idyll* 23. Might we, then, detect in this omission a hint of the 'fears of lithic agency' that Cohen discusses in his book?[75] Has the fearsome stone exerted its effect? Do we shy away from allowing stone its full power? This resonates with Cohen's discussion of the material generation of meaning. Stone does not use words – but in resisting putting it into words, is there something about its meaning-making that we are trying (and, inevitably, failing) to curtail? Our language about stone may be 'impoverished' – and perhaps the 'fearsome stone' just didn't ring right to the translator. Indeed, Gow describes this phrase as 'wretched writing', and notes the approach of Ahrens who 'altered λίθον to λίνον, connecting the noun, as his text allowed him to do, with σχοινῖδα: and as between stone and halter the latter seems the more grisly object'. But does it? It is not rope that has persisted throughout the poem as character and companion, actor and backdrop. The composer of *Idyll* 23 is using poetic language in such a way as to capture the stone as actant in his narrative. In this passage, the hanging is enacted through the network of human protagonist, rope and stone. More specifically: the protagonist, the rope and the *departure* of the stone. It turns out that it is not the stone we must fear, but its absence. Groundedness gives way to suspension, supportive stone to the nothingness of air. It turns out that there is something to be said for unyielding materiality, after all. In this atmosphere of fear and threat, tension and suspense, we might revisit the idea of dark ecology. The pessimistic tone Brockliss traces in Hesiod's *Works and Days*, which resonates with Morton's dark-ecological aesthetic, arguably raises its head in this *Idyll*. Yes, the overriding narrative is one of comeuppance, of a kind of poetic justice enacted through stone. But simultaneously there is an impression of unfathomable and unconquerable nature – of an inhuman agency that eclipses our own. Further, the sheer proliferation of stone in this *Idyll* approximates Morton's notion of the 'hyperobject', a pervasive materiality that permeates human narratives. Though Morton's idea is primarily focused on *manmade* materiality – that is, products created by humans coming, in turn, to influence us – it can be considered here in terms of a persistent material that is manifest in both crude and sculpted forms, nature and culture blurring, collapsing, with the human enfolded at the centre.

---

[75] Cohen 2015: 48.

The narrator claims he knows what will happen to the cruel youth (27): his beauty will fade, just as the rose and violet wither (28–32). Man is assimilated to flora, neither of which will flourish for long. The poet reflects on the transience of beauty – and, through the deaths about to unfold, on the ephemerality of man. What will last is not the human form, nor even the green landscape – but words etched in stone:

γράψον καὶ τόδε γράμμα τὸ σοῖς τοίχοισι χαράσσω·
'τοῦτον ἔρως ἔκτεινεν· ὁδοιπόρε, μὴ παροδεύσῃς,
ἀλλὰ στὰς τόδε λέξον· ἀπηνέα εἶχεν ἑταῖρον.'

The inscription should be the words I am writing on your walls:
'Love killed this man. Traveller, do not pass by, but
stop and say this: "He had a cruel companion."'

(*Idyll* 23.46–8)

This is an imagined epigram,[76] much like that envisaged by Hector for Andromache in *Iliad* 6:[77]

Ἕκτορος ἥδε γυνή, ὃς ἀριστεύεσκε μάχεσθαι
Τρώων ἱπποδάμων, ὅτε Ἴλιον ἀμφεμάχοντο.

This is the wife of Hector, he who was ever the best fighter
of the Trojans, breakers of horses, when they fought about Ilion.

(Homer *Iliad* 6.460–1)

---

[76] Fantuzzi and Hunter (2004: 185–6) look to Latin elegy, commenting that 'this passage, which is related to, though different from, the epigrammatic motif of the inscription left on the door of the beloved at the end of the *paraklausithyron* ... is a very rare Greek example ... of the elegiac motif of the lover who asks for his tomb to have a tombstone immortalising his commitment to love (e.g., Ovid, *Trist.* 3.3.71–6, [Tibullus] 3.2.27–30, Propertius 2.13.31–6)'. Hunter 2002: 100 uses the same connection to defend the poem and our study of it (against Gow's aesthetic criticism), arguing that 'this is a poem (and a poet) of the greatest interest for, *inter alios*, anyone concerned with Latin elegy, perhaps above all with the eroticization of death in Propertius'.

[77] The lines are called an epigram by [Plutarch] *On Homer* II ch. 215; see also the *Iliad* scholia *ad Il.* 6.460b (Erbse edition, bT scholia). On tracing the first allusions to epigram back to Homer see e.g. Baumbach, Petrovic and Petrovic 2010: 7. For detailed discussion of epigrams in Homer (and Homeric language in epigrams), focusing on the two epigrams imagined by Hector, see Petrovic 2016.

Or that which Hector imagines for himself:

'ἀνδρὸς μὲν τόδε σῆμα πάλαι κατατεθνηῶτος,
ὅν ποτ' ἀριστεύοντα κατέκτανε φαίδιμος Ἕκτωρ.'
ὥς ποτέ τις ἐρέει, τὸ δ' ἐμὸν κλέος οὔ ποτ' ὀλεῖται.

'This is the tomb of a man who died long ago,
whom, though he was once the best, shining Hector killed.'
So someone will say, and my fame will never perish.
(*Iliad* 7.89–91)

In both Homeric cases, Hector's memory eclipses that of the supposed subject of the epigram. In *Iliad* 6 Andromache starts off as the grammatical subject of the epigram, but she is quickly replaced by her husband as the real focus, becoming the channel for Hector's *kleos*. Similarly, in *Iliad* 7 the tomb that will memorialise Hector is not his own but that of another man:[78] as in Andromache's epigram, Hector's memory overshadows another's. Our idyllic lover, then, should perhaps have been more careful in his choice of words. He begins with himself, τοῦτον, though he is grammatically the object rather than the subject. Already he has become subordinated within his own story. Love is the agent, the subject, the focus. Then in the second line he brings in the cruel youth, as his ἀπηνέα ἑταῖρον. The cruelty may be memorialised, but so is the youth, and indeed in the words to be read out by the traveller the onus is primarily on the companion (our protagonist is relegated to the unarticulated subject of the verb). The wooer is eclipsed partly by love, and partly by the one he loves.

In *Idyll* 23, the material aspect of the epigram is emphasised. In an article of 2016, Jenny Clay uses Hector's sepulchral epigram in *Iliad* 7 to reflect on epic's awareness of writing – yet even if we take this passage as evidence of Homeric writing, it is still the case that it is not the act of writing that is foregrounded in either of the two Homeric examples I have offered. By contrast, in our Theocritean passage the writing, the inscribing, is featured. γράψον … γράμμα calls attention to both process and product, and χαράσσω closes the line with the reiterated action and emphasises its materiality (the verb means engraving, scratching, chiselling on a hard surface). Further, the narrator hopes that the words will be repeated in two written contexts: as he speaks, he is inscribing them on the youth's walls, and he imagines that they will be reinscribed at his gravesite. Within the conceit of the poem, one of these at least is brought into existence, while the latter does not fit with the youth's own plans. By inscribing this premature epitaph out of place, the protagonist predicts

---

[78] Clay (2016: 195) calls this 'the first example of *damnatio memoriae*'.

not only his own death – but ultimately that of the youth. There will be no grave for the narrator, no inscription at the gravesite. There is just this dislocated epigram, which is on the walls of the youth's house (they are not just any walls, but σοῖς τοίχοισι) so those seeing the words will connect them with that space. Passers-by will read correctly that love killed *this* man too; as we will see in our next passage, love kills the youth even more directly (and stonily) than it does our protagonist. But the inclusion of the 'companion' continues to backfire, as the youth's cruelty is reassigned to the erstwhile wooer. The words in stone may last longer than either mortal character – they may transmit a message across time – but that message is corrupt and misleading.

To complicate matters even further, as Hunter notes,

> The language of the lover's epitaph (47–8) has been anticipated by the final plea to the *erastes*: 'do not pass by me, but stop and weep a little …' (37–8). The very first 'passer-by,' the generalized addressee of all epitaphs, is indeed the cruel boy himself.[79]

The youth is cast in multiple roles. He is both the cruel companion *and* the traveller, creating a kind of feedback loop. He does pass the corpse by, ignoring the first plea – and within this parallelism, he is therefore also 'cast in the role of a very resistant "reader"'.[80] In one respect, this multiplication of the cruel youth is another example of him taking over the poem, commandeering the protagonist's story and his memory. The anticipating of 47–8 in 37–8 enacts a reading of the imagined epigram – but we find out later in the poem that this particular reading never happens. Perhaps none ever will. Yet despite the flaws showing in the protagonist's plan, Hunter rightly notes that 'the poem thus not only celebrates the power of *eros*, but also dramatizes the power of an epitaph, and indeed of poetry generally, to enact its will'.[81] In the spirit of this chapter, I would emphasise that the epitaph is not just poetry, it is poetry in stone – and these words in stone join a network of agents, which we will see gathering below.

Homer reflects on the limitations of objects.[82] He presents the memories encased in objects as transient, and consistently presents objects as inferior to the medium of poetry as memorialiser. Ian Hodder has written of objects being 'entangled' with

---

[79] Hunter 2002: 104.
[80] Ibid. p. 104.
[81] Ibid. p. 104.
[82] For full discussion of material memory in the Homeric epics, see Canevaro 2018b: 43–54.

the human world, and James Whitley has discussed 'Homer's entangled objects'.[83] The entanglement of things is presented by Homer as precarious, and the link between object and memory not inextricable. The two imagined epigrams are a case in point – the one, that of Andromache, conveys the transience of the mortal form (Andromache can preserve the memory of her fallen husband, but only for as long as she herself lives); the other, that of Hector in *Iliad* 7, shows that material meaning is malleable (a tomb to a fallen warrior becomes a monument to Hector). In our discussion of Theocritus, the very same considerations have arisen. According to *Idyll* 23, mortal memory is fleeting – it fades, just like beauty. We need material reminders, and we search to anchor these in steadfast stone; yet these cues are not without their pitfalls. They are open to misinterpretation and reinterpretation, negotiation and neglect. Memory, its mechanisms and durability, is something that preoccupied the ancient poets. They wanted their works to last, and embedded deliberations on the problem within their poetry. Tracing this hierarchy of memory media that they map, we learn something about this persistent preoccupation, and in doing so we walk a little way alongside these poets. It's just a shame we can't have them walk with us a while, if only to show them that somehow – against the odds of the intervening time, space and perils of transmission – they made it.

According to the epigram, love kills our protagonist. The death is brought about by a network of agents: as well as the two human characters and unrequited love, there are also the material actants of the threshold, the door, the noose and the (departing) stone. It is a collaborative effort, an assemblage, something emphasised by the narrator's recasting of suicide as murder. For the *Idyll*'s next death, stone takes centre stage, as a statue of Eros assumes the active role and kills (subject of ἔκτεινεν) the cruel youth:

καὶ ἔκηλα φίλων ἐπεμαίετο λουτρῶν,
καὶ ποτὶ τὸν θεὸν ἦνθε τὸν ὕβρισε· λαινέας δέ
ἵπτατ' ἀπὸ κρηπῖδος ἐς ὕδατα· τῷ δ' ἐφύπερθεν
ἅλατο καὶ τὤγαλμα, κακὸν δ' ἔκτεινεν ἔφαβον·

Without a care he made for the washing places he loved,
and went towards the god he had dishonoured. He leaped from the
stone ledge into the water – and the statue flew
from above and killed the wicked youth.
(*Idyll* 23.57–60)

---

[83] Hodder 2012; Whitley 2013.

This passage is littered with parallelisms and antitheses:[84] the youth is careless of what has just happened, but the baths are dear to him; he heads for the god of love though he has just offended against him; both the youth and the statue fly down from a height. We are not told exactly what the statue is made of, but the stony (λαινέας) outcrop from which the youth jumps leads us to the mental leap that he is stoned to death. I note that, again, Hopkinson omits the rocky environs, translating merely as 'pedestal'. But λαινέας is crucial, as the motif of lithic agency that has been latent throughout the poem now comes to the fore, in the figure of a vengeful god. The god does not appear in an epiphany; he does not visit in disguise; he does not even take explicit anthropomorphic form. He is τὸν θεὸν, and he is τὤγαλμα: lacking descriptive detail, the presentation is ultimately more petromorphic than anthropomorphic. What do we need to know of statues, in order to make sense of the death? That they are large, that they are hard and that they are heavy. The necessary details are the material. That the god is here specified as being a statue in fact contrasts with *Idyll* 1, in which the goatherd suggests the singers sit 'facing Priapus and the (Nymphs of the) springs' (τῷ πριήπῳ καὶ τᾶν κρανίδων κατεναντίον) – in this case we might suppose a statue of one or both figures (Priapus and Nymphs), but this is not made explicit. In *Idyll* 23, however, the materiality of the god is paramount. We might conceivably proceed towards anthropomorphic projection when we consider motive: offence, anger, vengeance. Yet at the same time this points towards Cohen's 'affect-laden' stone. And movement? That is not uniquely the province of the organic, as the geological record tells us and to which the mythological impetus consistently drives. If 'stone's reticence is tied intimately to its stillness', by witnessing stone in motion we remove that reticence and question the boundary between person and thing.[85]

The youth in *Idyll* 23 is killed by stone, but he comes to a watery end: 'the water turned red' (νᾶμα δ' ἐφοινίχθη, 61). This takes us back to the *Idyll* 1 passage with which we started this chapter, and the network between man, rock and sea. It also leads us to the end met by Daphnis in that first *Idyll*:

τά γε μὰν λίνα πάντα λελοίπει
ἐκ Μοιρᾶν, χὠ Δάφνις ἔβα ῥόον. ἔκλυσε δίνα
τὸν Μοίσαις φίλον ἄνδρα, τὸν οὐ Νύμφαισιν ἀπεχθῆ.

---

[84] These continue in the remainder of the poem, e.g. line 63: 'be kind, those who hate' (στέργετε δ'οἱ μισεῦντες).

[85] In the epilogue to *Objects as Actors*, Melissa Mueller directs our attention to a similar story told by Aristotle in his *Poetics* (1452a7–11). The statue of a murdered man, Mitys, one day falls on the man who murdered Mitys and kills him. Here we see another example of death by statue, vengeance through stone. Mueller asks: 'What manner of agency is, after all, responsible for the death of Mitys's murderer?' (2016: 191).

> All the threads from the Fates had run out,
> and Daphnis went to the stream. The pool engulfed the man
> dear to the Muses, he was not unwelcome to the Nymphs.
> (*Idyll* 1.139–41)

A mysterious death, and one of the most heavily discussed parts of the Theocritean corpus. Interpretations range from the prosaic (suicide in a pool) to the mythologically elaborate (Daphnis is in love with a water nymph),[86] and they eschew the simple equation of water with Underworld in favour of a concrete narrative. Particularly relevant to the material-ecocritical project is the argument offered by Segal (1981).[87] He reads a contrast between the two singer-herdsmen Thyrsis and Daphnis in *Idyll* 1, connecting one with the waters of life and the other with the waters of death. Segal suggests that Daphnis 'embodies a view of art as attempting to assert its autonomy, proudly but tragically, against the rhythms of nature's processes of birth, procreation, and death', whereas Thyrsis epitomises art 'harmonious with nature, celebrating a joyful responsiveness to and fusion with the energies that unite men with all living things'.[88] In this reading it is Daphnis' detachment from nature that is his downfall.

What the interpretations of this passage have in common is the tracing of a neat narrative trajectory with a particular watery resonance,[89] making this the 'right' death for Daphnis. This leads us to ask the question: is it the right death for the cruel youth of *Idyll* 23? The answer lies in the differences between the poems. Daphnis goes to the stream for no other purpose than to meet his end, and to that extent he goes willingly. He is overpowered by an inhuman agent, as the pool becomes the subject and Daphnis the object. Just as we have explored the agency of stone in this chapter, so too might water be seen as an agent, and so too can it be a hyperobject.[90] Yet despite being engulfed by the stream, Daphnis leaves a positive memory, his

---

[86] At Apollonius *Argonautica* 1.1239, a δίνη closes over Hylas. The connection can be made via *Idyll* 13, which tells the story of Hylas' fate. This too is a pessimistic poem that could be read through the lens of dark ecology.

[87] Segal 1981: 25–46.

[88] Segal 1981: 16–17.

[89] The theme of 'death by water' is explored in Segal 1981: 47–65.

[90] On the agency, hybridity and entanglements of water, see Edgeworth 2011; Ingate 2019 and 2020. On water (rivers, the sea) as a hyperobject, drawing on OOO, see Campbell 2020 (on the archaeological record more generally as a hyperobject, see Campbell 2021). There are potential dark-ecological readings of water, and rivers in particular: Edgeworth terms rivers the 'dark matter' of landscape archaeology, as they are often overlooked and we know little of what went on inside them.

affiliations (with the Muses and with the Nymphs) conveyed in two parallel phrases. In my earlier discussion of epigrammatic formulations I raised the issue of balance, of which party the epigram commemorates. A similar consideration holds here, with Daphnis living on in the line following his death. The cruel youth, by contrast, leaves only the moral of his demise, and that focused through the divine: 'for the god knows how to dispense justice' (ὁ γὰρ θεὸς οἶδε δικάζειν, 63). It is the god – known better to us, and to the youth, as the statue – who wins out, in agency and in memory. It is the statue, not the water, that has killed the youth – the water is there to take on, and ultimately wash away (not from the perpetrator but from his environs), the taint of his misdeeds.

In his commentary on *Idyll* 23, Gow declares: 'The narrative is bald, frigid, and improbable ... the poem is the least attractive of the whole Theocritean corpus.' In Chapter 1 (pp. 23–37) we discussed such aesthetic criticisms against the backdrop of suspect authorship and the ring-fencing of a poetic corpus. Shifting our focus, at this point it is worth spending some time on the specific adjectives Gow chooses to sum up this *Idyll*, to consider whether after this lithocentric reading we are left with the same impression and reach the same evaluative conclusion. Bald: true, the style is plain and the presentation often clumsy. But form reflects purpose, as the blunt poet tells the story of a failed wooing, a one-sided love affair destined to go nowhere. 'Bald' also suggests a lack of adornment or embellishment. It is indeed striking that this poem offers very little description – and the most descriptive part is that which mainly describes what the youth does *not* look like. It is emphatically and importantly not a poem about beauty, and so it is stripped bare. Its environs are hostile and unyielding, its characters savage and wounded.

Frigid? With stone's cold connotations, it seems likely that there is a rocky backdrop to this assessment. We might connect this back to fears of lithic agency – perhaps the poem's stony actants give us chills. In his chapter on 'ecophobia' in *Material Ecocriticism*, Simon Estok notes:

> Scholars and artists have long known and worried about the agentic capacities that reside well beyond and threaten the human ... These interactions and the fears they evoke about our own transience, about the transience of our corporeal materiality ... are the basis of material ecocriticisms.[91]

According to Estok, it is fear of the nonhuman that lies at the root of material-ecocritical analysis, and as such *Idyll* 23 provides an ideal subject for this exploration. 'Frigid' also raises again the question of affect, and here we might bring in Gow's

---

[91] Estok 2014: 131.

final blow: that the poem is unattractive. We fear stone, its obdurate magnitude, its durability, its contrast with our own ephemerality. Yet, contrary to Gow's verdict, we are also attracted to it. As Cohen writes,[92]

> Stone is the stuff out of which we fashion as fellow artists those architectures that we trust to convey story into futures we cannot imagine, futures for which we nonetheless yearn. We desire stone, and if we can allow stone its proper duration, its agency within the networks of restless, slow, relentless connection we form with it as companion ... we can see that stone desires in return.

The protagonist of *Idyll* 23 entrusts his story to a stone wall, commits his love affair to (he imagines) perpetuity, yearns for a future in which he might be remembered. We have seen that the mechanism is flawed, the message precarious, the meaning lacking fixity. In potential fluctuations of transmission, the narrator and the youth switch around as the 'cruel companion', and these lacunae in memory suggest that the stony companionship presented by Cohen is not always without its own cruelty. And yet, we do desire stone (and in more nuanced and complex ways than Pygmalion). We not only fear the longevity of the nonhuman, but desire the futurity that it offers: a lithic chronology beyond our evanescent comprehension. We desire stone's solidity in the face of our weakness and transience. Cohen concludes that 'stone desires in return', arguing this not from an anthropomorphic standpoint but through a consideration of what it means for a stone to desire.[93] Following this through, when we create statues of Eros – and poetic narratives that describe them – sculpting stone bodies that represent our human desire, perhaps this is not (or, at least, not only) an anthropomorphic act, but one that reveals an isomorphism. Stone acts and stone attracts.

Improbable? Well, the suicide might be over the top, and statues do tend to stay put. But a love so bluntly unrequited has a realistic colouring, a universality and a groundedness that the stony environs serve to reinforce. And the prevalence of the lithic in this *Idyll* is far from improbable – it is a representation of our constant companion, a sturdy materiality that outlives, outlasts and outwits us.

Margaret Atwood's bestseller *The Testaments*, published in 2019 as a sequel to the 1985 dystopian novel *The Handmaid's Tale*, begins with this startling paragraph:

---

[92] Cohen 2015: 249.
[93] Useful for this purpose is the term *virtus*, used in medieval lapidaries to 'designate innate lithic potency, rocky material agency, a trigger to worldly activity. *Virtus* is creatureliness without anthropomorphism, the life-force of stone' (Cohen 2015: 233).

> Only dead people are allowed to have statues, but I have been given one while still alive. Already I am petrified.

I offer this example to show that just as there is nothing new under the sun, so there is no end point for literature's exploration of the human relationship to stone. It continues to be a powerful literary trope. Atwood's opening sentences set the idea of petromorphism in relief, as they push beyond it, to petrification. Strictly speaking, petrification is both a geological process (organic matter turning into fossil over a long period of time as the original material is replaced by and the original pore spaces filled with minerals) and an embodied emotional state (extreme fear making you unable to move). But the rendering of the metaphorical literal is of course familiar to us from Greek mythology, in the figures of the Gorgons who turn anyone who looks at them (and by extension is afraid of them) to stone. But what is particularly compelling about Atwood's take in light of our discussion in this chapter is that it plays with temporality: 'still', 'already'. Statues are supposed to outlive and outlast people. Indeed, they are meant to come *after* a lifespan has already ended – separate timelines, almost. The narrator's case is the exception. And in bringing the temporalities of stone and human into conjunction, the one has had a transformative effect on the other. The 'I' of the narrator blurs with the persona of the statue, continuing through the chapter:

> [I] pulled the rope that released the cloth drape shrouding me; it billowed to the ground, and there I stood.
> ...
> That was nine years ago. Since then my statue has weathered: pigeons have decorated me, moss has sprouted in my damper crevices. Votaries have taken to leaving offerings at my feet: eggs for fertility, oranges to suggest the fullness of pregnancy, croissants to reference the moon. I ignore the breadstuffs – usually they have been rained on – but pocket the oranges. Oranges are so refreshing.

The statue may be anthropomorphic in form – but more than that, the narrator feels a palpable petromorphism, to the extent that woman and statue become indivisible, in her syntax, her imagination, her sense of self. Which raises some interesting readings and questions: for one, who is it that pockets the oranges?

From the old fisherman and his rugged rock, *Idyll* 1 then moves to the next scene on the cup:

> τυτθὸν δ' ὅσσον ἄπωθεν ἁλιτρύτοιο γέροντος
> περκναῖσι σταφυλαῖσι καλὸν βέβριθεν ἀλωά,

τὰν ὀλίγος τις κῶρος ἐφ' αἱμασιαῖσι φυλάσσει
ἥμενος·

Not far from the sea-worn old man
is a vineyard with a fine load of grapes ripe to eat,
and a small boy guards it, sitting on a drystone wall·
                                                    (*Idyll* 1.45–8)

With the new scene comes a new lithic backdrop, in the form of the drystone wall.[94] It is to the boy and his activities that I move in the next chapter – but as a final point in this section I take a tighter focus than my general discussion of stone so far, and zero in on the term αἱμασιά. Again adopting an intertextual approach keyed into materiality, I move between literary examples of the αἱμασιά, but with attention to its material existence. The αἱμασιά differs from the stony examples discussed so far, as its defining feature is not its solidity or its steadfastness, but its constituent parts. Here in the plural, it refers to the stones that make up a wall – here standing alone, in metonymy, the parts standing in for the whole. I consider contrasting examples: one in which the wall is mentioned along with the stones, and another in which the stones are not metonymic but rather hint at a wall struggling to be built. Through this examination I consider Theocritus' response to both real and imagined landscapes, and his own portrayal or creation of them; his deft use of material detail in carving out his own poetic space; and the implications for the network between man and his environs of a material assemblage put on show. Let us begin with a reflection on the vibrant materiality of not only the figures on the cup, but also their nonhuman surroundings.

The boy is sitting on the wall, elevated so that he can observe the vineyard: a little guard on his makeshift tower. The position and the preposition take us back to the Iliadic fisherman and his differentiating datives. Stone is not here cast as part of a hybrid agent. However, there are Homeric precedents that point us towards other readings interesting for the consideration of the boundary between the human and nonhuman in these poetic traditions. This passage has usually been compared with the vineyard depicted on the shield of Achilles in *Iliad* 18, and similarly that on the

---

[94] For the meaning of αἱμασιά, I point the reader to Steiner's note on *Od.* 18.359. To summarise some of her main points: the scholia and Eustathius suggest a fence of small stones; Herodotus 2.68 mentions the lizards living in such a wall, so it must be dry. I would note, further, that Theocritus too has lizards sleeping in the wall: σαῦρος ἐν αἱμασιαῖσι καθεύδει καθεύδει (*Idyll* 7.22). In that passage there is also a wonderful example of the lithic landscape responding to human movement: ὥς τοι ποσὶ νισσομένοιο | πᾶσα λίθος πταίοισα ποτ' ἀρβυλίδεσσιν ἀείδει (7.25–6), on which see Chapter 3 (pp. 111–13). See also Beekes 2010 *sub voce*: wall around a terrain, of stone or thorns.

shield of Heracles. In focusing here on the stone wall rather than the vineyard scene more generally, I shift away from these more immediate comparanda, and draw out some different elements of the passage. It is worth noting, however, that the vineyard of *Iliad* 18 and that of *Idyll* 1 operate on different material and thus imaginative levels. The scene on the shield of Achilles has movement in the youths gathering the grape harvest and dancing; it has sound in the lyre-playing and singing – it is an object featuring characters with a vitality that pushes beyond their material contours.[95] And yet, the poet reminds us of the shield's material details, preventing the landscape from achieving such independent vibrancy. The vineyard as a whole is made in gold (καλὴν χρυσείην); there are poles of silver (κάμαξι ἀργυρέῃσιν); a ditch of enamel (κυανέην κάπετον); and a wall of tin (ἕρκος κασσιτέρου): all of these are material markers of the shield's status as created object. The liveliness of the scene carries the audience away from the shield as shield, but the material elements of the environs remind us of the physical parameters.[96] This is a piece of metalwork, and not just any metalwork but that of the blacksmith god, so the vineyard's walls are, of course, made of metal.[97] Michael Squire draws our attention to this 'slippage':

> This 'slippage' of medium and recession of replicative levels are of the utmost importance. For all the vividness of the described scenes, audiences are reiteratively reminded of the medium's metal materiality … To my mind, the very emphasis on visual medium draws attention to the illusion and artifice that the replication involves – in terms of both the shield's own depictions, and the make-believe of poetic language as a medium for depicting that shield in words.[98]

The processes of representation are foregrounded, the illusory qualities of both visual and verbal representation put on display. Theocritus, by contrast, does

---

[95] For readings of the shield of Achilles that are especially relevant here, see Purves 2010; Brown 2015; and Canevaro 2018b: 222–8.

[96] Heffernan 1993: 32: 'By explicitly noting the difference between the medium of visual representation … and its referent … Homer implicitly draws our attention to the *friction* between the fixed forms of visual art and the narrative thrust of his words.'

[97] I focus specifically on the vineyard scene here, as the natural comparandum for *Idyll* 1. For other examples of such nods to material reality, see *Il.* 18.548–9: 'the earth darkened behind them, and looked like ploughed land, although it was gold' (ἣ δὲ μελαίνετ' ὄπισθεν, ἀρηρομένη δὲ ἐῴκει, | χρυσείη περ ἐοῦσα); *Il.* 18.574: 'the oxen were wrought of gold and tin' (αἳ δὲ βόες χρυσοῖο τετεύχατο κασσιτέρου τε). This is not to say, however, that the description of the shield never introduces materials more pertinent to its depictions – take, for instance, the elders sitting on stone benches (ἐπὶ ξεστοῖσι λίθοις, *Il.* 18.504) – though these instances are far fewer.

[98] Squire 2013: 159.

not insist on a wooden wall for the vineyard on his wooden cup. In his ekphrastic description it is not only the characters that transcend their physical constraints, but also the environs. Through this contrast we can see that the drystone wall is as vibrant (that is, as differentiated from its material makeup) as the boy sitting on it.

In *Iliad* 18 the vineyard has a wall, but it is made of tin, not stone – so for an intertextual reading at the material level we must look elsewhere. I begin with *Odyssey* 18, in which the suitor Eurymachus mocks Odysseus (κερτομέων, 'speaking cutting words', 18.350) in his beggar's disguise. He taunts him with an offer of 'honest' work on his land and contrasts it with Odysseus' current lowly occupation.

ἦ ῥ', ἅμα τε προσέειπεν Ὀδυσσῆα πτολίπορθον·
ξεῖν', ἦ ἄρ κ' ἐθέλοις θητευέμεν, εἴ σ' ἀνελοίμην,
ἀγροῦ ἐπ' ἐσχατιῆς μισθὸς δέ τοι ἄρκιος ἔσται
αἱμασιάς τε λέγων καὶ δένδρεα μακρὰ φυτεύων;

He spoke, and he said to Odysseus, sacker of cities:
'Stranger, would you wish to serve, if I were to take you on,
on a faraway farm – there would be reliable pay –
gathering stones and tending tall trees?'
(Homer *Odyssey* 18.356–9)

Eurymachus describes the work as 'gathering stones and tending tall trees': and here we find the first of only two Homeric occurrences of αἱμασιά, the drystone wall of Theocritus' *Idyll*. The imaginary setting is one distanced from the main action: it is ἀγροῦ ἐπ' ἐσχατιῆς, in contrast to Odysseus' begging, which takes him 'among the people' (κατὰ δῆμον). The implication is of separation: on two levels. First, Eurymachus suggests removing the beggar and the embarrassment he constitutes. This problematic figure is to be relocated to somewhere out of sight, out of mind. Second, Eurymachus' argument is that beggar-Odysseus does not belong here but could be fitted elsewhere. He will be transformed from a drain on resources (βόσκειν σὴν γαστέρ' ἄναλτον, 'you feed your insatiable belly', 18.364) to a productive member of society adequately provided for (ἔνθα κ' ἐγὼ σῖτον μὲν ἐπηετανὸν παρέχοιμι, 'there I would provide food sufficient for the year', 18.360) – though, as Steiner in her commentary notes, even the offer of μισθός is a slight, as it 'usually involves relations of subordination where the wage-receiver stands as social (and/or ethical) inferior to the one who pays'.[99]

---

[99] Steiner 2010 *ad loc.*

The negotiation Eurymachus attempts between separation and fit is then reflected in the environs, as the plan seems fleshed out (good pay, food, clothing and shoes), while the imaginary landscape is in fact elusive and fragmented.[100] It is an ἀγρός – meaning farm, or field, or countryside more generally. What kind of place are we to envisage? It is a marginal environment, loosely described.[101] The only details we get are of stones and of trees: and as such, both job and location are described through constituent parts, and these not sufficient for a clear picture of either. We have a generic rural landscape punctuated by generalised natural markers.

Separation persists as a theme in the stones that are to be gathered. Theocritus' young guard sits ἐφ' αἱμασιαῖσι; beggar-Odysseus is imagined as 'gathering stones' (αἱμασιάς τε λέγων). In the one case, the stones already make up a wall; in the other, they are the component parts, separated and needing to be gathered, and we have to project their future as a constructed whole. The fragmentation in the Odyssean passage hints at frustration, at futility: stones gathered without a goal reads as almost Sisyphean. The beggar is thrust into the midst of a process, and it is not clear where that process leads. All of this serves to undercut Eurymachus' ostensible philanthropy, to suggest that his offer belies his ulterior motives, and ultimately circles back to his mockery of the beggar. The subordination of achievement to endless process in this passage is brought out more clearly through its contrast with the other Homeric occurrence of the αἱμασιά:

οὐδ' εὗρεν Δολίον, μέγαν ὄρχατον ἐσκαταβαίνων,
οὐδέ τινα δμώων οὐδ' υἱέων· ἀλλ' ἄρα τοί γε
αἱμασιὰς λέξοντες ἀλωῆς ἔμμεναι ἕρκος
ᾤχοντ', αὐτὰρ ὁ τοῖσι γέρων ὁδὸν ἡγεμόνευε.

He did not find Dolion, when he went down into the great orchard,
nor any of his slaves or sons, but they were gone to gather
stones to be a wall for the garden,
and the old man was leading them on their way.
(*Odyssey* 24.222–5)

---

[100] This stands in contrast to Odysseus' subsequent description of his proposed ploughing contest. As Steiner notes *ad* 18.366–86, 'the beggar begins in calm, leisurely fashion with a wealth of ornamental details reminiscent of the language of similes and of scenery-depictions'.

[101] Steiner 2010 *ad loc.* notes that ἀγροῦ ἐπ' ἐσχατιῆς is 'a formula (cf. 4.517) used to designate land beyond the cultivated fields, a marginal space where hunting and herding occur … The ἐσχατιή lies between nature and culture, "a marginal environment" where men and wild beasts share a single space.'

In this second passage, Odysseus arrives at Laertes' farm and goes in search of his estranged father. Again, the setting is an ἀγρός (24.205); again, it is far removed (νόσφι πόληος, 'far from the city', 24.212). But it is described in detail: the land is worked; there is a house and huts; there are slaves and a Sicilian woman to care for Laertes. We are presented not with a fragmented picture, but with a system. There are a number of reasons we might posit for this difference – first, from a narratological perspective, we move from an embedded secondary setting loosely projected by a character, to a main narrative setting. Second, in terms of characterisation, a contrast is set up between Eurymachus and Laertes: simply put, the extra attention to detail gives the impression that the latter runs the better farm. Third, combining narrative trajectory and characterisation in relation to Odysseus, the contrast makes the point that he belongs in one landscape but not the other – in the role he finally regains through reunion with his father, not in that offered to him by Eurymachus. But what I would like to point out here is that the stony environs reflect the difference. Again the workers are gathering stones (αἱμασιὰς λέξοντες) – but this time, they are explicitly said to be stones 'that will be a wall for the garden' (ἀλωῆς ἔμμεναι ἕρκος).[102] The workers have a purpose, a goal, and in that respect, they are just like Odysseus, who through his eventual reunion with his father is about to fit the final piece in the puzzle. The poem is drawing to a close, and there is no more room for Sisyphean frustrations – at this point it is all about recognition and resolution.

Theocritus, then, cherry-picks from Laertes' orchard, establishing a *locus amoenus* that recalls this particular Homeric landscape. But it also reads as a middle ground between the two Odyssean examples, in that the stones stand in metonymy for the wall. There is no explicit goal, like we have in the Laertes passage, as the wall is not referred to as a whole but through its constituent parts – yet clearly we are not in the midst of process, as we are in the Eurymachus passage, given that the boy is sitting in his completed stony surroundings. The work that pervades both Homeric passages (the one, an unwanted suggestion of servitude with overtones of frustration and futility, the other, effective and harmonious teamwork) is sidelined in *Idyll* 1, as the wall is already functional and needing no construction. In this way, Theocritus takes the resolving trajectory of *Odyssey* 24 to its natural conclusion. So the boy can idle,[103] and get on with other tasks – and it is to these that I turn in the next chapter.

---

[102] I translate ἀλωή here as 'garden' to keep its multiple meanings open, but it is picked up in the ἀλωά of Theocritus' first *Idyll*, where it is more specifically a vineyard, and indeed at 24.221 we are in a πολυκάρπου ἀλωῆς, a garden with much fruit, so likely a vineyard or an orchard.

[103] Gow notes that ἥμενος 'at the end of the sentence and beginning of the line, as in *Il*. 5.356, *Od*. 4.596, 15.392, 21.425, suggests *sitting idle*'.

And yet, in its very material form this wall evokes parts, whole and process simultaneously. As Gow comments, the αἱμασιά is 'a wall composed of the loose stones cleared by the cultivator from the ground'. It is an evident assemblage; a loose construction in which the parts are never completely obscured by the whole, and which in its final composition continues to point back to creative process. We revisit the theme of separation, in a potentially disjointed edifice that retains something of its separateness even in its complete form. Furthermore, the connection of the αἱμασιά with the cultivator and the ground he cultivates evokes *in nuce* the network of man, material and landscape which Theocritus' *Idylls* explore.

Excursus: San Sperate

Walking through the quiet village of San Sperate, Sardinia, we are surrounded by art, by beauty, by imagination – and by stone. Murals adorn almost every building, transforming the walls from barriers and boundaries into irresistible invitations. And gardens of Sounding Stones call out to us, their voices as irrepressible as those of their human neighbours. It is a place of human and lithic companionship, where identity is constructed as much by the place as by the people.

San Sperate was home to the artist Pinuccio Sciola, who was born in 1942 and died in 2016, just one year before our visit to the village. As Sciola honed his craft and grew to prominence, he began to drift further and further away from his roots, and felt keenly the cultural chasm that had opened up between him and his home. He was faced with a decision: to leave his hometown for good in order to pursue his artistic endeavours, or to bring his creative world home with him. He decided to unite his two selves, and the transformation of San Sperate began. In June of 1968, a group of young people from the area converted the mud-brick walls of San Sperate's houses into white lime-washed expanses – tantalising blank canvases that have beckoned to artists ever since.

But the walls are not walls. Transmuted by *trompe l'oeil*, the brick and lime become wood, or metal, or textile, or living flesh. In a previously featureless stretch, doors open and curtains part, playing with our expectations, confusing our senses and challenging our world-view. With faces and figures crowding the scenes, the village finds new inhabitants – and remembers those now gone. At the foot of a low building is a skyline, taking the eye down to go up; ants of disconcerting dimensions march inexorably towards a crack that isn't. Time folds in on itself through materiality, as the mud brick underneath the white lime is depicted on its surface, with playful disregard for the chronological contours of preservation and decline. A lemon tree suspends its fruit over a wall as its painted correlate is uprooted and falls, the simultaneous unification of and antithesis between the two prompting reflection

THE FISHERMAN AND THE ROCK | 141

Fig. 3.1 San Sperate, Sardinia. Photo credit: Lilah Grace Canevaro

Fig. 3.1 (*cont.*)

on the durability of respective materials (which will outlast the other, nature or culture? And is there really a divide between the two?).

The murals belong to the village; they belong to the villagers. They *are* the village: part of its material makeup, its very fabric, participating in its identity. These are people's houses – people live and work in and around the murals, the walls not dividing but bringing together life and art, imagination and reality, representation

Fig. 3.2 San Sperate, Sardinia. Photo credit: Lilah Grace Canevaro

and materiality. When you visit, you can't help but feel part of something special – a collaboration that may begin with the human, but certainly doesn't stop there.

In the streets of San Sperate we really *see* the boundaries blur. Human and material agency merge, as the narrative of matter is inescapably apparent. The murals were painted by human hands – but to those experiencing the place with no guide or guidebook, no blue plaque or museum label, the murals now tell their own stories. Hands are a notoriously permeable and porous point between person and thing. Where does the blind man end and the stick he holds begin? Likewise the artist and her brush, the sculptor and his material? Can we always be so sure that we do not share our personhood with the things (objects, people, places) we touch? Hands recur as something of a motif in San Sperate. Most of all: the guiding hand of Pinuccio Sciola. It is a hand that has left its imprint on this place but that also emerges from it, set in stone yet ready to greet you (Fig. 3.2).

Leaving the colourful streets behind, we walk down a dust road that shimmers in the heat, looking for Sciola's other artistic imprint on this village: his Garden of Sounding Stones. We have already met some of these Stones – we have been staying in Cagliari, and there seems to be a Sciola sculpture in every park and piazza. They have an indisputable presence, and we have been intrigued by them, but up until now haven't known what they are, what they mean, what they do. We are visitors:

Fig. 3.3 Giardino Sonoro, Sardinia. Photo credit: Lilah Grace Canevaro

new, uninformed, uninitiated. That is about to change. The Garden opens out before us, cluttered with stones. Standing stones, sculpted stones, stones lying as though discarded. Foliage growing around the rubble, lemon trees shading their lithic companions. A guide takes us around and introduces us to some of Sciola's work. She keeps urging us to listen. To listen? To stones? Our eighteen-month-old son is the first one with his ear to the rock – nothing about this strikes him as strange. He is the first to hear (Fig. 3.3).

Our guide approaches one monolith that is covered in squares, raised and indented, and taps her fingers gently over the pattern. We listen. And we hear – music. Beautiful, delicate, haunting music. The voice of the stone as it responds to her touch. Who knew that obdurate mass could emit such sweetness? We are entranced. Another monolith, with narrow strips cut away, leaving rigid tendrils of stone reaching upwards. She strums across the stony slats as though they were strings – and they hum. And they *sway*, the rock mimicking something arboreal, malleable, *living*. Another monolith. This one doesn't sound. Its impact is visual, and haptic. Out of an unformed block of rough rock emerges a central shaft of smoothed, planed stone, the raw and the polished encountering one another in a kind of antithetical symbiosis. They are opposites, yet one and the same; separate in form yet joined together in a single entity. In this last sculptural type we are confronted by a viscerally material evocation of that persistent binary, nature/culture – only to be shown that it is not a dichotomy at all, but two parts of a whole.

4 The Plaited Trap

Idyll 1: Creative Matter

    ἀμφὶ δέ νιν δύ' ἀλώπεκες, ἁ μὲν ἀν' ὄρχως
φοιτῇ σινομένα τὰν τρώξιμον, ἁ δ' ἐπὶ πήρᾳ
πάντα δόλον τεύχοισα τὸ παιδίον οὐ πρὶν ἀνησεῖν
φατὶ πρὶν ἢ ἀκράτιστον ἐπὶ ξηροῖσι καθίξῃ.
αὐτὰρ ὅγ' ἀνθερίκοισι καλὰν πλέκει ἀκριδοθήραν
σχοίνῳ ἐφαρμόσδων· μέλεται δέ οἱ οὔτε τι πήρας
οὔτε φυτῶν τοσσῆνον ὅσον περὶ πλέγματι γαθεῖ.

Near him are two foxes; one goes among the vine rows
and plunders the grapes that are ready to eat, while the other
uses all its guile to get his knapsack, and is determined
not to leave the boy alone until he has only dry bread left for his breakfast.
He meanwhile is weaving a fine trap for grasshoppers by linking together
rushes and stalks of asphodel, and his care for his knapsack and vines
is much less than the pleasure he takes in his plaiting.
                                                             (Theocritus *Idyll* 1.48–54)

The final scene on the cup takes us back: back to the land, the farm, *oiko*-criticism and Hesiod, as we reconnect with our earliest Greek agrarian poem.[1] First, dualities

---

[1] Hunter (1999: 83) notes that 'epic colouring is appropriate in this *ekphrasis*, and ἀμφὶ δέ νιν is a Homeric verse-beginning'. Here, however, I would like to begin by tracing not the Homeric connections, but the Hesiodic.

and contrasts are integral to the scene: the two foxes with diverse behaviours; the actions of the foxes versus the attention of the boy; the boy's disregard for his knapsack and vines as contrasted with the pleasure he takes in his creative work. This recalls Hesiod's characteristic *Begriffsspaltung* – particularly his doubling or splitting of characters and concepts – and the use of animal figures reminds us of Hesiod's *ainos* of the hawk and the nightingale, as well as the fable tradition more generally, whose origin was often attributed to Hesiod in antiquity.[2] Second, to focus in on the material aspects of the scene, the stalks of asphodel and rushes (ἀνθερίκοισι … σχοίνῳ) recall the mallow and asphodel of Hesiod's famous riddling rebuke of the corrupt and ignorant kings in his *Works and Days*:

νήπιοι, οὐδὲ ἴσασιν ὅσῳ πλέον ἥμισυ παντὸς
οὐδ' ὅσον ἐν μαλάχῃ τε καὶ ἀσφοδέλῳ μέγ' ὄνειαρ.

Fools, they do not know how much more the half is than the whole,
nor how great is the value in mallow and asphodel.
(Hesiod *Works and Days* 41–2)

The boy's rural wisdom trumps that of Hesiod's kings, as he *knows* the value in these simple plants, and he can use them for the creation of something more complex. The echo of the Hesiodic riddle could also feed into the much-debated lines 50–1 of Theocritus' first *Idyll*, of which the final four words (ἀκράτιστον ἐπὶ ξηροῖσι καθίξῃ) have continued to defy explanation. In lieu of solving the textual and interpretational difficulties, we may posit some sort of riddling obscurity here, along the lines of Hesiod's τετράτρυφον ὀκτάβλωμον (the ambiguous sandwich of *WD* 442):[3] the idea of the worker's packed lunch connecting the two.

Third, the particular nexus of insects, weaving and, by metapoetic extension, song is established already in the *Works and Days*.

---

[2] On the 'origins' of fable, see Canevaro 2015a: 152–3. For a comparative reading, see Moyo 2019 on foxes in Kalanga wisdom poetry.

[3] This phrase is explained variously as: a quarter of an eight-scored loaf (West 1978); a four-piece eight-part loaf (Most 2006); an eight-part loaf kneaded four times (Hofinger 1967, alternative Most 2006); a four-piece loaf eaten in eight bites (see also the *Works and Days* scholia *ad* 422a (Pertusi edition, *WD* scholia); a loaf divided in four one way and in two another to create eight pieces (Paley 1861); a quarter-loaf divided into eight pieces to be eaten in eight pauses through the day (Ercolani 2010). It is a complex phrase, advertising insider knowledge and encouraging the audience to think, and with its use of fractions resembles the riddle language at line 40 (ὅσῳ πλέον ἥμισυ παντός); again, Hesiod is championing frugal living.

ἦμος δὲ σκόλυμός τ' ἀνθεῖ καὶ ἠχέτα τέττιξ
δενδρέῳ ἐφεζόμενος λιγυρὴν καταχεύετ' ἀοιδήν
πυκνὸν ὑπὸ πτερύγων, θέρεος καματώδεος ὥρῃ

When the golden thistle blooms and the chirping cicada,
sitting in a tree, pours out a dense clear-sounding song
under its wings, in the season of toilsome summer
(Works and Days 582–4)

The cicada is a singer, its sound a song which projects well (λιγυρὴν ... ἀοιδήν, 583).[4] The connection with the poet is foregrounded by Hesiod when he describes his own song as λιγυρῆς ... ἀοιδῆς at 659. But the cicada is an ambivalent figure, also used to represent idleness in the proverbs.[5] In combination, then, the cicada is a singer and *not* a worker. In the *Works and Days*, the result of this meeting point of traditions is midsummer: a time in which work must cease, and rest, feasting and *song* take its place. Similarly, in the *Phaedrus*, Plato tells the myth of the cicadas:[6] cicadas were once men who became so carried away by singing that they neglected to eat and drink and so died. From them the race of cicadas was born, with a gift from the Muses: from their birth they need no sustenance, but might spend their entire lives singing. Plato describes the same moment as that presented by Hesiod: a time of leisure and heat, which gives the potential for intellectual, creative activity (in this case: Platonic dialogue).[7] So Theocritus picks up this creative assemblage: the grasshoppers are to be caught in the woven object, in a *locus amoenus* in which agricultural labour is set aside.[8]

---

[4] At *Il.* 3.151–2 the Trojan elders are likened to cicadas with a 'silver' voice (ὄπα λειριόεσσαν; the cicadas there too sit in a tree, δενδρέῳ ἐφεζόμενοι). On the cicada and song, see LeVen 2021, Chapter 3.

[5] Petropoulos 1994: 54–6 gives examples of fables (such as Aesop fable 373 Perry) and demotic songs depicting the ant and the cicada. In the most common version of the story, the cicada does not take part in the harvest, as he is too busy singing, and is criticised by the hard-working ant. The cicada ends up being reduced to begging. This is sometimes expressed in terms of a curse; the cicada is cursed to sing in summer and starve in winter. This tradition is particularly relevant to the *Works and Days*, rendering the lines both a threat to Perses and an admonitory lesson to any other potential idler. Even the formula λιγυρὴν ... ἀοιδήν does not always have positive connotations: at *Od.* 12.44 and 183 it is used of the song of the Sirens which lures men to their doom.

[6] Plato *Phaedrus* 258e–259d.

[7] See further Canevaro 2015a: 154–6.

[8] Another intertext often discussed in relation to this passage is Callimachus *Aetia* 1 (though which came first is debated); see e.g. Goldhill 1987.

There are many connections between singing and weaving attested in the literary record and in what we know about the actual ancient practices of weaving. In woven objects, song finds a material manifestation: the rhapsode as sewer of song, likening poetry to a crafted object;[9] the semantic connection perpetuated through narrative, from Circe and Calypso at their looms, to the stories of Ariadne or Philomela. The terminological interaction between textile making and poetry making is explored by Harlizius-Klück and Fanfani 2016 and Fanfani 2017 – and indeed with much variety in Henriette Harich-Schwarzbauer's volume *Weben und Gewebe in der Antike: Materialität – Repräsentation – Episteme – Metapoetik*. It is only in a substantial book like this that we can even begin to get an idea of the complexity and pervasiveness of the associations between text and textile – from the conceptual to the practical. As Andrej Petrovic shows in his introduction to *The Materiality of Text*, in terms of etymology, materiality and text involve the same conceptual metaphors: those of weaving and entwining. 'Text' comes from Latin *texo, -ere*, 'to weave, construct', and 'matter' from Indo-European *mat, 'to entwine, twist, interweave'[10] – there is an affinity between them, as they intertwine. These particular conceptual metaphors are of the utmost relevance to this book, connected as they are with ideas of entanglement. And it is in bringing attention to the underlying commonalities between text and materiality (philology and archaeology; word and world) that we can begin to question boundaries, from the disciplinary to the ontological.

The specific activity we have in Theocritus' *Idyll* is that of plaiting (πλέκει ... πλέγματι).[11] The plaiting of song is attested in, for example, Pindar (*Olympian* 6.86, *Nemean* 4.94). Giovanni Fanfani discusses two passages, one from Pindar and one from the dithyrambographer Telestes in the fifth century BC (quoted by Athenaeus), that use compound forms of πλέκω (διαπλέκειν and ἀμφιπλέκειν respectively) in the context of programmatic declarations of musical poetics.[12] In Pindar's *Pythian* 12, Pindar describes the invention of *aulos* music by Athena, when she 'plaited' into music the deadly dirge of the fierce Gorgons (lines 5–6). In the passage of Telestes we are told, again, of the sound of the *aulos* and the invention of a certain type of music: the Lydian tune, rival of the Dorian Muses, made by 'plaiting' the fair-winged breeze of the breath around reeds of quick-moving forms. In her analysis of Telestes' archaeology of *aulos* music, Pauline LeVen here notes that he uses 'the materiality of language to evoke musical features' (through metaphor and paronomasia),[13] and in

---

[9] ῥαψῳδός derived from ῥάπτειν 'to sew' and ᾠδή song.
[10] Petrovic 2019: 9–10.
[11] On plaiting in Sappho, see Mueller forthcoming.
[12] Fanfani 2017: 427–8.
[13] LeVen 2014: 166. For the Telestes passage: Athenaeus (14.617b = *PMG* 806).

putting the two passages together Fanfani concludes that 'the craft of weaving represented a favourite source of techniques and technical terminology for illustrating innovations in instrumental music' – weaving here referring specifically to πλέκω ('plaiting'). Fanfani further specifies that

> the composite nature of the αὐλός, made of two reeds, resulted in a highly mimetic and variegated sound according to the sources, and the semantic domain of interlacing, plaiting, and weaving (especially the technique of pattern-weaving) may have been perceived as aptly conveying the complexity of the αὐλετικὴ τεχνή.

There is a strong metapoetic resonance to the verb – but equally forceful are its materiality, its mimetic quality and its use in mapping the material and the musical in language. Further, that πλέκω can be used more generally of being 'entangled' (LSJ) reaffirms our theme and points towards the multiple entanglements between person, object and song.[14] There is a hierarchy of things set up in the final lines of this scene: the bag, the vines, the plaiting – and it is the plaited creation (πλέγματι), and specifically its *process*, that comes out ahead, as the boy takes more pleasure in it (the comparison made explicitly: τοσσῆνον, ὅσον) than in either his breakfast or the environs of his labour.

Hunter notes that in lines 53–4 the boy is completely absorbed in his task, and that this 'captures both the "frozenness" of art and the innocent unconcern which is built into the pastoral vision from the earliest texts ... we are here close to an ancient expression of "art for art's sake"'.[15] We come back to Hunter's claims about the first scene on the cup: that 'such a stylised and controlled display [that is, the woman and her two suitors] is possible only in the freezing grip of pictorial art'. Indeed, it is appropriate that we come full circle, as Hunter argues that 'the two foxes echo and invert the two men who strove for the attention of the beautiful woman':[16] the foxes are likely trying to *evade* the boy's notice, and because his attention is exclusively elsewhere, they are succeeding. So we have another evocation of the 'frozenness' of art. Certainly, the boy's concentration makes for a more static moment of representation than, say, him chasing off the presumptuous foxes. But yet again we might invoke Bill Brown, and the ekphrastic capacity 'to undermine the opposition

---

[14] It is worth noting that Odysseus, master of both words and things, plaits in the *Odyssey*: 'plaiting a rope a fathom long, well woven in both directions, I bound together the feet of the terrible beast' (πεῖσμα δ᾽ ὅσον τ᾽ ὄργυιαν ἐυστρεφὲς ἀμφοτέρωθεν | πλεξάμενος συνέδησα πόδας δεινοῖο πελώρου, *Od*. 10.167–8).

[15] Hunter 1999: 84.

[16] Ibid. p. 83.

between the organic and inorganic, the vibrant and the inert'. There are elements of this description that elevate it beyond its 'freezing grip'. There are intentions, emotions: the fox has a plan (φατί; Hunter: 'thinks to herself'); the boy finds joy in his creation (περὶ πλέγματι γαθεῖ). Further, as we have already noted, in his discussion of the shield of Achilles, Brown brings out the ordinary lives embedded in an extraordinary object of war, drawing connections with Latour on assemblage and quasi-object, the human drama within the nonhuman. In shifting from the heroic to the bucolic, we swap an extraordinary object for an ordinary one – but the echoing entanglement of material and textual creation (weaving and song) continues to expose human lives within nonhuman things.

In this part of the cup, our focus shifts from those of the Homeric and Hesiodic examples I cited above. First, the foxes are introduced as if characters in a fable, one using all her trickery (πάντα δόλον) and plotting to herself (φατί). But they are ignored. Second, the viticultural environs are described: the vineyard, the vines, the grapes. But our protagonist doesn't care for them. His attention is on his grasshopper trap: yet, again, contrary to our expectations as generated by Hesiod's (and Plato's) cicada passages, the focus is not on the grasshoppers – who haven't even arrived on the scene yet – but on the trap.[17] The assemblage persists: person, thing, song. And we cannot forget that the cup, ultimately, is a prize for song, offered in exchange for it, treated as equivalent to it. But within this final scene, the balance sways in favour of the person and the thing, the boy and his creation. We can say that materiality is foregrounded over textuality, as we are drawn not to the song (the unheard utterance of unseen grasshoppers), but to the created thing (within the created thing). Metapoetics is an important theme here, but our reading should not obscure the prominence of materiality in the scene, which thus operates on two levels.

I would return also to Ruth Webb's 2018 article and her analysis of Odysseus' bed as an *ekphrasis tropou*: a detailed narrative of making. Webb notes that the focus of the ekphrasis in *Odyssey* 23 is not on the finished product but on the process, with the result that matter is more conspicuous than is form. This is an interesting perspective to read into this part of *Idyll* 1, as here we have an ekphrasis of a thing (the cup), and an ekphrasis of a process (the plaiting) embedded into it. We can think of this in a linear, narrative way, setting the final scene in its wider context. This is the last of three scenes: we have been immersed in the cup's decoration for a while. We have been drawn into it as a microcosm, a whole world unfolding through its

---

[17] Payne (2007: 126) draws the revealing parallel between the cage and Thyrsis' song, specifically in terms of materiality: 'As the boy's cage remains empty, so Thyrsis' voice is the material presence that cannot be enclosed within the poem's structure of words.'

characters, its stories, its objects. So far gone are we, that Theocritus can introduce an ekphrasis within an ekphrasis: a story of process rooted in a description of a product. And, to continue the linear trajectory, the subsequent lines shift us out of our material immersion:

παντᾷ δ' ἀμφὶ δέπας περιπέπταται ὑγρὸς ἄκανθος,
αἰπολικὸν θάημα· τέρας κέ τυ θυμὸν ἀτύξαι.

All around the cup is spread pliant acanthus.
A marvel of the goatherd's world; a wonder to amaze the heart.
(*Idyll* 1.55–6)

In the embedded *ekphrasis tropou*, Theocritus pushes us as far as we can go, before pulling us back to the 'reality' of the cup, its first-level materiality, its construction and form. We had reached a tipping point at which the materiality of the plaited trap might even vie with the materiality of the cup – and it is at this point that Theocritus allows the framing narrative to re-exert its force.

And yet, just as in the introductory lines, the conclusion of the framing narrative does not so much shut down vitalist readings as it does gesture towards them. We return to lively, pliant foliage – not the coldness of metal, nor the obduracy of stone, but the immediacy and vivacity of plant-life. Importantly, Theocritus does not here reiterate or emphasise the material of which the cup is made, but rather comments on the acanthus that encircles the cup. He does not jolt us out of the ekphrasis with a stark statement about materiality, of the sort that would shed a harsh light on our material immersion. Rather, he expands his description by presenting another element of the cup's form. Hunter suggests 'The acanthus design runs around the base of the cup';[18] though the broader discussion in Chapter 1 showed that such precise placement is difficult to prove, it is certainly the case that the scenes and the acanthus are separate and differentiated. This is an addition, then, rather than a correction or specification. Our response is not contradicted, but simply framed – and, indeed, the lively foliage supports a vitalist reading.

So what is the response to the cup? As Hunter points out, 'the language of "wonder" is standard in ancient *ekphrasis*'.[19] Just like δαίδαλμα at line 32, θάημα and τέρας mark out the marvellous nature of the cup and its decorations and situate this passage in its wider literary context. But while the second part of line 56 evokes

---

[18] Hunter 1999: 84.
[19] Ibid. p. 84.

a strong yet standard epic response,[20] the first part of the line is far more tethered to the particular rural context of the poem. The cup is αἰπολικόν θαῆμα: a marvel of the goatherd's world. The interpretation and translation of this phrase is debated, and what we take it to mean has an impact on how we understand the relationship between person and thing in this part of the *Idyll*.[21] I have followed Hunter's translation here, though he notes an alternative reading: '"a thing at which a goatherd would marvel" seems less natural, although the difference is slight'. Hopkinson translates as 'a wonderful product of the pastoral world', and adds a note offering 'a marvel for a goatherd to behold' as an alternative. So the phrase is either marking out the wondrous within the pastoral context – or the wonder experienced by the goatherd. For our understanding of the entanglements in this poem, and especially for our appreciation of the affective response the central object initiates, the difference is more than 'slight'. In the latter interpretation, the goatherd is singled out as a particular party with a particular reaction of wonder. He is especially struck by the object, because it is alien to him and his lifestyle. The object drifts towards the second, more emphatically epic, part of the line, and a boundary is set. In the former interpretation, by contrast ('a marvel of the goatherd's world', or 'a wonderful product of the pastoral world'), the object is *claimed* by its bucolic context. It is part of the goatherd's world, even produced by it. The entanglements hold, the ivy and acanthus tether the object to the land and the people working it. This interpretation fits better with the subsequent lines, which present an equivalency that precedes that between the cup and the song:

τῷ μὲν ἐγὼ πορθμῆι Καλυδωνίῳ αἶγά τ' ἔδωκα
ὦνον καὶ τυρόεντα μέγαν λευκοῖο γάλακτος·

As payment I gave the ferryman from Calydna a goat
and a great cheese made from white milk.

(*Idyll* 1.57–8)

The goatherd received the cup from a ferryman and paid for it with a goat and a cheese. We do not learn of the cup's creation; we are not told where the ferryman

---

[20] Hunter 1999 *ad loc*. 'ἀτύζειν is a strong word of high poetry' – take, for example, baby Astyanax bewildered at the sight of his father (ἐκλίνθη ἰάχων πατρὸς φίλου ὄψιν ἀτυχθείς, *Il*. 6.468), or Andromache frightened nearly to death by the news of Hector's defeat (ἀτυζομένην ἀπολέσθαι, *Il*. 22.474).

[21] The text, too, is debated: αἰολικόν is offered in the scholia in place of αἰπολικόν, and τι θαῆμα and θαῦμα are circulated as variants.

got the cup; but at some point in its narrative of circulation, it was judged to have an equivalency with 'products of the pastoral world'. This ostensibly straightforward economic exchange grounds the cup within the goatherd's sphere. The cup has been drawn into the goatherd's world, and the terms of the exchange verify that. And yet, there is something more than straight economics going on here. Throughout the poem the cup is marked out as something special, something far beyond a goat and a cheese. The ferryman's role in mythology is essentially a liminal and potentially transgressive one: we might think of Charon manning the crossing of the river Styx, or the ferryman Phaon who encountered Aphrodite. Perhaps he did receive the cup from the gods after all (setting in context τι θεῶν δαίδαλμα at line 32). The cup circulates, and its circulation plays a vital role in the poem's worldmaking. The cup is always given, and its giving seems to thematise incommensurability: a goat and a cheese for a cup, a cup for a song. It is given, but it is not used, a point the goatherd makes clear:

οὐδέ τί πω ποτὶ χεῖλος ἐμὸν θίγεν, ἀλλ᾽ ἔτι κεῖται
ἄχραντον.

It has never yet touched my lips: it still lies
unused.
      (*Idyll* 1.59–60)

He has brought the cup into his world, but though it has been admired, marvelled at, responded to as an immersive entity, it has not been incorporated into the goatherd's sensory experience. He hasn't tasted from it – and the choice of θίγεν, an essentially haptic word, exaggerates the claim. The goatherd draws a line for the assemblage, showing that his ownership of the cup is not immutable, that though it is part of the pastoral world, it is not unique to *his* world. The goatherd's cup is recast as a work of art rather than a use object, and this is to revisit our earlier conception of the cup as tangible and multisensory.[22]

In Chapter 1 suggested that the entire ekphrasis should be read as the goatherd's response to the cup, told to elicit Thyrsis' response, engendering a response in the reader – and this all conducted by Theocritus, himself responding to an imagined object. The focus on response, rather than on description, directs us to a dynamic interaction with the cup, instead of a static contemplation of it. A consideration of response can also be useful in these lines, in terms of both the internal and external audience/viewer/reader (the divisions between these aspects are frequently

---

[22] See further Chapter 5 (pp. 195–201) on the silver-gilt Theocritus Cup.

obscured by the multisensory nature of the passage). Hunter writes: 'As cup and song are reciprocal artefacts, so the effect of the cup upon Thyrsis will be the same as that of Thyrsis' song upon the goatherd.'[23] This raises questions of materiality, and of affect.[24] First, that the song can be cast as an artefact is particularly powerful. This is an exchange: the cup offered as a prize for song, the one equated in some way with the other. The song is treated as a quantifiable, even a *tangible* thing: an object in itself. That the final scene is one of material creation is, then, key to the equivalency and the proposed exchange: the plaiting of the cage, the creation of an object to capture a creature and a sound, resonates with the invitation to sing, to create another 'object' of wonder. And both cup and song are intended to evoke responses, to initiate affect. To this too it is pertinent that the ekphrasis ends with a scene of material creation, and, importantly, of a character taking pleasure in that creation. In both ways, then, the assemblage is staged within the scene; amplified by the concluding lines and framing narrative; and, ultimately, extended outwards to the reader. As Hunter notes,

> The expression of admiration refers to the acanthus, but colours the description of the whole cup, to which it forms the conclusion; after the section-by-section account, we learn that the *whole* cup is a τέρας, as acanthus surrounds the *whole* cup.[25]

In these lines the film-strip presentation of the cup is brought together in terms of aesthetic and affective response. The acanthus connects up with the ivy tendrils with which we started, encircling the cup and drawing the object together.

Idyll 28: Emigration and Collaboration

Creation, and in particular the equation of material object and poetry, takes centre stage in another poem of the Theocritean corpus: *Idyll* 28. In this *Idyll*, the narrator apostrophises a distaff, an object he plans to give as a gift and whose future life the narrator envisages. Whereas in *Idyll* 1 two 'artefacts', the cup and the song, are judged equivalent and exchanged, in 28 two artefacts work in tandem towards the same goal, as we imagine the poem to accompany the distaff on its journey to Miletus. This poem offers an essential focal point for a material-ecocritical analysis,

---

[23] Hunter 1999: 85.
[24] The two aspects work naturally together, as shown by the contributors to Telò and Mueller 2018.
[25] Hunter 1999: 84.

concerned as it is with entanglements (actor networks, even hybrid agents), with both human and nonhuman creativity and with personification and anthropomorphism. Focusing on the wider theme of creation, these are all aspects I work through in this chapter.

Γλαύκας, ὦ φιλέριθ' ἀλακάτα, δῶρον Ἀθανάας
γύναιξιν νόος οἰκωφελίας αἶσιν ἐπάβολος,
θέρσεισ' ἄμμιν ὑμάρτη πόλιν ἐς Νείλεος ἀγλάαν,
ὅππα Κύπριδος ἶρον καλάμῳ χλῶρον ὑπ' ἀπάλῳ.

Distaff, friend of spinners, gift of grey-eyed Athena
to women whose minds are skilled in running the household,
come with me boldly to the splendid city of Neleus,
where the precinct of Aphrodite lies green in its soft rushes.
(*Idyll* 28.1–4)

The distaff is asked to come with the narrator, with the poem, to the city of Neleus, legendary founder of Miletus. The poet wishes to see his friend Nikias: to see him with pleasure and be welcomed by him in return (ὅππως ξέννον ἔμον τέρψομ' ἴδων κἀντιφιληθέω, 6). We are immediately transported to a context of travel, hospitality, guest-friendship and reciprocity. Nikias is no stranger to the Theocritean corpus: a doctor, he is also addressed in *Idylls* 11 and 13, and the scholia even quote two hexameter verses which were said to have been the opening of a reply to *Idyll* 11 by Nikias himself.[26] The recurrence of characters is one definite way in which Theocritus' poems are drawn together: a clear attempt to create, add to and integrate with a unifying framework. But the close associative relationship between material object and poetry is another thread that ties this *Idyll* to others, in particular to *Idyll* 1 and the scene discussed above. In this case, however, the poem and the object are not to be exchanged one for the other, but are cast as travelling companions, two artefacts working together as guest-gifts, combining to praise Nikias' wife.

Yet there are equivalencies in the poem, these being between the distaff and the human characters. This is our first pointer towards the strong entanglement between human and nonhuman actors in *Idyll* 28. First, there is an alignment between the

---

[26] ἦν ἄρ' ἀληθὲς τοῦτο, Θεόκριτε· οἱ γὰρ Ἔρωτες
ποιητὰς πολλοὺς ἐδίδαξαν τοὺς πρὶν ἀμούσους.

This then was true indeed, Theocritus: the instruction of the Loves
turns many, who knew not the Muses before, into poets.

poet and the distaff. As the distaff is a travelling companion to the poem, so is it to the poet. They are travelling from the same place:

οὐ γὰρ εἰς ἀκίρας οὐδ᾽ ἐς ἀέργω κεν ἐβολλόμαν
ὄπασσαί σε δόμοις, ἀμμετέρας ἔσσαν ἀπὺ χθόνος.
καὶ γάρ τοι πάτρις ἃν ὤξ Ἐφύρας κτίσσε ποτ᾽ Ἀρχίας,
νάσω Τρινακρίας μύελον, ἄνδρων δοκίμων πόλιν.

I would not have liked to give you into the house of a weak or idle woman,
since you are from my own country:
your hometown is that which Archias of Ephyra once founded,
marrow of the Trinacrian island, a city of famous men.
(*Idyll* 28.15–18)

We learn about Theocritus while we learn about the distaff, compatriots emigrating together from Syracuse.[27] That the distaff's hometown is described as the 'marrow' (μύελον) of Syracuse adds further depth to the story's entanglements, as the town is portrayed as being at the core of the island: its delicacy but also its lifeblood. The distaff comes from a city of famous men (ἄνδρων δοκίμων πόλιν); in the use of ἄνδρων here, this is an assertion of Theocritus' worth as much as that of the object (the extent to which ἄνδρων might also apply to the distaff is something we will return to in our discussion of anthropomorphism below). And coming from such a place makes the distaff unsuited to 'the house of a weak or idle woman' – just as (by extension) Theocritus is unsuited to unimpressive acquaintances. The proximity between Theocritus and the distaff, in their point of origin, their destination and the journey itself, is mutually reinforcing of fame and prestige. Indeed, the inextricability of poet, poem and distaff becomes clear in the final lines of the *Idyll*:

ὡς εὐαλάκατος Θεύγενις ἐν δαμότισιν πέλῃ,
καί οἱ μνᾶστιν ἄει τῶ φιλαοίδω παρέχῃς ξένω.
κῆνο γάρ τις ἔρει τὤπος ἰδών σ᾽· 'ἦ μεγάλα χάρις
δώρῳ σὺν ὀλίγῳ· πάντα δὲ τίματα τὰ πὰρ φίλων.'

So that Theugenis may be famous for her distaff among her townswomen,
and you may always give her remembrance of her friend.

---

[27] Trinacria, 'the three-promontoried', is the island of Syracuse, founded in 734 BC by Archias of Corinth (original name: Ephyra).

Someone will say when they see you, 'Indeed great goodwill goes with
this slight gift; and all things that come from friends are precious.'

(*Idyll* 28.22–5)

The distaff will bring good repute to Theugenis, the wife of Nikias. It will also remind her of the giver, Theocritus. Further, in the envisaged epigrammatic response to Theugenis and her distaff, it is both the gift and the giver (the friend and the token of friendship) that are commemorated. The inalienability of the gift – the memorialisation of the giver embedded in the process of giving – is something with which we are familiar, from Homeric examples to modern anthropological research.[28] What is particularly striking here, however, is the way in which this is achieved through equivalency. The distaff does not commemorate Theocritus primarily because of its status – its costly creation, its precious materials, its cultural biography. We are told that it is 'made out of ivory, with great care' (ἐλέφαντος πολυμόχθω, 8), but its creation is not greatly emphasised (it is not attributed to a particular artisan, for instance – or, even better, to a god, as often in Homer), and indeed it is judged to be a small gift (δώρῳ σὺν ὀλίγῳ, 25) and takes its value, rather proverbially, from the friendship (πάντα δὲ τίματα τὰ πὰρ φίλων, 25). Instead, the distaff commemorates the poet because it has something in common with him. It will remind Theugenis of Theocritus partly because it is *like* him.

From the perspective of gender roles, the reader might be surprised at this equivalency between Theocritus and the distaff. A tool for spinning, the distaff is an object of the female domestic sphere, and its gender allegiances are reiterated throughout the poem: it is a gift for women (δῶρον γύναιξιν, 1–2), specifically in their domestic role ('whose minds are skilled in running the household', νόος οἰκωφελίας αἷσιν ἐπάβολος, 2), and it is to bring a woman fame among other women (ὡς εὐαλάκατος Θεύγενις ἐν δαμότισιν πέλῃ, 22). And yet, the distaff shadows Theocritus' movements. On the one hand, this can be explained in terms of male and female complementarity in the social mechanism of *xenia*. In the Homeric poems, for instance, 'female' gifts (especially textiles) are offered along with 'male' objects (those of metal, in particular) to complete a picture of guest-friendship. In this way, it is the whole household that contributes to forging ties with another household. We can thus read the distinction between male and female garments set out in lines 10–11: Theocritus already embeds in his poem a differentiation yet parallelism between male and female objects (emphasised by repetition: πόλλα ... πόλλα), which we can map onto the different elements of gift-giving. On the other hand, we can go beyond the practicalities of social norms to the level of metapoetics, and return to

---

[28] See e.g. Mauss 1967 (the gift as *immeuble*); Weiner 1992.

the strong connection between textile production and poetry. To put it simply, the weaving of cloth and the weaving of words are interlinked in the wider literary tradition (and, indeed, in the way we think – consider the conceptual metaphors for matter and text cited above), so the affinity between the poet and the tools of the textile trade bypasses or transcends expectations of gender norms. Homer displays a nuanced awareness of and sensitivity to the details of textile production, even to the gender-coded messages transmitted by women through their weaving.[29] This gives us another way to read the gender distinction in lines 10–11: Theocritus knows that the clothing code is marked in terms of gender. But in this chapter I would like to go beyond the general correlation between text and textile, and take a more materially inflected approach. Much as I explored the specific connotations of plaiting in the first section of this chapter, here I turn to the specificities of spinning – of the distaff. What is it that Theocritus is trying to achieve through this object in particular? Why the distaff and not the loom? Or, why the tool and not the textile?

In her landmark article of 1993, 'Spinning and weaving: Ideas of domestic order in Homer', Maria Pantelia makes the point that 'although modern scholarship has appropriately recognized the symbolic or metaphorical function of weaving in literature and in the Homeric poems in particular, no distinction has yet been made between weaving and spinning'.[30] In discussion of metapoetics, the details of the materiality (the processes, the techniques, the equipment) had been elided. However, the material turn has brought with it a more sustained interest in these neglected elements, with Harlizius-Klück and Fanfani 2016 and Harich-Schwarzbauer 2015, both mentioned above, as prime examples. To return to Pantelia's point, though spinning and weaving are undeniably interlinked, they are different processes of creation, and should be treated as such – in terms of their materiality, and in their literary connotations, from metapoetics to characterisation. Pantelia explores the 'symbolic functions' of spinning and weaving in the Homeric poems, concluding:

> Women who feel uncertain about their future or identity ... use the creativity of their weaving as an escape from reality or as the means through which their identity will be preserved beyond the physical limitations of their mortal existence. On the other hand, women ... in the later and established stages of their lives, do not have the need for such expression ... From a position of power and security, they are able to redirect their energies towards others by producing the thread, that is, the material other women may use in order to 'weave' their own lives.[31]

---

[29] Canevaro 2018b.
[30] Pantelia 1993: 493.
[31] Ibid. p. 500.

The material aspect of this analysis is crucial to our understanding of the spinning motif in poetry – and to our exploration of the distaff in *Idyll* 28.[32] The key point here is that the distaff is designed for the production of *material* – still an early stage in a production process, rather than the conclusion of a finished product. As Pantelia puts it, 'spinning produces only the thread, that is, the raw material which makes weaving possible and, most importantly, allows the weaver to speak and express herself through the specific artifact she produces on her loom'.[33] I would draw attention to the complete picture *Idyll* 28 draws: from the shearing of the sheep (12–13), through the spinning, to the making of 'robes for men' (ἀνδρείοις πέπλοις) and 'flowing garments such as women wear' (οἷα γύναικες φορέοισ' ὑδάτινα βράκη, 10–11), Theocritus puts in motion the entire creative process, enacted through the gift of the distaff. The role the distaff will play as agent in this process will be discussed further below, but here it is worth drawing some preliminary conclusions about the distaff as a well-positioned object, and its implications for this poem's entanglements. The distaff is not, in fact, at the root of the process – thread is *not* the 'raw material', as Pantelia would have it, but just one created stage in a larger creative design. Theocritus takes us back to the real raw materials – the sheep, and specifically the sheep in the pastures. The creative process is explicitly tied up with human hands; manmade objects of technology; materials, both transitional and raw; animals; and, ultimately, the land. We are taken from the rarefied picture of spinning and weaving as we have it in Homer – both activities depicted largely in the palace setting – and reconnected with the wider context of land and labour. So spinning is not the beginning of the creative process – but nor is it the end. The glimpse forward to the projected finished product, the clothing, gives a teleological view of the enterprise (ἐκτελέσῃς, 10), and sets the distaff at its mid-point. The distaff is perfectly positioned, then, to look both forward and back, and as such to act as the encapsulation of the entire process of creation. It is for all these elements in unison that the most flattering epithet Theocritus can bestow upon Theugenis is εὐαλάκατος (literally 'well-distaffed', 22).

Another key distinction Pantelia makes between the loom and the distaff is in terms of portability: the upright loom is large, heavy, difficult to move (it is the weaver who walks to and fro), and in Homer it is situated fixedly in the inner rooms; the distaff, on the other hand, is portable, can be used sitting or standing and can be moved around, perhaps while the spinner engages in other tasks. In this section I have focused on the equivalency between Theocritus and the distaff, in terms of

---

[32] Though I have disputed some details of this in my work on Homer, particularly Pantelia's characterisation of Helen in the *Odyssey*: see Canevaro 2018b: 71n43.

[33] Pantelia 1993: 494.

travel and emigration – and this is upheld by the nature of the object Theocritus chooses. It is an object whose primary differentiating characteristic is its portability – its flexibility, which makes it suited to multiple locations, contexts and users.[34] This is a further way in which the object, the poem and the poet come into alignment: it is not just that the distaff is being moved, but that its construction, its very nature, facilitates movement. It is suited to its status as emigrant object.

The parallelism of distaff and poet is not the only equivalency between human and nonhuman characters we encounter in *Idyll* 28. There is also that between the distaff and Theugenis, as the gift parallels not only the giver, but also the recipient. That Theugenis will be εὐαλάκατος epitomises the proximity between woman and distaff, as the human and nonhuman converge in this adjective. The distaff will make its home with Nikias (οἶκον ἔχοισ' ἄνερος, 19), will make its home with the Ionians (οἰκήσεις, 21) – will live as Theugenis does. Theocritus has a plan for the distaff:

καὶ σὲ τὰν ἐλέφαντος πολυμόχθω γεγενημέναν
δῶρον Νικιάας εἰς ἀλόχω χέρρας ὀπάσσομεν,
σὺν τᾷ πόλλα μὲν ἔργ' ἐκτελέσῃς ἀνδρείοις πέπλοις,
πόλλα δ' οἷα γύναικες φορέοισ' ὑδάτινα βράκη.

So that I may bestow you, made out of ivory with great care,
as a gift into the hands of Nikias' wife,
with whom you will create many pieces of work for men's robes,
and many flowing garments such as women wear.
(*Idyll* 28.8–11)

Much like the textile's trajectory traced above (from sheep to garments), the distaff's life story is mapped out. It began as ivory; was shaped with great care (though by whom, we are not told – the labour is concealed at that stage); is to be given from Theocritus' hands to those of Nikias' wife; and will create clothing. What is most striking about these lines from a new-materialist perspective, and will be the focus of this part of my discussion, is the collaborative nature of the work envisaged. 'With whom' (σὺν τᾷ): this is a resounding signal of an actor network, an assemblage, an entanglement, even a hybrid agent, as human and nonhuman actors join together to work in tandem. The distaff is not an inanimate tool that Theugenis will use to make

---

[34] Ibid. p. 494: 'the spinning of wool could easily be done by all women, regardless of age', in contrast with weaving, which 'required a certain amount of physical energy, which probably made weaving an occupation more suitable for younger women'.

her textiles; nor is the distaff separated out as the prime actor in the process – it is the combination, the collaboration, of the two that will result in the creation of garments.

In line 9 the distaff is to be given into the hands (εἰς χέρρας) of Nikias' wife. In the following line, the apostrophised distaff is to complete 'works' (ἔργ' ἐκτελέσῃς). It is important to note here that 'hands' and 'work' are the fundamentals of the creative process – and particularly women's creations[35] – in Greek poetry. Women in Homer are prized for their *erga*: for example, when Agamemnon appeases Achilles with gifts in *Iliad* 19, they include seven women whose works were blameless (ἐκ δ' ἄγον αἶψα γυναῖκας ἀμύμονα ἔργ' εἰδυίας ἕπτ', *Il.* 19.245). These *erga* are usually textiles, made 'by the hands of women': at *Iliad* 22.511 the grieving Andromache vows to burn the clothes (τετυγμένα χερσὶ γυναικῶν); even goddesses work garments with their hands, with Athena putting on a robe 'which she herself made and worked with her hands' (ὅν ῥ' αὐτὴ ποιήσατο καὶ κάμε χερσίν, *Il.* 5.735, 8.386). Women's hands might be remembered for their work, as when Helen gives Telemachus a textile gift as a 'reminder of the hands of Helen' (μνῆμ' Ἑλένης χειρῶν, *Od.* 15.126). More generally, the hand can be a key locus of agency, and a focal point for questions of boundaries and our relationship with the world.[36] Hands are central in the 2018 special journal issue of *Art History* on 'The Embodied Object', with Milette Gaifman and Verity Platt pointing out in their introduction that 'hands constitute a critical site of engagement between human bodies and the worlds that they inhabit. A locus of sensation, creation, communication and collaboration, they are arguably as vital as the eye when considering dynamic relations between persons and things'.[37] It is crucial here, then, that the hands are those of Theugenis – but the works are those of the distaff. The actor network is established by separating out this key creative nexus, setting it across two lines and dividing it between two agents. A hybridity is established, with woman and distaff not only co-operating but acting as two parts of a whole. The circle is then completed when the *erga* are transferred to Theugenis in the characterisation of her as ἀνυσίεργος (14), a 'work-finisher' (i.e. industrious). The work that began with the distaff becomes a part of Theugenis' very identity, as the two agents merge and transfer their attributes.

---

[35] To stick with Homeric examples, there are occasional passing references made to male creators in Homer. One example is Phereclus, the smith, killed at *Il.* 5.59, 'who knew how to make all sorts of intricate things with his hands' (ὃς χερσὶν ἐπίστατο δαίδαλα πάντα | τεύχειν, *Il.* 5.60–1), and who can in fact be blamed for the entire Trojan War, as he was the one who built Paris' ships. See also *Il.* 7.220–3 for one Tychius who made Ajax's shield.

[36] Having been through every occurrence of hands in Homer (Canevaro 2018b: 129–42), I have become particularly preoccupied with them. See also Worman 2018 and 2021, Chapter 2.

[37] Gaifman and Platt 2018: 404.

And this team will be a productive one. So productive, in fact, that sheep will need to be shorn twice yearly, just to keep up:

δὶς γὰρ μάτερες ἄρνων μαλάκοις ἐν βοτάνᾳ πόκοις
πέξαιντ' αὐτοέτει, Θευγένιδός γ' ἕννεκ' εὐσφύρω.

The mothers of lambs in the pastures might be shorn of their
soft fleeces twice a year as far as fair-ankled Theugenis is concerned.
(*Idyll* 28.12–13)

A material-ecocritical approach to literature extends our attention beyond the literary object, beyond the isolated thing, to read systems and processes. This is to propagate relational new-materialist paradigms, in which people are only ever one component in an assemblage (here, the 'finisher' of a long process). *Idyll* 28 is really a poster child for this approach, as systems readily open themselves up to our reading. In these lines, Theugenis and the distaff collaborate, their agency overlapping, towards the same creative goal – and they are simultaneously linked back to raw material, animals and the land. The periphrastic expression for sheep is more than an allusive formulation – it is an opportunity for further entanglement, for mention of the pastureland (ἐν βοτάνᾳ) as well as the animal. As a result, the created clothing is not held up as a discrete entity, a literary thing to be contemplated in splendid isolation. It is not even just presented as an extension of its human creator. It is part of a full system that stretches from raw material to finished product, and involves land, animals, both human and nonhuman agents – and, of course, the poet.

In these lines, human creativity is linked with the creativity of nature, all encapsulated in a poetic creation. The theme of creativity with which this chapter is concerned really comes to the fore in an emphatic and all-encompassing way. In his chapter 'Creative matter and creative mind: Cultural ecology and literary creativity', Hubert Zapf draws on the approaches of cultural ecology and Material Ecocriticism to show that 'creativity is beginning to newly move into the focus of attention not alone as an exclusionary feature of human culture but as a property of life and … of the material world itself'.[38] Zapf argues that 'the creative potential of imaginative literature is intrinsically related to its power to actualize in always new forms the fundamental relationship between matter and mind, nature and culture, as a source of its creative processes'.[39] And further, 'literary creativity can be described in one important sense as a self-reflexive staging and aesthetic transformation of those processes

---

[38] Zapf 2014: 51.
[39] Ibid. p. 51.

of emergence and creativity that characterize the sphere of material nature itself'.[40] These propositions are key to the material-ecocritical colouring of my reading here, as they show how Theocritus' creativity can combine with that of his imagined characters and imagined landscape, in an emergent process. In this understanding, creativity is not something imposed top-down by humans; it is not something unique to us. Rather, we are surrounded by creative matter. From geological processes (as we explored in Chapter 3, pp. 113–40) to atmospheric conditions, our material world is constantly creating. This kind of lively ecopoetics is at the heart of David Abram's book *Becoming Animal: An Earthly Cosmology*, which explores in parallel the wild mind of the planet and the wild intelligence of our bodies. As Zapf shows, we might add yet another approach to the mix: that of biosemiotics and the suggestion that '*all* life – from the cell all the way up to us – is characterized by communication, or semiosis'.[41] In this interpretation, improvisation is foregrounded – that is, the improvisational flexibility that allows both natural and cultural creative processes to respond to the changing demands of their environments. And cultural ecology in particular emphasises the interconnectedness and dynamic feedback relations between culture and nature, mind and matter, text and life.

Louise Westling has identified the motif of the 'human-animal dance',[42] which has pervaded literature from its earliest incarnations to modern times. Zapf presents this as epitomising the way in which literature 'has presented human experience as part of a shared world of bodily natures and embodied minds'.[43] In this way we can sometimes see this 'shared world' finding its expression in literary motifs, tropes and even genres. Certainly the parallel elements of creativity we have seen in this chapter (from poet, to character, to object, to animals, to the land) point us towards this 'shared world'. We need only think of the ivory from which the distaff is made: a material that originates in the animal world, turned into an object for human use. And what is it that points Theocritus in this particular direction in *Idyll* 28? 'Fair winds' from Zeus (τυίδε γὰρ πλόον εὐάνεμον αἰτήμεθα πὰρ Δίος, 5). This is relevant to Zapf's chapter, in which he presents the four elements as an 'especially significant source domain for tropes of creativity' and includes examples of the air and winds as 'signifiers translating natural into cultural creativity'.[44] Though *Idyll* 28 foregrounds creativity primarily in other ways (first and foremost the parallelisms and equivalencies between human and nonhuman agents), it is interesting in light of

---

[40] Ibid. p. 51.
[41] Wheeler 2011: 270
[42] Westling 2006.
[43] Zapf 2014: 57.
[44] Ibid. p. 60.

Zapf's argument that the winds are needed to propel Theocritus and the distaff on their creative way.[45] And the poem continues to fit the fundamental pattern, as the earth features in the pastureland, and the animal world (another recurrent source domain for creativity) in the shorn sheep. Though these aspects are not evidently metaphorical, this does not preclude us from reading into them some creative patterns that cross between domains, with the elemental and animal worlds echoing and supporting human creativity.

In this same article, Hubert Zapf moves through physicist David Bohm's claim that 'the latent creativity of the mind' corresponds to the 'presence of creativity in nature and the universe at large',[46] and philosopher Manuel De Landa's description of 'matter's inherent creativity'[47] – to Jane Bennett's reference to reality as an '"onto-tale", in which everything is, in a sense, alive'. The material-ecocritical discussions of creative matter, then, represent a convergence of numerous disciplines and approaches – all exploring the affinities between different manifestations or expressions of creativity. Zapf also cites Bennett on anthropomorphism, and it is to anthropomorphism and isomorphism that I now turn.

Anthropomorphism is a 'symptom' of the overarching new-materialist approach that has come under scrutiny, and is something with which Material Ecocriticism, in particular, has to engage. In the introduction to their *Material Ecocriticism*, Serenella Iovino and Serpil Oppermann write:

> We are well aware that 'stories' or 'narratives', if applied to matter, might be read as metaphor. We want, however, to challenge the criticisms of anthropomorphizing matter and use this human lens as a heuristic strategy aimed at reducing the (linguistic, perceptive, and ethical) distance between the human and the nonhuman. So understood, anthropomorphism can even act against dualistic ontologies and be a 'dis-anthropocentric' stratagem meant to reveal the similarities and symmetries existing between humans and nonhumans.[48]

And they too cite Bennett, in particular her suggestion that 'anthropomorphism can reveal isomorphism'.[49] The first thing to note here is the mention of metaphor. I mentioned Zapf's points about elemental metaphor – but I used his arguments also

---

[45] It is worth noting that both sailing and weaving are technologies that are heavily dependent on natural processes, more so than other technologies that are more alienated.
[46] Bohm 1998: i.
[47] De Landa 1997: 16.
[48] Iovino and Opperman 2014: 8.
[49] Bennett 2010: 99.

to discuss parts of *Idyll* 28 that involve the elements yet are not obviously metaphorical. The stories of matter range more widely than just being manifest in metaphorical language, and though metaphor is an interesting and productive site for material-ecocritical analysis, it is not where this approach stops. The second point to address is the range and scope of anthropomorphic narrative, in particular the productive distinctions between anthropomorphism and personification, which I believe help to reveal the potential of the former for a new-materialist reading. Both anthropomorphism and personification are, to put it simply, literary devices used to assign human characteristics or qualities to nonhuman entities. Anthropomorphism's etymological meaning points towards something being made to appear human, to take on human form. Personification, rather, involves assigning typically human actions or emotions to the nonhuman. Though similar and related devices, personification is more slanted towards the figurative, anthropomorphism towards the literal; personification creates visual imagery, while anthropomorphism allows the nonhuman to *act* human. Both are arguably anthropocentric devices in that they involve the human creator (poet, author, etc.) ascribing human traits to the nonhuman world in an ostensibly top-down fashion. And yet, it is indicative for a material-ecocritical reading that the focus in scholarship has been on anthropomorphism rather than personification: on the literal rather than the figurative, the *morphing* rather than the visually descriptive or imagistic. Through anthropomorphism in particular we can explore the shape of the nonhuman, its form and its potential proximity to the human. We can blur the boundary, and start to ask why it was ever there to begin with: 'anthropomorphism can reveal isomorphism'.

In his chapter on the 'semiotization of matter' (again, in Iovino and Oppermann's volume), Timo Maran discusses the 'so-called morphisms':[50] metaphoric ascriptions including biomorphism, technomorphism, sociomorphism – and anthropomorphism. Maran argues that morphisms are about comprehension: 'Different morphisms allow us to comprehend things that are rather unknown to us, based on their analogies to things that are more common'. The New Materialisms and Material Ecocriticism have a heuristic as well as a philosophical remit: they are both ways of thinking about the world and our place in it, and tools for making sense of these. In this way, morphisms supply another heuristic tool: a way for us understand, to reframe, to relate. However, this article is important in that it draws attention to morphisms as analogy-based modelling strategies, and highlights the necessity of recognising the difference between anthropomorphic modelling and the agency of matter.[51] Though both

---

[50] Maran 2014: 148.

[51] Ibid. p. 149: 'Though conceptually and typologically indispensable, the distinction between matter (which may afford natural signs …) and the semiotic realm (which may have an

are valid perspectives on materiality, they are not always one and the same: the one is (or, at least, can be) an anthropocentric heuristic tool, which has benefits such as introducing 'empathy in humans for understanding and appreciating environmental processes'; the other can operate independently of our models, and might emerge in ways we haven't even thought to model. Anthropomorphism and other types of analogy-based modelling can result in semiotised matter – that is, matter which bears the imprint of an organism or culture. But as Maran points out, this is not the end of the story:

> Semiotized matter is not fully accessible or decodable without the human [or other organisms'] codes used in its creation, but nevertheless the semiotized matter has its own semiotic potential, which can creatively or distractively interact with new semiotic processes or debar them.[52]

My point here is that anthropomorphism is intrinsically anthropocentric, has a strong metaphorical component and is a modelling strategy – but it can be a useful heuristic for finding analogies and engendering empathy, and it does not have to close down routes to uncovering the agency of matter. Though we should distinguish between matter's semiotic potential and our semiotisation of matter, it is important to note that both do exist, and indeed co-exist.

The question of anthropomorphism is of relevance to *Idyll* 28, as we have here not simply an apostrophe to an object, or the personification of it in some isolated instances of figurative language, but a sustained anthropomorphic narrative that includes the distaff among the poem's cast of characters. The distaff is a friend; it is a gift (this does not necessitate inanimacy: we need only think of the whole host of women foregrounded in Homeric gift exchange, or indeed the transactional nature of Greek marriage); it has a hometown and will make a new home for itself; it will be a companion to Theocritus, a collaborator of Theugenis. Though it is not described as taking on specifically human form, its behaviours clearly approximate those of the poem's human characters. But to look at this from another perspective, do we really need to read anthropomorphism into *Idyll* 28? Is a human 'form' or 'shape' or 'character' really the only way we can think about the multiple agencies and alliances tracked in this chapter? Or has an exploration of anthropomorphism actually led us to Jane Bennett's point: a revelation of isomorphism? Perhaps all of these interpretive gymnastics we have to do in order to highlight the anthropomorphic reading obscure

---

effect on matter) has become increasingly blurred and unstable within contemporary, human-influenced environments.'

[52] Ibid. p. 151.

the underlying realisation – that the poem makes complete sense without them, and that we can explain the distaff's behaviour equally well as an equation of agents: a parallelism between distaff and Theocritus, between distaff and Theugenis. In using anthropomorphism as a heuristic strategy, as an interpretive lens through which to approach this poem, we have ended up right back where Material Ecocriticism would have us: reading across the porous, permeable boundary between person and thing, human and nonhuman. Furthermore, levelling the playing field in this way might allow us also to read the alignment in reverse – that is, to see Theocritus and Theugenis as somehow not-human, as part of a material and natural process that is greater than them.

I would add here a further example of an anthropomorphic scene in the Theocritean corpus, and an anthropocentric reading of it.

> Κόως δ' ὀλόλυξεν ἰδοῖσα,
> φᾶ δὲ καθαπτομένα βρέφεος χείρεσσι φίλησιν·

> Cos gave a joyful cry when she saw him,
> and clasping the baby with loving hands she spoke.
> (*Idyll* 17.64–5)

Idyll 17 is an encomium to Ptolemy II. It tells of his birth on Cos, and in this part of the poem the island receives Ptolemy from his mother and cares for him. As in the poems to which Theocritus possibly alludes (the *Homeric Hymn to Apollo* and Callimachus' *Hymn to Zeus* and *Hymn to Delos*[53]), this has been treated as an anthropomorphic scene, with the island taking on voice, emotion and agency. We can detect hints of discomfort with this reading, however. In his Loeb edition, Hopkinson adds a footnote to the line about Cos giving a joyful cry: 'I.e., the eponymous nymph of the island'. But what is there in the poem to point us in this direction? Why do we need to move beyond anthropomorphism to direct manifestation in the form of a human-like entity? There is more in *Idyll* 17 than in *Idyll* 28 to guide us towards an anthropomorphic reading: that the island has hands, for instance, and that she speaks in a human tongue. Her agency is exercised through human means. This sets the distaff of *Idyll* 28 in even greater relief, as it does not necessitate this particular standard and rigid interpretation. And yet, there is no reason for which we should

---

[53] The relative chronology in relation to Callimachus' hymns is uncertain, but they seem to be roughly contemporaneous. There are clearly connections there, but which poet has been influenced by whom is up for debate.

make a further anthropocentric shift, away from anthropomorphism. We don't need a nymph here – the island is quite capable of saying it all.

Though this argument has come full circle, on its way it has challenged those 'criticisms of anthropomorphizing matter' mentioned by Iovino and Oppermann. Anthropomorphism may have an anthropocentric element in its etymological meaning, and indeed if we stop at step one of the argument, we limit our reading to a comparison between person and thing that is weighted towards the person. And yet, if we continue the argument, if we push past our initial preconception about anthropomorphism, about personification – the ring-fencing of figurative language as something characteristically human – we come to the more interesting stuff: the opening up of metaphor and other types of figurative language to affinities with creative matter, and the revelation in anthropomorphism of similarity, of resistance to a top-down model that prioritises human creativity, in favour of a material narrative with a cast of equal characters more diverse than we realised.

From Distaffs to Guineas

Before moving to what is arguably the most compelling comparandum and intertext for Theocritus' *Idyll* 28, let us take a wider arc – to the eighteenth century, Britain, and the 'it-narrative'. Working through this more far-flung connection will lead us in a roundabout way to Erinna: but en route it will allow us to think about trends or turns in literature and in literary criticism, from the perspective of material agency and, specifically, the animated object.

The 2004 edited volume *Things*, from Bill Brown of 'Thing Theory' fame (a frequent reference point in this book so far),[54] considers the cyclical modishness of 'things' as an academic and artistic subject. Brown focuses on the twentieth century, which, he claims, had a 'thing about things'. But he does not claim that this mode came out of nowhere, that there is something unique about the twentieth century – rather, he suggests that it is one in a series of material 'moments', a resurgence of interest in materiality and a new manifestation of it. In the opening of his 2007 edited volume *The Secret Life of Things*, Mark Blackwell revisits Brown's assertion, giving a very similar account for the eighteenth century – and, as this book and others like it show, we can take the cycle back to antiquity.[55]

---

[54] The 2004 volume was preceded by a 2001 *Critical Inquiry* special edition. Thing Theory takes its impetus from Heideggerian distinctions between 'object' and 'thing', on which see the essay 'The Thing' in Heidegger 1971.

[55] This tendency of materiality to move in and out of focus is essential to our understanding of the current material turn: both a turning towards the material and ontological, away from

But to turn to 'the secret life of things': in eighteenth-century Britain (and soon after this in France) a type of prose fiction rose to prominence, variously called the 'it-narrative', the 'novel of circulation' or the 'object tale'. In these stories, inanimate objects (coins, waistcoats, pins, corkscrews, coaches) or animate entities (dogs, fleas, ponies, body parts) are cast as the central characters, often enjoying a consciousness and perspective of their own. An object gives rise to a story. The narrative agency of the object vies with that of the human narrator, or eclipses it altogether. The nexus of the material-discursive comes to the fore, in a type grounded in multiple entanglements. Many of the eighteenth-century it-narratives are indeed novels of circulation: they are primarily about the object as commodity, its movements and exchanges. In studies of them, this has been identified as a generic self-consciousness by which the story parallels realities of property and specifically the print market. The stories tell the tale of their own consumption: the passing from hand to hand of circulating popular print is enacted in stories of clothes shifting from back to back (such as the *Adventures of a Black Coat*, 1760) or vehicles moving from place to place (the *Adventures of a Hackney Coach*, 1783). Yet as Jonathan Lamb notes in his book *The Things Things Say*, 'the best it-narratives chronicle an emancipation that divides the portion of their earlier lives as property from their later lives as an unowned thing'.[56] At some point, the thing breaks free, and governs its own story.

In his book, Lamb turns to Alexander Pope's *The Rape of the Lock* (a text to which we keep returning), arguing that in this poem things say nothing, and that the poem is about 'surface'. In her article 'The things things don't say' (discussed in Chapter 2, pp. 47–8), Elizabeth Kowaleski Wallace has gone beyond this argument, making a number of points that are of particular relevance to our consideration of poetic and material creation, and in particular the potential tension between the agency of the poet and the agency of the thing. Wallace argues that it is not that things say nothing in *The Rape of the Lock*, but that Pope is doing a very complex contortionist act by presenting 'vital' objects only to mock them. If there were no risk of things saying anything, why would Pope go down this route in the first place? The poem epitomises the eighteenth-century antithesis between mechanist and vitalist thought (as discussed in Chapter 2), and in its exploration of vitalism actually 'engages seriously with the natural philosophies it appears to reject through its comedy'.[57] Wallace continues:

---

a postmodern focus on the discursive and epistemological – *and* a moment in which the material, once again, takes its turn. For more on the material turn in Classics, see Canevaro 2019a.

[56] Lamb 2011: xxviii.
[57] Wallace 2018: 105.

Coming down clearly and decisively on the side of the doctrine of mechanism, the poem is designed to mock those who would believe in dancing teacups, sylphs, or even the agency of women themselves as vital matter. Yet in the very process of disavowing the capacity of matter to move, to express, or to possess agency, Pope calls forth the presence of what he denies.

Though the conclusion is firm, the process has the secondary effect of giving some degree of credence to the very idea Pope ostensibly resists. And that is the key point: resistance. In *The Rape of the Lock* there *is* vital materiality, though this is supposedly curtailed by Pope through mockery. Disavowal and presencing prove to be interrelated.

As Brown notes, we can also trace a cyclical focus on things in academic treatments, and this applies to Eighteenth-century Literary Studies, where consideration of these it-narratives has burgeoned: conference panels like 'The Agency of Objects without Subjects' or 'The People Things Make' suggest the direction of the discourse. There is a growing interest in this field in the relationship between literature and materiality, and this is something we can see happening also within Classics. The it-narrative has been spotted, discussed, displayed – in particular because of scholarship's resurgent 'thing about things'. A focus on 'the things things say' (or indeed, 'the things things don't say') – a sustained consideration of the nonhuman that gives full weight to material agency – is timely, in the current wave of New Materialisms, with the palpable effects of the material turn, the growing interest and expertise in reading across material-discursive narratives. Bill Brown has written a review of Mark Blackwell's volume, in which he highlights as key 'such moments in the collection where accounts of the it-narrative disrupt received wisdom about English literary history'.[58] These are moments when the it-narrative is shown to be more important than is usually assumed; when the it-narrative is shown to be more prevalent than we realised; when, indeed, elements of it-narrative are found where they were not expected to be. The it-narratives are often emphatically advertised as such, Charles Johnstone's *Chrysal; or, The Adventures of a Guinea* (1760–5) being the most popular example at the time. But sometimes they are narrative elements embedded in stories that are known for reasons other than their object orientation. These embedded it-narratives offer a particular comparandum for the broad spectrum of material agency I have traced in the Theocritean corpus, in that they encompass a wide swathe of object narratives. And yet, the 'advertised' it-narrative takes on special relevance to *Idyll* 28, known in some collections as Ἠλακάτη or Ἀλάκατα, 'The Distaff'. Its object narrative is foregrounded, its material agency

---

[58] Brown 2009: 635.

even becoming titular.⁵⁹ The distaff, however we are to categorise its entanglements, is indisputably placed centre stage.

In Chapter 4 (p. 158) I presented lines 24–5 of *Idyll* 28 as an epigram:

κῆνο γάρ τις ἔρει τῶπος ἴδων σ'· 'ἦ μεγάλα χάρις
δώρῳ σὺν ὀλίγῳ· πάντα δὲ τίματα τὰ πὰρ φίλων.'

Someone will say when they see you, 'Indeed great goodwill goes with
this slight gift; and all things that come from friends are precious.'
(*Idyll* 28.24–5)

As Jesper Svenbro puts it, an epigram acts as 'a machine for producing *kleos*'.⁶⁰ By setting these lines in an epigrammatic mode, Theocritus generates *kleos* for the distaff (ἴδων σ'), and for himself (πὰρ φίλων): we return to the equivalency established between poet and object. But there is much more we can say about these epigrammatic lines if we approach them from the perspective of materiality and material agency. As a final point in this chapter, I will set Theocritus' epigram in *Idyll* 28 in the wider context of Hellenistic epigram, and use the comparanda provided by the period to help interrogate the interplay between the themes that have proven central to this chapter: materiality, creation – and gender.

As an introduction to the question of epigram in the Hellenistic period, Michael Tueller offers the following:

> These foundational poets [Callimachus, Theocritus, Asclepiades, Posidippus and others] were particularly concerned with the ability of writing to construct reality, and with whether an artistically constructed object can be said to *be*, or only to *represent*, its model. They explored these ideas by making enigmas out of the formerly conventional questions of inscribed epigram: 'Who is talking?' 'Who is being addressed?' 'What is the object to which they point?'⁶¹

Tueller's chapter is part of *The Materiality of Text*, the book I mentioned at the start of this chapter: a volume of great relevance to many of our themes, as it brings the material turn to bear on classical texts. In his introduction, editor

---

⁵⁹ 'The titular object' is the topic of Mario Telò's current book project, with a focus on Plautus and comedy.
⁶⁰ Svenbro 1993: 164.
⁶¹ Tueller 2019: 187.

Andrej Petrovic notes that 'in all literate societies textuality is predicated on materiality'.[62] The ring-fencing of 'material culture' is broken down with the realisation that materiality underpins all of our textual evidence too, and as such is at the heart of every branch of classical study. The book offers a comprehensive survey of themes, covering epigraphic, literary and architectural spaces – though it is simultaneously demarcated by a focus on epigraphic texts, which drive all of the contributions and continually bring us back to the physicality of the inscribed text.

The question 'Who is being addressed?' has loomed large in the current chapter, because of the opening apostrophe to the distaff itself: the foregrounding of the material object, and the material agency that emerges from this narrative choice. In this case, the object to which the epigram points overlaps with the addressee, as the distaff is both the subject of the poem and the object that initiates the epigrammatic reading. Tueller goes on: 'The early, foundational epigrams that were most influential in promoting these themes are ascribed to women: to Nossis, Anyte, Moero, and especially Erinna'; and 'the epigrams of Erinna played a key role in adjusting the relationship between the writer, the written, and woman'.[63] As a final point in my exploration in this chapter, then, I turn to Erinna: to her own *Distaff*, and the epigrams derived from it. In doing so, this section brings together questions raised by those preceding it: on gender, and the agency of the female object; on equivalency between poet and material actor; on the speaking object; and on the broader theme of creation, both material and literary.

In Chapter 2 I introduced the approach, advocated by the Material Feminisms, of reading across the body. This is something we might pick up in a consideration of epigrams – specifically those associated with women. Tueller explores the Freudian line of criticism pursued by Page DuBois, which sees women as surfaces that receive writing.[64] There is an equation between women and written text, which we might trace outside the strict parameters of inscribed epigrams to literary manifestations of the epigrammatic mode like that in *Idyll* 28. An early example of the type is Andromache as a living epigram in *Iliad* 6 (see Chapter 3, pp. 126–7), and I quote the lines again:

Ἕκτορος ἥδε γυνή, ὃς ἀριστεύεσκε μάχεσθαι
Τρώων ἱπποδάμων, ὅτε Ἴλιον ἀμφεμάχοντο.

---

[62] Petrovic 2019: 4.
[63] Tueller 2019: 187.
[64] Ibid. p. 190. See DuBois 1988: 130–66.

> This is the wife of Hector, he who was ever the best fighter
> of the Trojans, breakers of horses, when they fought about Ilion.
> (Homer *Iliad* 6.460–1)

In *Idyll* 28, the distaff is to be the instigator of the imagined epigram: the *lieu de mémoire*. Read at one level, this is a simple function of the object: the thing gives rise to the story. And yet, the picture is complicated by the equivalencies we have seen throughout this *Idyll*, between person and thing. By these final lines of the poem, we no longer see the distaff as just an object: its material agency has been emphasised; it has been equated both with Theocritus and with Theugenis; it has been cast as collaborator, as an active participant in the household creation. Further, in its domestic and female allegiances it has been cast primarily as a feminine object. As the line between human and nonhuman blurs, these epigrammatic lines become akin to those of *Iliad* 6: an epigram 'written' on a woman.

Tueller argues that 'Erinna's key contribution in her epigrams is to move away from the idea of a feminine speaking object, and insist that women displace their speech onto other objects'.[65] She 'drove a wedge between the women in her poems and the objects that are allowed to speak. She showed a clear desire to reveal the silence of women, and not to downplay that silence by acting as if objects are a sufficient substitute'.[66] How does this relate to Theocritus' distaff? First, the double equivalency in *Idyll* 28 is one way in which Theocritus follows Erinna's example of problematising the easy substitution of woman/object. The distaff is primarily a female object, but by casting it as emigrant, as travelling companion of Theocritus himself and his poem, as creator akin to the poet, Theocritus too 'drove a wedge', complicating the substitutions by multiplying the equivalencies and having them straddle the gender boundary. Second, it is notable that the epigram itself does not give voice to the distaff. It does not even focus on the qualities, or function, or creative output of the distaff. Rather, it offers a generic, proverbial-sounding sentiment, deflected onto 'the gift' in general rather than the specifics of the thing. It can be argued, therefore, that Theocritus, like Erinna, avoids the speaking object here in order to praise and elevate the female object without downplaying the question of female silence.

In Erinna's poetry, the issue of female silence is inextricably bound up with the theme of loss. In her *Distaff*, as well as in the epigrams that are modelled on it, Erinna takes her cue from the loss of Baukis, her companion from childhood. Her poems incorporate elements of lament and are vehicles of commemoration. In this,

---

[65] Tueller 2019: 199.
[66] Ibid. p. 203.

they have much in common with the Andromache epigram cited above: though Andromache will remain, she will be a physical reminder of her own loss, a living memorial for her dead husband and a vessel for his memory. Both the Homeric example and Erinna's poems are trained on loss and on commemoration. Theocritus' *Idyll*, however, uses memory in a very different way. The distaff is not a prompt for memory of a lost loved one, a window into the past, but rather an object anchored in the present (the journey, the guest-friendship) and looking hopefully towards a positive future. Andromache's epigram, too, contemplates the future – an enacting of Hector's memory as her body is 'read' – but it is a future that involves the constant revisiting of her own grief. Theocritus transposes the embedded literary epigram into a neutral context of hospitality and guest-friendship, and instead of using the distaff as a focus for lamentation, he enlists it to encapsulate a continuing friendship. This is another manifestation of the theme of creation: that of memory creation. In the Homeric poems, women use objects to establish a prospective model of memory: they take an object that does not have a long-standing cultural biography (unlike high-profile circulating male objects) and imbue it with resonance in the present, propelling it into futurity.[67] This may be an object they themselves have created; it may be part of their domestic environs; it may be their body as object (as in the case of Andromache). Similarly, as Diane Rayor notes, 'Erinna preserves Baukis' memory through her poetry – the poet remembers and ensures that the memory of the deceased lives on.'[68] And more specifically, Erinna uses an object as the vehicle for that memory. Theocritus too utilises this prospective, instigative, *creative* aspect of memory through objects, as the distaff is to be something seen, noted and commented upon, thus cementing the friendship for posterity. Rayor makes an important distinction between Erinna and Sappho in terms of the functioning of memory: 'Memory is one-sided here, compared to the reciprocal workings of memory in Sappho's poems. Obviously, Baukis cannot carry on the memory of their shared experience, and Erinna gives no hint of any women's community in her poems.'[69] There is a similar truncation of memory in the Andromache epigram, though differently triangulated. Andromache will monumentalise Hector, who will be remembered by those who see her. While her bodily survival is required for this process to work, she is not the primary focus of the epigram she instigates: though the grammatical subject, she is quickly sidelined in favour of a description of her husband's prowess. And as this epigrammatic scenario is envisaged as following Hector's death, there will be no reciprocal commemoration on his part.

---

[67] See further Canevaro 2018b: 43–54.
[68] Rayor 2005: 61.
[69] Ibid. p. 61.

Theocritus' poem, by contrast, deals firmly with the living, and with a full and continuing relationship. It is about the 'reciprocal workings' *par excellence*: those of gift-giving and guest-friendship.

There are, then, essential differences in perspective and focus between Erinna's *Distaff* and related verses, and Theocritus' distaff-*Idyll*. Working through these has helped us clarify the function of Theocritus' literary epigram, as well as raising other aspects of the broader theme of creation. As a final point in this section, I would like to use the poetry of Erinna to revisit a set of questions that have persisted throughout this book, particularly in consideration of *Idyll* 1 and the scenes on Thyrsis' cup. My primary focus on materiality – on material-ecocritical approaches, on material agency – has generated a perspective on the cup's images that enlivens them, that follows Theocritus' strategies for reducing or problematising ontological and interpretive boundaries. It is relevant, then, that Erinna explicitly *reflects* on the vitality of art in the first lines of her epigram 3:

Ἐξ ἀταλᾶν χειρῶν τάδε γράμματα· λῷστε Προμαθεῦ,
ἔντι καὶ ἄνθρωποι τὶν ὁμαλοὶ σοφίαν.
Ταύταν γοῦν ἐτύμως τὰν παρθένον ὅστις ἔγραψεν
αἰ καὐδὰν ποτέθηκ᾽ ἧς κ᾽ Ἀγαθαρχὶς ὅλα.

This picture is the work of sensitive hands. My good Prometheus,
there are even human beings equal to you in skill.
At least, if whoever painted this maiden so truly
had just added a voice, you would have been Agatharchis entirely.

This has been classed as the earliest Greek ekphrastic epigram, and as such it ties together our formal focus on epigram in this section and the theme of ekphrasis which has been prevalent throughout the book. In this epigram, Erinna praises the lifelike quality of a portrait of one Agatharchis. That she compares the painter responsible for it to Prometheus is telling: Prometheus moulded the human race from clay, and in doing so he created not merely an illusion of life but life itself.[70] And yet, there are limits. Because the portrait lacks 'voice', it cannot fully embody Agatharchis. Had voice and image been combined, true vitality would have been achieved, and the human woman replicated. Prometheus is not the only Hesiodic figure this passage brings to mind. Here we might return to Pandora and her connections both to vital materiality and ekphrasis, as explored in Chapter 2. The first woman lacks animacy

---

[70] We have discussed Prometheus also in Chapter 2. It seems he is central to a consideration of ancient vitalist thought.

in the *Theogony*, described as 'like' a maiden but given no character, agency or, importantly, voice. By contrast, the creatures depicted on her diadem and given ekphrastic description are arguably more lively, and specifically they are 'like living *speaking* beings'. However, in the *Works and Days*, Pandora *does* have a voice: αὐδὴν (*WD* 61); φωνὴν (79).[71] She is more animated than her Theogony counterpart, and her ability to speak is an essential component of that. In this passage from Erinna, we are confronted head-on with an equation, a comparison, between the creation of the human and the creation of the nonhuman, the animacy of (wo)man and the animacy of matter. Though the portrait ultimately falls short, there is the suggestion that it *could* have been fully animate matter, had it possessed all the correct ingredients. Art not only imitating life but becoming it.

---

[71] On the different vocabulary here, see Canevaro 2015a: 114–15.

5 Beyond the Cup

Idylls 6 and 11: His Monstrous Materials

Theocritus' cast of characters spans men and women, elite and non-elite, people and things, human and nonhuman nature. A focus on 'herdsmen's lives' as representative anecdote, or on the elite context of the poems' composition, chooses but one firmly anthropocentric lens. A material-ecocritical reading, by contrast, has decentred the conventionally foregrounded male human protagonist and has given us a view of the margins, a view from below: a view that has clarified the dark undercurrents of pastoral poetry. Again and again in this book we have seen the rural idyll punctured by a menacing materiality. Harmony between man and nature is precarious and questioned as material agency moves to the fore. Not only does our foot hurt because we stubbed our toe on a stone, but it was the stone that did it. The landscape becomes agentic, threatening – monstrous. Where better to focus this reading than on Theocritus' monster himself?

Polyphemus is the central character of both *Idyll* 6 and *Idyll* 11. The latter poem tells the story of Polyphemus' love for the sea nymph Galatea. The Cyclops' love song is framed by an address to the doctor Nikias, whom we have met in our reading of *Idyll* 28. The frame recommends song as a remedy for love while also being a symptom of it. *Idyll* 6 then presupposes 11 and forms a sequel. It is a singing contest between Daphnis and Damoetas, in which the first song admonishes Polyphemus for being a lazy lover and the second assumes Polyphemus' voice and defends his neglect of Galatea as a wooing strategy. Both *Idylls* are prequels to the Polyphemus episode with which we are familiar from book 9 of the *Odyssey*, and as such the 'future' narrative arc looms large. We know what will happen to Polyphemus, and Theocritus hints at the Cyclops' gruesome fate throughout these *Idylls* in repeated references to Odysseus' 'Nobody' trick (*Idyll* 11: οὖτις, 38; τις ξένος, 61; κἠγών τις φαίνομαι ἦμεν, 79) and the possibility of Polyphemus losing his one eye (11.51, 6.22–4). The Theocritean response to Homer has been interpreted as comedy and as tragedy, as a positive bucolic twist and as dramatic irony. A material-ecocritical reading can offer another interpretation. This is not tragic irony, but dark ecology. By the end of *Idyll* 11, is Polyphemus cured of his lovesickness? Hunter argues that 'there is in fact nothing in 80–1 to suggest a final "curing" or *katharsis*'.[1] There is a prevailing tone of pessimism here, and in my reading I aim to show that it is enacted specifically through material agency.

Let's start at the end of the story: with Polyphemus in Homer's *Odyssey*. Homer's Polyphemus is primal; he is destructive, uncivilised and 'other'. In his book *Monster Theory*, Jeffrey Jerome Cohen classes Polyphemus as the prototype in Western culture for the 'geographic' monster: dissociated from community, showing a rugged individualism.[2] In Cohen's 'Monster culture (seven theses)', this comes under his Thesis V: 'The Monster Polices the Border of the Possible'. This formulation is compelling for our reading, as we have been concerned throughout this book with (ontological, interpretational, generic) borders and boundaries and with the realms of possibility and impossibility, reality and fiction. The Cyclopes are characterised by their lack of civilising objects: they have no tools for agriculture ('they do not plant or plough', οὔτε φυτεύουσιν ... οὔτ' ἀρόωσιν, *Od.* 9.108), and none for seafaring ('for the Cyclopes have no red-cheeked ships', οὐ γὰρ Κυκλώπεσσι νέες πάρα μιλτοπάρῃοι, *Od.* 9.125). Polyphemus only has objects that function for storage of milk, cheese and whey (e.g. ἄγγεα, *Od.* 9.222 and 248; τάλαροι, 247), indicative of a simple, self-sufficient lifestyle. Yet this is no bucolic idyll – because Polyphemus is no ordinary famer.[3] He might care for his flock and store some standard foodstuffs, but there is room on his monstrous menu for more gruesome items too.

Homer's Polyphemus is emphasised with natural objects, but specifically in ways that suggest power and threat: a pile of wood he drops with a crash (*Od.* 9.233–5), a door stone that twenty-two wagons could not lift (*Od.* 9.240–3), the mountain peak and the stone he throws after Odysseus (*Od.* 9.480–6, 537–42). He is even assimilated to the natural landscape:

καὶ γὰρ θαῦμ' ἐτέτυκτο πελώριον, οὐδὲ ἐῴκει
ἀνδρί γε σιτοφάγῳ, ἀλλὰ ῥίῳ ὑλήεντι
ὑψηλῶν ὀρέων, ὅ τε φαίνεται οἷον ἀπ' ἄλλων.

---

[1] Hunter 1999: 220.
[2] Cohen 1996b: 14.
[3] As I argue in Canevaro 2018b: 145–6.

> For he had been made a monstrous wonder, not like
> a man who eats bread, but like a wooded peak
> of high mountains that appears apart from the others.
>
> (Homer *Odyssey* 9.190–2)

This description encapsulates Polyphemus' size, strength and isolation. He is explicitly othered, being emphatically not like a man – and in this othering he is distanced not only from human but also from animal or 'humanimal' and is associated rather with his environment. It is from this perspective that we can view Polyphemus as he is picked up by Theocritus in his pastoral poems.

Theocritus' Polyphemus is often treated as a positive bucolic twist on the Homeric monster. But how positive is this version really? Has the threat of Homer's Polyphemus truly been neutralised?[4] Mark Payne argues that the Polyphemus of *Idyll* 11 is:

> neither the representative of all that is opposed to civilization, as he is in the *Odyssey*, nor the monstrous manifestation of all the excesses of civilization, as he is in the comic tradition. He is instead a young lover, a herdsman, and a singer. While he has shed all the traits of the Homeric Cyclops other than his one eye and his flock, the new ones that he has acquired do not make him a vehicle for contemporary satire, but identify him with the herdsman of the other bucolic poems.[5]

I will come back to this identification with the herdsman and its implications in terms of a reading from below, but first I would argue that a focus on materiality can in fact reveal other Homeric Cyclopean traits that Theocritus' Polyphemus retains – traits that are charged with threat, and specifically the threat of the landscape. As Cohen puts it, monsters 'serve as the ultimate incorporation of our anxieties – about history, about identity, about our very humanity. As they always will.'[6]

ἀλλὰ τὸ φάρμακον εὗρε, καθεζόμενος δ' ἐπὶ πέτρας
ὑψηλᾶς ἐς πόντον ὁρῶν ἄειδε τοιαῦτα·

---

[4] Cohen (1996a: 18) notes this as a possibility for monster narratives: 'The co-optation of the monster into a symbol of the desirable is often accomplished through the neutralization of potentially threatening aspects with a liberal dose of comedy'.
[5] Payne 2007: 71.
[6] Cohen 1996b: xii.

But he found the remedy, as sitting on
high rocks and looking out at the sea he sang in this way.
(Theocritus *Idyll* 11.17–18)

Polyphemus sings to soothe his lovesickness. He sings for the sea nymph Galatea, and so he sings to the sea. His love interest and her environment are inextricable. And Polyphemus has brought with him his Homeric environs. Sitting alone on a high rock looking out to sea, he still resembles the isolated mountain peak to which he was assimilated in *Odyssey* 9.[7] He brings his cave with him too, and its transformation into a *locus amoenus* is hyperbolic:[8]

ἐντὶ δάφναι τηνεί, ἐντὶ ῥαδιναὶ κυπάρισσοι,
ἔστι μέλας κισσός, ἔστ' ἄμπελος ἁ γλυκύκαρπος,
ἔστι ψυχρὸν ὕδωρ, τό μοι ἁ πολυδένδρεος Αἴτνα
λευκᾶς ἐκ χιόνος ποτὸν ἀμβρόσιον προΐητι.

There are laurels, there are slender cypresses,
there is black ivy, there is the sweet-fruited vine,
there is cold water which wooded Etna produces for me
from its white snow, a divine drink.
(*Idyll* 11.45–8)

The proximity between Polyphemus and the mountain is reinforced here by the cold water which wooded Etna produces for the Cyclops as if in cooperation. We know that this cave will be the site of a grim scene in the *Odyssey*, and the contrast with the pleasant and peaceful Theocritean cave has important dark-ecological ramifications for Theocritus' bucolics more generally, in that it ruptures the very idea of the *locus amoenus*. The fate of Polyphemus in the *Odyssey* is portended by reference to fire, burning and wood, all of which will be components of his Odysseus-engineered downfall:

---

[7] See the discussion of man and rock in Chapter 3 (pp. 113–40) – here the syntax with preposition ἐπὶ does not suggest as close a hybridity as is the case with the fisherman and his rock in *Idyll* 1, and yet Polyphemus' position on the cliff does bring the Cyclops-as-mountain to mind. Hunter 1999 *ad loc.* notes that 'the primary model is the unhappy Odysseus on Calypso's island (*Od.*5.84, 158)' – in the former example Odysseus is sitting on the shore (ἐπ' ἀκτῆς); in the latter he is sitting on the rocks and banks (ἐν πέτρῃσι καὶ ἠιόνεσσι).
[8] Hunter 1999 *ad* 4–58: 'The pairing of virtually every noun with an adjective ... suggests the effort which goes into this set piece.'

αἰ δέ τοι αὐτὸς ἐγὼν δοκέω λασιώτερος ἦμεν,
ἐντὶ δρυὸς ξύλα μοι καὶ ὑπὸ σποδῷ ἀκάματον πῦρ·
καιόμενος δ' ὑπὸ τεῦς καὶ τὰν ψυχὰν ἀνεχοίμαν
καὶ τὸν ἕν' ὀφθαλμόν, τῷ μοι γλυκερώτερον οὐδέν.

But if I myself seem to be too shaggy,
I have oak logs and undying fire under the ash,
and burned by you I would give up my soul
and my one eye, than which nothing is dearer to me.
(*Idyll* 11.50–3)

The Cyclops' future is embedded in material detail, his narrative written across landscape and body, the one eye and shaggy brow soon to be burned by the very fire of which he boasts. Here he is burning with love or burned by the one he loves – it is a fine line. And the line blurs even further, as in the landscape of the cave his fiery Odyssean fate is superimposed on his blazing lovesickness.

At lines 56–9 Polyphemus wishes that he had been born with gills so that he could go to Galatea and kiss her and bring her flowers. He suggests white snowdrops[9] or red poppies – but in a jarring moment of realism he notes that poppies grow in summer and snowdrops in winter, so he wouldn't be able to bring them both together. Hunter *ad loc.* notes that 'his naïve pedantry is obviously amusing, but it also lays bare the artificially conventional nature of "love poetry," which has no place for simple ideas of "realism"'. I would shift our interpretation from the comedic to the pessimistic, however. There is a strong sense of futility and limitation here, manifesting through nature. First, Polyphemus *wasn't* born with gills. His own material makeup imposes limits, limits which are spatially demarcated in the division between land and sea. Second, the gifts he *would have* given *if* he were born with gills couldn't all be given simultaneously anyway, as nature's rhythms stand in the way. This recalls Asphalion in *Idyll* 21 questioning and blaming the seasons, setting up the environment as adversary.[10]

Polyphemus' limitations continue in the next lines (60–2), as he resolves to learn to swim so that he might visit Galatea. He *cannot* swim, and he needs a teacher – some stranger who might arrive in a ship. There is a clear Odyssean resonance to these lines: the stranger (τις ξένος) points towards Odysseus and *xenia*, with Polyphemus now *inviting* the expert swimmer who, we know, will ultimately sail away leaving

---

[9] 56 κρίνα λευκά – Gow *ad loc.* suggests these might be narcissi, as snowdrops are not common in Greece.

[10] See the first section of Chapter 3 (pp. 91–113).

him blind.[11] Polyphemus' resolution and practical consideration inject another dose of pragmatism into his love song. Though Polyphemus then goes on to blame his mother, ultimately it is the divide between land and sea that is the issue. He is *somebody* on land (δῆλον ὅτ' ἐν τᾷ γᾷ κἠγών τις φαίνομαι ἦμεν, 79); but away from land, he is all at sea. There is a boundary in nature that he cannot cross, and this dislodges the agency from the Cyclops and distributes it between the sea nymph and her environs. This divide is perhaps at its clearest in line 43, bringing with it an indication of agentic nature:

τὰν γλαυκὰν δὲ θάλασσαν ἔα ποτὶ χέρσον ὀρεχθεῖν·

Let the grey sea roar upon the shore.

The phrase γλαυκὰν θάλασσαν occurs in Homer only once, at *Iliad* 16.34. There Patroclus is reproaching Achilles for holding back from battle and is asking to go into the fray himself. He depicts Achilles as pitiless by claiming he was born not from Peleus and Thetis but from the grey sea and steep rocks (γλαυκὴ δέ σ' ἔτικτε θάλασσα | πέτραι τ' ἠλίβατοι). We have seen in Chapter 3 (pp. 113–40) the intransigent nature of stone, and a posited lithic parentage transfers this quality to the obdurate Achilles (another petromorphic move). But the grey sea is part of his characterisation too, and the connotations are likely to be recalled in this passage of *Idyll* 11. Achilles is harsh, and so is the sea. Polyphemus might think he wants swimming lessons, but he does not paint a positive picture of the sea. The Cyclopes have no ships; Polyphemus cannot swim; his downfall will come to him across the sea; and the sea itself is pitiless. The pessimistic tone is marked here as a strong dark-ecological aesthetic breaks through Polyphemus' words of love. Further, the grey sea in *Idyll* 11 has a say in the matter. ὀρεχθεῖν is a verb of uncertain and disputed meaning, but it is often taken to mean 'roar'. At *Iliad* 23.30 it seems to be the death rattle of oxen being slaughtered (cognate with ῥοχθέω), though it might rather refer to their struggle (cognate with ὀρέγομαι). In either case, this is a grim connection, with suggestions of roaring, groaning, resisting. The sea acts, and it talks back. Later poets use the verb of the swelling (like ὀρίνομαι) of the heart in anger, sorrow or pain. The sea feels, too – and it does not feel good.

In *Idyll* 6 the divide between land and sea again acts as a constitutive symbol of failed wooing. This time the tables have turned: Polyphemus is playing hard to get, while Galatea pelts his sheep with apples. She gazes on his caves and flocks 'from

---

[11] Hunter 1999 *ad loc.*: 'The Cyclops chooses (unwittingly) an expert swimmer as his teacher, perhaps in fact the *protos heuretes* of the art'.

the sea' (ἐκ δὲ θαλάσσας, 27), the spatial limitations having more of an impact on the sea nymph this time. Though she is in a frenzy (τάκεται, 27), the sea seems to have calmed (perhaps because Galatea is *becalmed*, unable to get to Polyphemus). There are 'fair waves' (καλὰ κύματα, 11) that reflect an image of Polyphemus' dog as he barks at the sea, and these waves are not roaring but 'gently sounding' (ἄσυχα καχλάζοντος, 12). Polyphemus too considers his reflection in the calm sea (35–8) – and is pleased with what he sees. As Galatea's control of the situation wanes, so too does the agency and voice of the sea (agency is distributed between them, shared in a hybridity that captures the nature of the nymph). But threat lurks in the depths, nonetheless. First, there is the threat of Polyphemus – he might take on the comical persona of the dandy as he preens before the mirroring sea, but he does draw attention to his reflected teeth (37–8), and we know what those teeth will do. Second is the threat *to* Polyphemus – he gazes into his one 'fair' eye (καλὰ δέ μευ ἁ μία κώρα, 36), which won't be fair for long. And Polyphemus knows something isn't quite right. He can sense the peril, and tries to avert it with some apotropaic spitting (39–40). His gazing upon his reflection is prideful and dangerously narcissistic. Galatea hasn't managed to tempt him – will the water do it for her?

Cohen's Thesis III is 'The Monster is the Harbinger of Category Crisis'. Again this resonates with the current book, which has at its core a blurring of ontological boundaries, a picking apart of those entrenched dichotomies called into question by the New Materialisms. Cohen writes: 'Because of its ontological liminality, the monster notoriously appears at times of crisis as a kind of third term that problematizes the clash of extremes'.[12] Odysseus is in the midst of crisis, enduring trials at sea and striving for a *nostos* that seems forever out of reach. He is trying to resolve his own identity, passing through fantastical lands, the hands of women divine, magical and otherwise, and creatures that defy definition. What, then, is the herdsman's crisis? And a related question: if Homer's Polyphemus is the 'other' in terms of civilisation and geography, policing the borders of the possible, then what is Theocritus' Polyphemus? Readers have treated Theocritus' Polyphemus as neutralised, civilised, humanised. What I hope to have shown, however, is that there is still an underlying threat to these *Idylls*, and it comes through the landscape (and even more so through the seascape). Polyphemus is less monstrous in Theocritus than in Homer – but there is nothing neutral about his environs.

Let's return to Payne's identification of Polyphemus with the herdsman. Again, we can start at the end – with the *Odyssey*. Homer's Polyphemus is the 'other', a monster Odysseus must defeat – but he is also *aligned* with Odysseus. There is a pervasive similarity between the Cyclops and the suitors, but with the theft of the sheep

---

[12] Cohen 1996a: 6.

it is Odysseus and his companions who become like the suitors, until finally on Ithaca Odysseus takes his Cyclopean vengeance on those who have abused his hospitality.[13] A material focus of this association between man and monster is Polyphemus' staff: the object on which the narrative centres. The Cyclops has a club of green olive wood as big as the mast of a ship with twenty oars (*Od.* 9.319–24), and it is this object that Odysseus refashions and uses against its former owner (*Od.* 9.325–8). Odysseus acculturates Polyphemus' rough and ready club into an object of technology – yet the process of craft did not start with Odysseus. Polyphemus has cut and dried the wood, with the explicit purpose of using it (τὸ μὲν ἔκταμεν, ὄφρα φοροίη | αὐανθέν, *Od.* 9.320–1). Odysseus and Polyphemus, then, are not only set up in contrast to each other, but through this object are presented as in a sense co-operating, just as Odysseus' companions help with smoothing the stake while Odysseus sharpens it, and with lifting it while Odysseus twists it. As in the strange case of Dr Jekyll and Mr Hyde, the monstrous 'other' is not as far away as it might seem.

If Polyphemus is identified with the herdsmen, where does the monstrous fit in, where is the 'othering'? It is no longer geographic, as the Cyclops is 'our countryman' in *Idyll* 11.[14] But the darkness that we have detected in these ostensibly light and parodic *Idylls* negates, I think, a straightforward interpretation of a neutralised pastoral Polyphemus. One possibility is that what is monstrous in the Homeric episode is separated out from the Cyclops and is instead revealed through materiality: objects and environment. The land, and even more so the sea, are the 'other'.[15] This resonates with dark ecology and has compelling implications for the experience of the herdsman, or indeed the fisherman (on whom we focused in Chapter 3, pp. 91–113). They may work with and on the land and sea, but they do not control it. The environment acts, and not always in the way we want it to. However, this separation is not clear-cut. We have seen that Theocritus' Polyphemus does bear marks of the monstrous: sitting on his rock like the mountain he resembles, with his eye that is always looking to his grim future. We might, then, arrive at a more distributed interpretation, with the monstrous shared between the Cyclops and his environment. But what of the herdsman? He shares agency with the land, his animals, his environs. The fisherman, meanwhile, shares agency with his rugged rock, his nets, the sea. In both cases, the line between man and material environment is porous, influence flowing in both directions. This adds a potential further level to

---

[13] On the parallels between Odysseus and Polyphemus, see Bakker 2013: 67–73.
[14] *Idyll* 11.7: ὁ Κύκλωψ ὁ παρ' ἁμῖν – Theocritus, Nikias and the Cyclopes are all associated with Sicily.
[15] Given the antithesis that we have traced between land and sea, we might even go a step further and say that each is the other's 'other'.

the 'othering' in these *Idylls*, and one that fits with our reading from below: perhaps the *herdsmen* pose a threat, too. As Cohen puts it, we have 'a cultural fascination with monsters – a fixation that is born of the twin desire to name that which is difficult to apprehend and to domesticate (and therefore disempower) that which threatens'.[16] Disempowerment as a strategy bears the hallmarks of a class divide. Just as the menacing materiality in these *Idylls* shows the cracks in the bucolic *locus amoenus*, so too might the threat distributed across man and land show cracks in the elite's comfort with the working men on the margins of their world.

The Pipes Are Calling

Polyphemus can play the pipes like no other Cyclops (*Idyll* 11.38). He sits piping sweetly (*Idyll* 6.8–9), and the telling of his tale results in an exchange of *aulos* and syrinx between herdsman-singers Damoetas and Daphnis. This object type may seem banal, obvious and ubiquitous in the bucolic context. But when considered through an intermedial lens and with the tenets of Material Ecocriticism in mind, it allows further targeted reflection on the central assemblage of this book: that of human, material and narrative. In Theocritus' pastoral *Idylls*, we have seen song equated with or offered in exchange for material goods, Thyrsis' cup in *Idyll* 1 being our anchoring example. But there is one object that is so emblematic of bucolic song that it inspires, supports and, in one *Idyll*, is even used as a wager for it.

> ἔνθ᾽, ὦναξ, καὶ τάνδε φέρευ πακτοῖο μελίπνουν
> ἐκ κηρῶ σύριγγα καλὸν περὶ χεῖλος ἑλικτάν·

Come, lord, and take this pipe, sweet smelling of honey
from its compacted wax, with a good binding around its lip.
(*Idyll* 1.128–9)

In *Idyll* 1 Daphnis calls to Pan himself as part of his bucolic song, and offers him a material equivalent for song: the panpipes or syrinx. As Hunter comments on these lines, 'the syrinx shares the sweetness of cup (ἑλικτάν recalls 30–1) and poem ... The sweet aroma of the binding wax forms an associative unity with the sweet breath of the syrinx-player and the sweet sound of the musical "airs".' There is a multisensory quality to the description, and an assemblage is created that intertwines singer, song and instrument – and a further material extension in the form of the cup that has been so central to our analysis throughout this book. The description evokes

---

[16] Cohen 1996b: viii.

freshness, a pipe that has just recently been made: much like the cup in *Idyll* 1 that is still 'fragrant from the chisel'.[17] There is an evocation of vital materiality here: a lively object that recalls its creation, that is still linked to its material composition, its raw materials, while also being fit for purpose (and, indeed, fit for a god). Further, the connotations of creation and craftsmanship here resonate with our discussion of created and creative matter in Chapter 4. Indeed, a musical instrument is an ideal focal point for consideration of creativity, as it is both a crafted object in and of itself, and a vehicle for musical (and literary) creation.

In *Idyll* 4 we see quite the opposite of this fresh image: a scene in which the *disuse* of the pipes is emphasised in terms of their material state.

φεῦ φεῦ βασεῦνται καὶ ταὶ βόες, ὦ τάλαν Αἴγων,
εἰς Ἀίδαν, ὅκα καὶ τὺ κακᾶς ἠράσσαο νίκας,
χἀ σῦριγξ εὐρῶτι παλύνεται, ἄν ποκ' ἐπάξα.

Oh no, your cattle too will go down to Hades, wretched Aegon,
because you too are in love with evil victory,
and the panpipe you once made is spotted with mould.
(*Idyll* 4.26–8)

This *Idyll* consists of a conversation between Battus (speaking here) and Corydon, who is looking after Aegon's cattle while he is away at the Olympic Games. Here Battus laments in mock-tragic fashion that Aegon has abandoned both his cows and his music, the moulding pipes standing as a constitutive symbol of Aegon's absence. This provides a stark contrast with the sweet-smelling wax of *Idyll* 1. It has much in common, however, with other poetic images of material disuse that stand in for human absence or neglect, such as the presence of spider webs: at *Odyssey* 16.35 Telemachus worries that spider webs might be covering his parents' abandoned marriage bed in place of bedclothes, and at *Works and Days* line 475 spider webs appear in empty storage jars, conveying a lack of sustenance. This emphasises the importance of the assemblage as a component, or perhaps the source, of an object's vitality: when separated from their human interactors, use objects may languish and fade. In just such a way does Odysseus' bow need to be checked for damage when he first takes it up again on his return to Ithaca.

Archaic epic displays a persistent concern with the perishable: from the mortal body, to material things, to one's fame. Homer sets up a hierarchy of durability,

---

[17] *Idyll* 1.28 – we have come full circle and are now back to our opening passage in Chapter 1 (p. 11).

in which man is ephemeral, nonhuman material lasts only slightly longer and both are trumped by song.[18] Homeric durability is the title topic of Lorenzo Garcia's 2013 book, where he argues that epic operates in the realm of the 'not yet', with κλέος ἄφθιτον not meaning 'imperishable glory' but merely 'glory that has not yet perished'. In his discussion Garcia focuses on the theme of decay, of materials that crumble and collapse. There is a dark-ecological aesthetic here. In *Idyll* 4 the image of decay isn't evident for long, as Corydon quickly counters that the pipe is fine: Aegon left it to him as a present, for him to play. The *locus amoenus* snaps back into place, but not before we notice the crack.

The 'newness' of the syrinx is an image revisited in another poem in our corpus, here with striking effects:

Μενάλκας
σύριγγ' ἃν ἐπόησα καλὰν ἔχω ἐννεάφωνον,
λευκὸν κηρὸν ἔχοισαν ἴσον κάτω ἴσον ἄνωθεν·
ταύταν κατθείην, τὰ δὲ τῶ πατρὸς οὐ καταθησῶ.

Δάφνις
ἦ μάν τοι κἠγὼ σύριγγ' ἔχω ἐννεάφωνον,
λευκὸν κηρὸν ἔχοισαν ἴσον κάτω ἴσον ἄνωθεν.
πρώαν νιν συνέπαξ'· ἔτι καὶ τὸν δάκτυλον ἀλγῶ
τοῦτον, ἐπεὶ κάλαμός με διασχισθεὶς διέτμαξεν.

Menalcas
I have a panpipe I made, a fine nine-reed pipe,
with white wax equal at the top and bottom.
I will wager this – but what is my father's I will not wager.

Daphnis
I too have a nine-reed pipe,
with white wax equal at the top and bottom.
I made it just recently, and this finger is still sore,
because a reed split and cut me.

(*Idyll* 8.18–24)

---

[18] For a full discussion, see Canevaro 2018b: 181–201 and 234–44.

Idyll 8 is another example of a poem now thought not to have been composed by Theocritus, but appearing in our standard corpus.[19] The main argument against Theocritean authorship is that it is imitative, with its opening lines resembling those of *Idyll* 6 and parts of the framing narrative recalling *Idyll* 5. In this poem, Daphnis and Menalcas meet while herding their sheep, and Menalcas challenges Daphnis to a singing contest. They discuss the stake, finally deciding on the wager of panpipes. A neighbouring goatherd, summoned as judge, proclaims Daphnis the winner. When listing the points against the *Idyll*'s 'authenticity', Gow mentions as an argument (though one with little force) that 'the language of 11–24 with its frequent repetitions has been adversely criticised, as has the stake of a pipe on either side. A contest which leaves Daphnis with two pipes and Menalcas with none certainly seems odd'. It is on the pipes that I would focus here.

In using pipes as a stake in this contest, the song is reified: symbolised by a material equivalent that is not chosen by chance. Calves and lambs are rejected as options before the pipes are suggested. These pipes belong to the contestants – were in fact *made by* them – so they trump the livestock that is their fathers'. There is a strong sense of ownership, craftsmanship and creation here, which makes the pipes an ideal wager for song. Through this object we see again the nexus between singer, song and object, but it is modulated slightly as the pipes take centre stage. Whereas in *Idyll* 1 there is a material equivalence established between song and cup (both created and crafted 'objects') and the pipe appears as a supplementary offering in the midst of Daphnis' song, in *Idyll* 8 the pipes form the crux of the exchange, intensifying and encapsulating the proximity between song and object because of their musical nature. The bets of Menalcas and Daphnis parallel one another (to the critics' apparent disdain), but Daphnis – who we must remember will be the winner – emphasises and elaborates his making of the pipes. There is an exertion of material agency here, a wrestling for cooperation, for hybridity, as the pipes resist their creator. Daphnis still has the wound to prove it, a sore finger. The 'freshness' of the pipes recalls the passage from *Idyll* 1 cited above – but here with a more visceral slant. From a new-materialist perspective it reminds us of Heidegger's broken hammer, of the stone that stubs our toe: an object that comes into focus when it acts out. And the material agency is signalled by the syntax of the final line, in which the reed is in the nominative and governs two verbs, and Daphnis is relegated to the concise accusative με.

I turn away from Theocritus' *Idylls* to his epigrams for a final example. Though I discussed epigrammatic features of the *Idylls* in Chapter 3 (pp. 113–40) and drew on other epigrammatic texts from the Hellenistic period in Chapter 4 (pp. 169–77),

---

[19] It was accepted in antiquity, also being included in a second-century AD papyrus of Theocritus' poems.

I have not yet integrated Theocritus' own epigrams in my reading. This is one way, however, in which we might probe those boundaries of genre and tradition explored in Chapter 1 (pp. 23–37), taking our analysis into a different mode of literary production entirely. I give in full here a fascinating epigram, along with Hopkinson's 2015 translation.[20]

Οὐδενὸς εὐνάτειρα Μακροπτολέμοιο δὲ μάτηρ
μαίας ἀντιπέτροιο θοὸν τέκεν ἰθυντῆρα,
οὐχὶ Κεράσταν ὅν ποτε θρέψατο ταυροπάτωρ,
ἀλλ᾽ οὗ πειλιπὲς αἶθε πάρος φρένα τέρμα σάκους,
οὔνομ᾽ Ὅλον, δίζων, ὃς τᾶς μέροπος πόθον
κούρας γηρυγόνας ἔχε τᾶς ἀνεμώδεος,
ὃς μοίσᾳ λιγὺ πᾶξεν ἰοστεφάνῳ
ἕλκος, ἄγαλμα πόθοιο πυρισμαράγου,
ὃς σβέσεν ἀνορέαν ἰσαυδέα
παπποφόνου Τυρίας τ᾽ ἐ<ξήλασεν>.
ᾧ τόδε τυφλοφόρων ἐρατόν
πῆμα Πάρις θέτο Σιμιχίδας·
ψυχὰν ἇ, βροτοβάμων,
στήτας οἶστρε Σαέττας,
κλωποπάτωρ, ἀπάτωρ,
λαρνακόγυιε, χαρείς,
ἁδὺ μελίσδοις
ἔλλοπι κούρᾳ,
καλλιόπᾳ
νηλεύστῳ.

The bedfellow of Nobody and mother of Far-war gave birth to the swift director of the nurse who stood in for a stone, not the Horned One who was once nurtured by a bull father, but he whose mind was once set on fire by the p-lacking shield rim, Whole by name, double in nature, who loved the voice-dividing girl, swift as the wind and with human speech, him who put together a shrill wound for the violet-crowned muse to represent his fiery love, who extinguished the might that sounded like a man who murdered his grandfather, and drove it out of the Tyrian

---

[20] I give Gow's text for consistency across the book, and have therefore made some minor changes to Hopkinson's translation (mainly capitalisation). I use a published translation rather than my own here because the epigram is highly allusive and nigh-on impossible to translate, and I don't fancy my chances.

girl. To him Paris son of Simichus dedicated the lovely possession of the carriers of blindness. May it please your soul, man-treading gadfly of the Lydian woman, son of a thief and son of no one, coffer-limbed, and may you play it sweetly to a girl who has no voice of her own but is an unseen calliope.

([Theocritus] *Syrinx* (or the Panpipe))[21]

This epigram is arranged in ten pairs of lines, each pair one syllable shorter than the one preceding. The resulting visual effect is the shape of a panpipe with ten reeds. The epigram describes its own inscriptional context: it claims to be inscribed on a pipe dedicated to Pan by Simichidas, a name usually taken to refer to Theocritus (see Chapter 3 pp. 91–113 for discussion of Simichidas in *Idyll* 7) – we return to questions not only of authorship but also of autobiography. Yet the name has a further riddling element to it, as Paris joins Simichidas as one of Theocritus' alter egos. As Hopkinson explains in his notes, Theocritus 'means "Chosen by God", but here it is assumed to mean "chooser of a god"; Paris judges the famous beauty contest of the goddesses and stands for the name of the poet'. The potential self-referential quality, then, is combined with an allusivity that links Theocritean and Homeric poetry, much as the intermediality traced throughout this book has inevitably compelled us to do.

This epigram is immensely allusive – but when picked apart, it turns out that it neatly brings together many of the key themes explored in this book. In terms of entanglement, enmeshment, assemblage and similar conceptualisations of relationality and intra-action, there is something irresistibly compelling about the density and allusivity of the riddling language in this epigram. Everything is connected, everything is gesturing to something else, and what I hope to show is that many of the pointers and links cross those categorical and ontological boundaries we have been interrogating throughout this book.

First to note are of course the Homeric allusions. We have already mentioned Paris, but there is also Odysseus (Nobody),[22] Telemachus (Far-war) and Penelope (bedfellow of the former, mother of the latter). Homer has been a constant presence throughout this book, as Theocritus' *Idylls* evoke a material narrative that stretches back to archaic epic. We might even posit a further intermedial gesture here, in the shield rim that takes us back to our recurrent discussion point: the shield of Achilles. Second, there is the mention of a 'stone replacement' (ἀντιπέτροιο). The reference is to Amalthea suckling Zeus on Crete, when Kronos believed he had swallowed his son but had been given a stone instead. The formulation ἀντιπέτροιο is a particularly relevant one to the second section of Chapter 3 (pp. 113–40), as

---

[21] This is another text with a titular object – see discussion in Chapter 4 (pp. 169–77).
[22] See the Cyclopean Nobody references in the first section of this chapter (pp. 178–86).

it equates an animate with an inanimate agent, specifically a lithic actor, the one standing in for the other in an equivalency that crosses ostensible ontological divisions. In its constituent parts we might also detect in the word a hint at *resistance* to rock – that fear of lithic agency also explored in Chapter 3 (pp. 113–40). Certainly Kronos is not a fan. The latent presence of stone may then continue in βροτοβάμων ('man-treading'), as Hopkinson explains: '"Man-treading" (*brotobamona*) apparently refers to Paris' running over the mountain rocks, *brotos* being similar in meaning to *laos* (people), which sounds like *laas* (stone).' I find this interpretive jump especially appealing, as people and stone actually cross over through aural proximity. The lithic companionship that was the focus of much of Chapter 3 is extended here to an overlapping of human and lithic agency, and the aural element brings to my mind the Sounding Stones described on pp. 140–5. However, J. M. Edmonds in his 1912 Loeb translation of this epigram renders βροτοβάμων as 'clay-treading', commenting 'lit. man-treading; Prometheus made man of clay'. This adds a further element of mythological background to the allusion, explaining the link between man and stone as literal, narrative and mythologically grounded, rather than simply aural. We explored Prometheus' creative act in Chapter 4 (pp. 169–77) in the context of an epigram from Erinna – here the effect of its presence as posited by Edmonds is to make material and tangible the link between human and nonhuman agents. It is worth emphasising, then, that the complex relationship between people and stone that we explored at length in the second section of Chapter 3 is in Greek thought anchored in a mythological aetion.

I have focused so far on Homer and on stone, but there are a range of themes covered in this epigram that connect with our discussions of passages from the *Idylls*. For instance, the 'Horned One', Κεράσταν, is thought to refer (through a shift from 'horn' to 'hair') to Comatas, 'Long-haired', who was kept alive by bees (*Idyll* 7, discussed in Chapter 3, at pp. 99–105) – and we might note another material link with this story in 'coffer-limbed' (λαρνακόγυιε), evoking the chest and its containment discussed in Chapter 3. Hopkinson explains the elaborate riddling allusion here: '"Coffer-limbed" (*larnakoguie*), because another word for *larnax* (coffer) is *chelos*, which sounds like *chele* (hoof).' Such riddles are a wonderful example of multiple entanglements manifested in language and literature through materiality, as here we see in the composite epithet 'coffer-limbed' a hybridity of man and material, in the allusion a further addition of specifically animal body parts and in the whole manoeuvre an expectation placed on the reader to decode and decipher this negotiation between 'categories'.

To come back to the pivotal object in this discussion, there is an overarching presence of both Pan and the pipes in the *Syrinx* epigram. Not only is the poem in the shape of a set of pipes, but the syrinx is also alluded to obliquely in the text:

'he who put together a shrill wound for the violet-crowned muse' (ὃς μοίσᾳ λιγὺ πᾶξεν ἰοστεφάνῳ ἕλκος, 7–8). The subject here is Pan himself, and the 'shrill wound' is a reference to the syrinx, as another meaning of the word is 'suppurating wound'. Again, this is to play not only with words but also with materiality, as by moving between pipes and wound the poet creates a material narrative that we must read across the body as much as across an object. Moreover, as with the potential Promethean underpinning of βροτοβάμων, there is a mythological backdrop here, and whereas Prometheus is linked with creation, this example is about metamorphosis. The pipe is described as 'a dedication of fiery desire' (ἄγαλμα πόθοιο πυρισμαράγου) – and this refers to the aetion story of the pipes, in which Pan pursued the nymph or maiden Syrinx, who was transformed into the reeds from which he made the first pipes so that he could sing about his love.[23] According to mythology, the syrinx is more than an inanimate object: it is a metamorphosed woman, a material thing with a vital story.

According to Achilles Tatius in his *Leucippe and Clitophon*, Pan cuts down the reeds thinking they stole his beloved, but then realises she had *turned into* the reeds and that in fact he has cut her down:

συμφορήσας οὖν τὰ τετμημένα τῶν καλάμων ὡς μέλη τοῦ σώματος καὶ συνθεὶς εἰς ἓν σῶμα, εἶχε διὰ χειρῶν τὰς τομὰς τῶν καλάμων καταφιλῶν ὡς τῆς κόρης τραύματα· ἔστενε δὲ ἐρωτικὸν ἐπιθεὶς τὸ στόμα καὶ ἐνέπνει ἄνωθεν εἰς τοὺς αὐλοὺς ἅμα φιλῶν·

Collecting the cut pieces of reed as if they were the limbs of a body and putting them together as a body, he held the stumps of reeds in his arms and kissed them as if they were the wounds of the maiden. He groaned and set his desiring mouth to breathe across the pipes as he kissed them.[24]

The reeds are treated like limbs, they are put together like a body, they are kissed like wounds. Here the 'shrill wound' mentioned above is integral to the story, the narrative of the body one of hurt and injury (recalling our discussion of Simaetha in Chapter 2, pp. 66–81). The fact that μέλη can mean both 'limb' and 'song' points us towards a material-semiotic narrative that crosses between body and instrument, voice of Syrinx and voice of the syrinx. This myth explores different vitalities, as the cutting down of the reeds (plant-life) is equated or conflated with the cutting

---

[23] Longus 2.34.3, Ovid *Met.* 1.690–712, Ach. Tat. 8.6.7–10. For discussion, see LeVen 2021, Chapter 5.
[24] Ach. Tat. 8.6.10.

down of the maiden. The syrinx is made from a maiden and from a plant, two lives enmeshed through metamorphosis. Pan then 'breathes life' into the object, recognising its vital origins and perpetuating them, the kiss animating the pipes as they come to 'have a voice' (ἡ σύριγξ εἶχε φωνήν). As LeVen shows in her 2021 book *Music and Metamorphosis in Graeco-Roman Thought*,

> there is more to a musical instrument than its being a material object, a tool, a thing: like a body part, it is thought of in terms of its task and its affordances in 'blended agency' with its user, and as part of an assemblage. This simple observation shifts the emphasis from the will of the instrument's inventor to other forces and agencies, including that of the instrument itself and the combination of performer and musical organ.[25]

In the case of the syrinx the agencies are complex. The maiden Syrinx was objectified and had her agency curtailed by a pursuing and predatory god. She turns into plant-life, which (as we have seen throughout this book) has its own kind of agency – but that too is cut short when Pan cuts the reeds down. Put back together, she can take on a new agency in the assemblage of instrument and musician – but she cannot be an independent agent. Pan has her.[26] Yet the 'voice' with which this passage ends opens further possibilities. Can the woman's voice ultimately break through? Further, is Pan any different from her, now that he is part of the same assemblage and 'the boundaries of their autonomous selves vanish into those of the whole they compose'?[27] And can the multiplicity of agencies in this story – the woods, the land, the reeds, the woman, the god, the instrument – blur the boundaries in which Syrinx was caught? As LeVen puts it,

> This new ontology deployed in the myth renders obsolete the dichotomies of active/passive and object/subject and is the best able to do justice to the status of the musical instrument, an object with an agency of its own ... Metamorphosis is a way of illustrating the endless potentiality of beings.[28]

---

[25] LeVen 2021: 138. The noun ὄργανον can refer to a musical instrument or a body part. LeVen describes the story of the syrinx in Achilles Tatius as 'a rich locus of meditation on the status of the instrument as vegetal material endowed with extraordinary power and nonhuman agency' (143).

[26] LeVen 2021: 146: 'A parody of a male being, she is now an extra-phallic appendage to Pan, a continuation of *his* body, a prosthesis to his desire.'

[27] LeVen 2021: 163.

[28] LeVen 2021: 159. The syrinx 'blurs the categories of natural/cultural, object/subject, male/female' (156).

Theocritus' *Syrinx* epigram evokes this complex assemblage of human, nonhuman and song in a particularly visual and material way. The poet and dedicator is one agent, though he is named in an obtuse way, adding his identity to the riddling bent of the epigram. The reader is another human agent; with such a dense, allusive and obscure poem, construction is largely in the eyes of the beholder, and the reader's role is crucial. Furthermore, the poem itself exerts a strong agency – and what I find intriguingly apposite here is that this agency is as much material as it is narrative. Though we can emphasise the (possible and posited) physicality of all epigrams to a certain extent, the visual dimension of this pattern poem, combined with its epigrammatic dedicatory claims, renders it especially compelling in material terms. Here we really see the material-discursive or material-semiotic in operation, as meaning is made not only through language, but through materiality. And, as we have seen in the previous paragraphs, there is much in the detail of the poem itself that speaks to the overlaying of agencies and the slippage between ontological categories. Against the backdrop of the examples explored in this section, we can see a form that not only epitomises musicality in a generic and generalising way, but also can be mobilised in specific circumstances: to convey vital materiality and multisensory affect (the fresh fragrance of the pipes); to question that vitality (threatening decay); even to reify song, becoming materially constitutive of it.

Slàinte

In this book we started from the cup in Theocritus' first *Idyll*: its form and its material, its decoration and its vitality, its characters and its agency and its affect. The scenes on the cup have structured the chapters in this book, a literary object guiding this exploration of material agency in literature. As the book draws to a close, then, it is natural that we return to the cup, to its entangled placement of intertwined motifs, to the vital materiality of its ivy wood and pliant plants. And as our discussion has taken us to other periods and across media, it is inevitable too that we now look at the cup from a different angle.

Theocritus' cup is a literary object. A thing conjured up by words, created in and for the imagination, mapping onto real-world objects yet something separate from them. Its decorations come alive through their descriptions, the line between person and thing blurring as ekphrasis foregrounds material agencies. We are required to read between the lines, figuring out disputed aspects like size and shape and placement and arrangement and putting a picture together that follows Theocritus' cues but has a lot of our own imagination in there too. But what happens when this literary object becomes real, or when it is made material? What

196 | THEOCRITUS AND THINGS

Fig. 5.1 The Theocritus Cup, Paul Storr and John Flaxman. Photo credit: National Museums Liverpool

about when the scenes are fixed, the placement is decided and the size, shape and composition are no longer up for discussion?

In 1811–13 the renowned silversmith Paul Storr made a series of silver-gilt cups, following a design by John Flaxman and retailed by the London firm of gold- and silversmiths Rundell, Bridge and Rundell.[29] One is in the Walker Art Gallery, having been acquired by the City of Liverpool Museums in 1974 (Fig. 5.1).[30] This cup was given to Alderman Thomas Earle, and is engraved with the arms of both Earle and Liverpool.[31] A second is in the Royal Collection.[32] This was made for Queen Charlotte, who presented it to George IV when he was Prince Regent. Another was commissioned by the Prince Regent for the Bishop of Winchester.[33] The various versions are known as the 'Theocritus Cup'. The design for the Theocritus Cup makes a lot of decisions, by necessity. As W. Geoffrey Arnott puts it in his discussion of the Liverpool cup,

> The Regency cup is at one and the same time an artistic and a scholarly attempt to realise Theocritus' literary vision in terms, admittedly, not of the goatherd's wood but of precious metal. The cup, unlike a scholar's paper, is not built on unverifiable hypotheses. It solves problems dogmatically but realistically.[34]

The multiplicity of the literary object, its openness to interpretation, is fixed and reified by the pragmatic decisions that have to be made by the artist. As soon as the literary object is made material, it can no longer fluctuate. To start with, rendering the cup in metal fixes the scene in terms of its materiality. This contrasts with Theocritus' strategy of keeping interpretive and imaginative options open. We have seen this in particular in the drystone wall (Chapter 3, pp. 134–40): it is not explicitly said to be made of wood (the material composition of the cup is, crucially, not reiterated), so we are not jolted out of our immersive reading of the second-level materiality in the passage. This is a shift away from Homer's material specifications

---

[29] Each cup measures c. 23.9 × 24.8 × 24.8cm, not including the various stands.
[30] Available at <https://www.liverpoolmuseums.org.uk/artifact/theocritus-cup> (last accessed 21 November 2022).
[31] It has a further inscription: 'The zeal, judgement and unremitting attention which he displayed during a long and arduous attendance on Parliament in the progress of the Act for the improvement of the port and town of Liverpool AD 1811.'
[32] Available at <https://www.rct.uk/collection/51538/the-theocritus-cup> (last accessed 21 November 2022).
[33] Virginia Museum of Fine Arts. Available at <https://www.vmfa.museum/piction/6027262-12977939> (last accessed 21 November 2022).
[34] Arnott 1978: 130.

on the shield of Achilles, where we are continually reminded that we are dealing with figurations in metal.

That the cup is fixed in *metal*, and more specifically in *precious* metal, takes it to the other end of the material spectrum from the goatherd's rustic wooden cup. Storr's creation to Flaxman's design fixes Theocritus' cup in a milieu far removed from its original description. It is interesting that Flaxman's interpretation of Theocritus' cup was made for nobility and royalty. The transposition of the 'humble' cup into a royal setting highlights the paradoxes that we have seen at the Hellenistic roots of pastoral literature, from elite patronage and an urban backdrop to the artifice of the *locus amoenus*. Theocritus' use of materiality leads us into the herdsman's world; Storr's use of materiality points to its contradictions.

As discussed in Chapter 1 (pp. 11–23), the cup in *Idyll* 1 is fragrant and sweet and entwined and entangled and vibrant. The wood and the plant motifs make this an organic object, its liveliness emphasised. When the description is rendered in metal, therefore, there is a shift in both materiality and material agency. Yet metal need not be cold and obdurate. Just as we have seen stone to be active but on its own terms, so too can metal exhibit vibrant characteristics.[35] The quintessential example is, of course, Achilles' shield, which is metal and repeatedly marked as such and yet has a vitality that has shone out to readers and scholars for millennia. We might note that Flaxman also created a design based on Achilles' shield, again for Rundell, Bridge and Rundell.[36] The choice to reify, to materialise these two iconic literary objects suggests that Flaxman was interested in the creative and representational challenges posed by ekphrasis. It is the ability of the figures on the metal shield to *seem alive* that makes it so striking to Homer's readers – artistry overcoming ostensible material limitations. By translating Theocritus' wooden cup into a silver-gilt piece, then, Flaxman and Storr arguably set themselves the definitive creative challenge, pushing material agency to its limits.

However, this is where the assemblage becomes paramount. In Greek literature, there is a blurring of boundaries between man and arms, between flesh and metal, as heroes wear their armour as a second skin, the two become hybrid agents and qualities are shared between them. As Lather puts it, 'bronze armour serves as both an aggressive and a defensive force to protect the flesh underneath, and figures wrought in metal seem to bring this material to life by making it seem as supple as human

---

[35] This is explored in Lather 2021, Chapter 2, which focuses on the vitality of metal in Greek literature and specifically archaic armour.

[36] Commissioned around 1810, design completed 1817, first cast in 1821 and prominently displayed at George IV's coronation banquet. Other versions were made in the 1820s.

flesh'.[37] It is primarily in the *engagement* between person and thing that the divisions disappear. These are dynamic interactions predicated on movement and action. Even when the focus shifts to a moment of contemplation, as when the Myrmidons gaze on Achilles' shield, there is still a compelling momentum that crosses between narrative and object. In the case of Flaxman and Storr's cup, however, we might question whether physical engagement is the primary intention for the object. The Liverpool cup was created along with a highly decorated stand, suggesting that this object is for display first and foremost.[38] It is a precious item made for admiration, so it is difficult to set it firmly in a context of material engagement. Similarly inappropriate to this object are other dynamic frameworks such as that of the embodied object (Gaifman et al. 2018), 'a form of engagement [that] is both visual and haptic, and concerns the material qualities of the object, its functional potential and its representational components'.[39] Gaifman and Platt (2018) discuss an Argive hydria and its dynamic entanglements: 'As soon as the water-carrier is conceived of as a handled vessel within a context of active use, rather than as an inert object of aesthetic contemplation, its innate vitality comes to the surface.' In the case of the Flaxman and Storr cup, however, aesthetic contemplation is likely to be the dominant paradigm.

What do we make, then, of the cup's handles? How active is the object's haptic potential? It is a two-handled cup. The handles are incorporated into the design, as a frame of vines winds round the cup and extends down to become the handles. There is an invitation to engage with the cup in terms of its practical elements, and through its design this invitation extends to an engagement between person, thing and *nature*. Were we to pick up the cup, our hands would be entwined in the vines that encircle the object and frame its scenes. Perhaps this is one type of interaction intended for the recipient of the cup. And yet, the stand and the precious nature of the object pose questions about this interaction. Furthermore, there are extant designs by Flaxman that show the vessel *without* handles,[40] suggesting that haptic entanglement is not integral to the composition. This recalls *Idyll* 1, lines 59–60 (discussed in Chapter 4, p. 154), in which the goatherd specifies that the cup has never touched his lips but lies unused. Perhaps the Flaxman/Storr cup picks up on this motif of distanced wonder, extrapolating it from the cup's life so far and projecting it into its future.

---

[37] Lather 2021: 94. On Homeric heroes and their armour as hybrid agents, see also Canevaro 2018b: 11–27 and Purves 2015.

[38] I do not claim to be an expert on the use of silverware in Regency dining. I am making some assumptions: namely, that the cup *may* have been used at a banquet or similar, but that it would more often and more likely be on display.

[39] Gaifman and Platt 2018: 404.

[40] Available at <https://collections.vam.ac.uk/item/O502478/design-for-a-flaxman-john-ra> (last accessed 23 November 2022>. It has been posited that this is a design for a wine cooler.

While the goatherd's cup has not been used so far (οὐδέ τί πω ποτὶ χεῖλος ἐμὸν θίγεν) and operates in the realms of the 'not yet', the noble/royal Theocritus Cup may rarely be used at all. Again we are dealing with paradoxes and contradictions, suggestions and misdirections, all of which reify the complexities of Theocritus' poetry as much as they prompt reflections on the interaction between man, object and nature.

As well as fixing the metal material makeup of the Theocritus Cup, Flaxman and Storr's creation also fixed the cup's scenes. All of those disputed placement markers (how the scenes are positioned, how they are framed) we have discussed throughout this book are resolved in a decisive act of design. One of the challenges faced by Flaxman was to make three scenes fit onto a cup with two handles that effectively divide it in half. His decision was to devote one side to the woman with her two admirers, and divide the other side between the fisherman hauling his net and the boy sitting on the wall. As Arnott notes, there is movement and dynamism in the first scene:

> Flaxman's woman is turned to the suitor on the right, whose shoulder her left hand touches; but the woman's head looks back over her right shoulder to the suitor on the left, who tries to catch her left hand. Plastic art here comes as near as it can to the suggestion of movement.[41]

The movement to the design is made even clearer through a comparison with its likely model, the Orpheus relief in the Villa Albani in Rome.[42] This too has three figures: Eurydice flanked by Hermes and Orpheus. There, however, the woman's stance, gesture and gaze all face in one direction: towards Orpheus. Hermes holds her hand, but her legs and body and face are turned towards Orpheus as she touches him on the shoulder. In the Theocritus Cup, by contrast, the woman seems to be turned and turning in both directions simultaneously, just as Theocritus describes her.

The other side of the cup is perhaps the more intriguing, in terms of Flaxman's design decisions and their implications for our reading of the Theocritus passage. There is a wealth of detail here: the fisherman's net, the boy making his trap, the foxes surrounding him. The vine motif that encircles the cup stems from the scene of the boy in the vineyard, and is integrated most fully into it as one of the foxes raises himself up to reach the grapes. We are reminded that the plants are not detached decoration but a part of the story, as the human characters interact with their environs and the environs become the object.

---

[41] Arnott 1978: 133.
[42] Available at <https://museum.classics.cam.ac.uk/collections/casts/three-figure-relief> (last accessed 21 November 2022).

Arnott draws our attention to the angle of the fisherman's net as he describes 'his net sweeping down in an arresting diagonal which continues the line of his left arm'.[43] The net and arm are used to demarcate space: to divide this side of the cup into two distinct scenes. But there is more going on here than just the practical. The continuation of arm into net, as well as the fisherman's leg and gaze all following the same line, creates a hybridity between man and tool as both muscles and cords strain in their toil and purpose. Interestingly, this picks up on the close alignment of man and material in this part of *Idyll* 1 – and yet it does so by foregrounding the net, *not* the rock. The old fisherman and his rugged rock are pictured *without* the rock. Our discussion in Chapter 3 (pp. 113–40) of human/lithic entanglement is not realised in Flaxman's design, despite a clear sensitivity on the part of the artist to the dynamic interactions between animate and inanimate in this passage. This is a rather stark omission in an otherwise thorough rendering of the lines. Stone as a material is not entirely absent: the boy is sitting on what looks like a wall. But even there the details are hazy, and the conglomeration of stones that make up a drystone wall are not evident. As we found in Chapter 3, the merging of human and lithic agency is far more evident in the case of the fisherman than that of the boy: so it is puzzling that the boy gets his wall but the fisherman doesn't get his rock. The rugged rock shares its nature, its identity, with the old fisherman, but Flaxman separates them. Are the fears of lithic agency exerting themselves once again? Perhaps design decisions are made not only to handle space and placement and character and narrative, but also to manipulate material agency.

---

[43] Arnott 1978: 133.

A Concluding Excursus: Marsden

THREE MILES SOUTH of South Shields, on the coast of North East England, lies Marsden Bay (Fig. 6.1). Overlooked by cliffs 80 to 100 feet tall, it is accessible only at two points: at the north by the shallow 'Velvet Beds' steps, and at a mid-point by 128 steep steps (don't let this put you off, though – there's a lift). There is a pub built in and around the cliffs: the Marsden Grotto. There are caves and coves along the beach and, most famously, the towering sea stack Marsden Rock. The stack was once an arch, with an archway it was once possible to sail through – until in 1996 the arch collapsed, scuppering the local postcard industry and giving the gulls a fright. The Bay, the Grotto and the Rock are the stuff of stories and legends, adventures and schemes, hermits and smugglers. There was Jack the Blaster, an ex-lead miner who is said to have blasted a home for himself into the cliff in the eighteenth century to break free from overzealous landlords; the Hairy Man, a young sailor who was jilted by his girl and moved into Smuggler's Cave, took to dressing in skins and grew his hair long; Peter Allan, nineteenth-century founder of the Grotto and host extraordinaire, who was thought to be onto a hoard of Roman coins. The place is full of colourful characters and tall tales. For centuries, curious tourists, geologists and holidaymakers came to Marsden by boat, navigating the treacherous coastline (with mixed results), entranced by the entanglement of people, place and story.

Marsden is layered. The cliffs and rocks are soft magnesian limestone, formed in strips of collapsed breccia. As local historian Bill Greenwell aptly puts it, 'the limestone rocks are like Ryvita crispbread slices'.[1] These limestone strata are layered with the seascape, in different ways across different timescales: Camel's Island

---

[1] Greenwell 2020: 3.

Fig. 6.1 Marsden Rock and Grotto, Marsden Bay, South Shields. Photo credit: Lilah Grace Canevaro

is separate from the beach at high tide but connected at low tide, the relationship between rock and sea shifting throughout one day; and the Marsden Rock sea stack has been shaped and reshaped over centuries (a long process, though the falling of the archway has an immediacy to me, as it happened within my memory). The rocks and the sea are layered with animal life. Marsden Rock is now a bird colony, home to cormorants and kittiwakes, and birds squawk and nest along the cliffs. At one point Peter Allan populated the Rock with white rabbits, and later he kept goats there, though it is an unlikely place for grazing (according to *Chambers's Journal*, the rabbits 'often fall over the edge to meet a certain death'). In the Grotto itself, Allan bred and tamed ravens, most notably one-legged Ralphy (who met his end in the jaws of a pet greyhound but was immortalised in taxidermy). He also kept Jack and Jessie (named after Jack 'the Blaster' Bates and his wife): two Russian pigs he bought from a sailor and trained like dogs. The Allans' bees flew freely around the Grotto (until customers complained), blurring the divide between the natural and human worlds just as they do in Comatas' and the goatherd's chests in Theocritus *Idyll* 7.

The agency of the landscape and of the nonhuman is palpable at Marsden Bay. Humans may have shaped the rocks, but the sea has done so more. Humans may have taken up residence in the cliffs, but they are outnumbered by the gulls. The stories that emerge from Marsden are truly material-discursive narratives, coming from the intra-action of human creativity and the narrative agency of matter. We can see this in the smallest of details, such as place names. The northern end of the Bay is known as the Velvet Beds, for the moss that makes the unyielding rock seem soft. The name is a story of stone as much as it is of picnics and sunbathing. And at the other end of the scale we can see it in the many poems composed about Marsden, in which agentic nature looms large and threat interplays with idyll.

Peter Thompson's 1773 poem of 247 lines, *Marsden Rock, & c.*, is thought to be the first extant poem about Marsden. As florid and romanticising as this poem is, it is one of many stories of Marsden in which the people are only part of the cast of characters. The rocks, the cliffs, the sea and their inhabitants, human and nonhuman, all combine in an assemblage of place. The poem tells the tale of a group of young men and women ('Each blooming damsel to her guardian swain') having a day out by boat to 'Marsden's rocky shore'. It is full of classical references: the Idalian boy (Eros), nymphs, Naiads, muses, Parnassian flowers, doric reeds, rosy Aurora, Phoebus gleaming, Nect'rous juice, Venus, Ida's top, ruling Jove, Elysium, Pomona (Thompson doesn't seem unduly concerned with differentiating between Greek and Roman mythology). Before setting out on their trip, the merrymakers pour a libation to Neptune 'to seek the favour of the wat'ry god'. At first all is well, thanks to our poet/narrator/helmsman:

> Safe bounds the vessel o'er the heaving tides,
> While beauty animates, – and Thompson guides!
> (lines 90–1)

But disaster threatens in the form of Sunderland (if you were from South Shields you would understand):

> Last gradual from the jutting cliffs expand
> The dreary, shelving shores of Sunderland;
> Obdurate shores, from whose horrific gloom,
> The bark assiduous sheers, or meets her doom.
> (lines 123–6)

A messenger from Venus – a white butterfly – comes to the crew and guides them along the treacherous coastline, until they come to land safely at Marsden Bay. They eat, they drink, they sing, they dance, they court, they explore Pan's haunts. They marvel at the land- and seascape, and they admire agentic Nature:

> Here Nature's hand unrivall'd acts her part,
> And mocks the chisel's – mocks the pencil's art;
> Here turns her arch, here bids her columns rise,
> Here scoops the gelid grot's capacious size,
> And piles the cliff tremendous to the skies.
> (lines 187–91)

The features of Marsden Bay are depicted as a product of art, but they come from Nature's artistry rather than that of humans. Nature trumps both the chisel and the pencil, controlling both the design and its execution. This image breaks down the nature/culture dichotomy, suggesting that nature *is* culture or, further, reimagining nature altogether. It is interesting that the human has faded so far into the background of Thompson's thought that the eclipsed human agency is represented by its tools. We don't see the human artist, or even the human hand. In San Sperate the hand of the artist is imprinted on stone in the village's murals. At Marsden, it is the hand of Nature that emerges from the rock. We have seen in this book that hands are a notoriously permeable and porous point between person and thing. Here they denote a porosity between agentic nature and features of the landscape.

Fig. 6.2 Lot's Wife, Marsden Bay, South Shields. Photo credit: Lilah Grace Canevaro

Thompson comments on another of Marsden's rocks, called Lot's Wife (Fig. 6.2),[2] in ways that resonate with our discussion of anthropomorphism, petromorphism and isomorphism:

> Lo, here Lot's wife, her petrid statue rears,
> And her wan cheek disdains with marble tears.
> (lines 192–3)

---

[2] The name is now given to a tall, leaning pinnacle to the north of Marsden Rock, only a few feet from the cliffs. However, according to Bill Greenwell (2020: 3), this was perhaps originally the name given to a larger rock further north which has long since collapsed, and the pinnacle was instead called the Needle.

The story is of course that told in Genesis, in which Lot's wife is turned into a pillar of salt. At Marsden she is a pillar of limestone (take it with a pinch of salt). The story is one of many lithic metamorphoses in ancient and medieval literature, and the detail of the tears perhaps most evocatively recalls the tale of Niobe, as her stone form was said to weep. Niobe had fled to Mount Sipylus, and a rock formation there has been associated with Niobe since antiquity and is described by Pausanias. This limestone rock formation is also known as the 'Weeping Rock', because rainwater seeps through its porous structure. The limestone is porous, but so is the boundary between human and nonhuman in these stories of petrified women. According to Thompson, Lot's wife doesn't cry watery tears but tears of marble. It is not an effect of rainwater or melting snow but purely of stone. So strong is the vital materiality in this image that the rock might even flow.

Marsden is beautiful and idyllic. But it is also fraught with danger. The coastline is difficult, and even the most experienced sailors have struggled with the squalls and currents. In Peter Allan's time, before the lighthouse was built, wrecks were common and drownings frequent.[3] Even the Hairy Man nearly drowned in his cave when a strong wind blew in a heavy tide. As Greenwell writes, 'It was no ordinary seaside spot. It was still wild.'[4] The Allans were forever having to mount rescue missions, and various members of the family were associated with lifeboats and with trials of lifesaving equipment. The Grotto itself was entangled with the shipwrecks that surrounded it, according to an article in *Chambers's Journal* of 11 September 1875, written by a Grotto guest:

> The outer buildings of the Grotto are constructed entirely of the debris of numerous wrecks, which testify by countless mementoes of these dire calamities. Wreck, wreck is everywhere – it pervades the chamber, the kitchen, and even the rifle-yard, in which were a store of floatabilities, each possibly with its history of some struggling wretch who had grasped it in the frenzied effort at rescue from a fearful death, and, mayhap after all, gone down in sight of my snug and cosy lodging.

Snug versus struggle, cosy verses calamity: it is a place of antitheses, where the meeting points are material. In this description the nautical clutter is biographed as the objects contain the stories of their perished possessors. The visitor is embroiled in

---

[3] In more recent times, Marsden cliffs have seen a number of suicides (the phone number for the Samaritans is now given on signs along the cliff path). And the cliffs themselves pose a threat, as rockfalls become increasingly common: so much so, in fact, that the local council are planning to move back the cliff path and the road that follows it.

[4] Greenwell 2020: 77.

these stories through haptic engagement with the mementoes: 'I could not ascend a step without grasping portions of masts or clinging to a port-hole, while figure-heads met me at every turn.'

Poems were composed about the risks and the rescues too. *The Mercy at Marsden Rocks: A True Tale* by the Reverend Richard Charles Coxe, 1844, shows dark ecology at work through Marsden's material agency. The paradox of the threatening idyll is epitomised in this menacing stanza:

> Did'st ever visit Marsden bay?
> 'Tis wondrous fair to view –
> Yet many a craggy peril's there
> And Cavernous horror too!

In this story, a group of young lads ('The senior sage twelve years has told – The youngest barely nine!') play hide and seek at Marsden. Little do they know they are venturing into 'the jaws of Death'. The game is at odds with the environs, as some of the boys hide in a cave:

> Their friends are gone – all's safe without –
> But ah! what's this within?
> They're found by one they heeded not! –
> The Sea comes hungering in!

The boys fight, they flee, they lament – all with the rocks and the sea as their powerful foes.[5] Luckily, Peter Allan steps in with his 'trusty rope' and pulls them to safety.

Marsden features prominently in *Moredun: A Tale of the Twelve Hundred and Ten*, a novel supposedly written by Walter Scott and published after his death. Though it was largely condemned as a forgery soon after publication in 1855, its attribution does rather propel Marsden to the heights of literary fame. The Marsden of *Moredun* is agentic and sinister (and classical):

> The rocks, which rose perpendicularly and to a considerable height on his right, were not content to form a solid wall to resist the encroachments of the tide and the lashing of the waves, but appeared to have stepped out of their places, and to have advanced upon the beach, and into the very waters, in all imaginable forms and sizes ... At the locality to which he was advancing, the rocks had not been satisfied

---

[5] This resonates with our family, as our youngest son is scared of waves. You might just see him in Figure 6.1, trying to get as far away from the sea as possible.

with marching forth in individual masses against the encroaching waves – they had gone in a body, so to speak, into the sea, where ruined castles, towers, and triumphal arches, seemed to indicate the site of an early Tyre or Carthage of the north.

Moredun's rocks have movement, affect, vitality. Again we return to the idea of isomorphism: that the rocks 'have stepped out of their places' and have been 'marching forth' might be interpreted anthropomorphically and as metaphor, but equally we might see in these descriptions a perceived proximity or affinity between the human and the lithic. That the rocks do not have a body does not stop them moving 'in a body', the language of corporeality evoking the material-ecocritical idea of transcorporeality, of the porousness of the body to the more-than-human world.

It is relevant to our consideration of Theocritus 'from below' that Marsden and the Grotto were not just the playground of the elite, as some accounts would have it. As Greenwell writes,

> artisans and tradesmen are making their way to Marsden. So are the poor. At a time when Roker, and indeed Whitburn, were in the process of being gentrified, Marsden was the one place where everyone could go, and the Grotto's master of ceremonies catered for them all.[6]

Peter Allan himself came from a complicated class background. His father, Peter Allan Sr, was a gamekeeper for a baronet: a relatively well-paid job, but one that was often unpopular. 'Men like Allan Sr were separated from their class by the company they kept, but separated from the company they kept by their class.'[7] Peter Allan Jr 'cocked a snook at authority. Where the Grotto was concerned, the rules were his'.[8] He had somehow managed to establish a right to the Grotto land, circumventing the local landowners just as Jack the Blaster is said to have done. In 1794 Newcastle radical Thomas Spence writes about Jack 'the Blaster' Bates, claiming to have coined the phrase 'the Rights of Man' (some twenty years before) inspired by this anarchic figure. Spence had visited Bates, and

> exulting in the idea of a human being, who had bravely emancipated himself from the iron fangs of aristocracy, to live free from impost, he wrote extempore with chaulk above the fireplace of this free man, the following lines:

---

[6] Greenwell 2020: 55.
[7] Ibid. p. 34.
[8] Ibid. p. 66.

> Ye landlords vile, who man's peace mar,
> Come levy rents here if you can;
> Your stewards and lawyers I defy,
> And live with all the Rights of Man.[9]

The proximity and porousness of man and environs that we see in Marsden's history has the effect we have traced in material-ecocritical approaches of decentring the elite and moving marginalised characters to the foreground. This reaches its peak when a colliery is opened in nearby Whitburn in the 1870s, and Marsden becomes a coal-mining village. There is arguably no closer meeting point between human and land than in a mine; no more urgent site of dark ecology; no more compelling case for a study from below. But that's another story.

I began thinking about this book in a field of cows, but I finished it on Marsden's stony beach. Marsden's stories allow us to reflect on the entanglements and porosity we have seen in Theocritean poetry between people, things and song; between the human and nonhuman worlds; between poetry and place. They allow us to reflect on the agency we have seen across all different types of materiality, from nature and environs, to the body, to objects; on the threat that material agency can pose, and how this threat lends a dark-ecological cast to the material-discursive narratives of which it forms a part; and on the reading of Theocritean poetry from below: a Marxist Ecocriticism that follows material agency across class, gender and ontological divides.

This book is about Theocritus. But it is about much more than elite cultural production, or the *locus amoenus*. It is about the underrepresented agents at the margins, and it is about environments that are not always amenable. It is also not just about Theocritus. I have called this Conclusion and the last section of Chapter 3 'excursuses', but they are not really digressions. They bring home the shifts this book has explored in the way we think about agency, about materiality, about nature and our environs. For me, Marsden brings this book's entanglements home quite literally. Where might your test case be?

---

[9] Ibid. p. 19. Spence claims to have beaten Paine to it. These lines are now written on a chalkboard in the Grotto pub. The revolutionary movements do not stop with Jack Bates and Peter Allan, however. A later landlord of the Marsden Grotto, Sydney Hawkes, was an active supporter of Mazzini, Garibaldi and the Italian revolution.

Bibliography

Abram, D. (2010), *Becoming Animal: An Earthly Cosmology*, New York: Vintage Books.
Ahmed, S. (2008), 'Imaginary prohibitions: Some preliminary remarks on the founding gestures of the "New Materialism"', *European Journal of Women's Studies*, 15: 23–39.
Alaimo, S. (2008), 'Trans-corporeal feminisms and the ethical space of nature', in S. Alaimo and S. Hekman (eds), *Material Feminisms*, Bloomington, IN: Indiana University Press, 237–64.
Alaimo, S. (2010), *Bodily Natures*, Bloomington, IN: Indiana University Press.
Alaimo, S., and S. Hekman (eds) (2008), *Material Feminisms*, Bloomington, IN: Indiana University Press.
Alpers, P. (1996), *What Is Pastoral?* Chicago, IL: University of Chicago Press.
Arnott, W. G. (1978), 'The Theocritus Cup in Liverpool', *Quaderni Urbinati di Cultura Classica*, 29: 129–34.
Bakker, E. J. (2013), *The Meaning of Meat and the Structure of the Odyssey*, Cambridge: Cambridge University Press.
Barad, K. (2007), *Meeting the Universe Halfway: Quantum Physics and the Entanglement of Matter and Meaning*, Durham, NC: Duke University Press.
Baumbach, M., A. Petrovic and I. Petrovic (eds) (2010), *Archaic and Classical Greek Epigram*, Cambridge: Cambridge University Press.
Becker, A. S. (1995), *The Shield of Achilles and the Poetics of Ekphrasis*, Lanham, MD: Rowman & Littlefield.
Beekes, R. (2010), *Etymological Dictionary of Greek*, Leiden: Brill.
Bennett, J. (2010), *Vibrant Matter: A Political Ecology of Things*, Durham, NC: Duke University Press.

Bennett, J. (2012), 'Systems and things: A response to Graham Harman and Timothy Morton', *New Literary History*, 43.2: 225–33.

Bevan, A. (2018), 'Pandora's pithos', *History and Anthropology*, 29.1: 7–14.

Bianchi, E., S. Brill and B. Holmes (eds) (2019), *Antiquities Beyond Humanism*, Oxford: Oxford University Press.

Billings, J. (2018), 'Orestes' urn in word and action', in M. Telò and M. Mueller (eds), *The Materialities of Greek Tragedy: Objects and Affect in Aeschylus, Sophocles and Euripides*, London: Bloomsbury, 49–62.

Blackwell, M. (ed.) (2007), *The Secret Life of Things: Animals, Objects, and It-Narratives in Eighteenth-Century England*, Lewisburg, PA: Bucknell University Press.

Blouin, K. (2019), 'Classics, antiquity and the Anthropocene: some thoughts', *Everyday Orientalism*, 30 April 2019, <https://everydayorientalism.wordpress.com/2019/04/29/classics-antiquity-and-the-anthropocene-some-thoughts/> (last accessed 25 November 2022).

Bohm, D. (ed.) (1998), *On Creativity*, London: Routledge.

Bowie, E. L. (1985), 'Theocritus' Seventh Idyll, Philetas and Longus', *CQ*, 35.1: 67–91.

Brockliss, W. (2018), '"Dark Ecology" and the *Works and Days*', *Helios*, 45.1: 1–36.

Brown, B. (2001), 'Thing theory', *Critical Inquiry*, 28.1: 1–22.

Brown, B. (ed.) (2004), *Things*, Chicago, IL/London: University of Chicago Press.

Brown, B. (2009), '*The Secret Life of Things: Animals, Objects, and It-Narratives in Eighteenth-Century England* (review)', *Eighteenth Century Fiction*, 21.4: 631–8.

Brown, B. (2015), *Other Things*, Chicago, IL/London: University of Chicago Press.

Cameron, A. (1995), *Callimachus and His Critics*, Princeton, NJ: Princeton University Press.

Campbell, P. (2020), 'The sea as a hyperobject: Moving beyond maritime cultural landscapes', *Journal of Eastern Mediterranean Archaeology & Heritage Studies*, 8.3–4: 207–25.

Campbell, P. (2021), 'The Anthropocene, hyperobjects and the archaeology of the future past', *Antiquity*, 95.383: 1–16.

Canevaro, L. G. (2013), 'The clash of the sexes in Hesiod's *Works and Days*', *Greece and Rome*, 60.2: 185–202.

Canevaro, L. G. (2015a), *Hesiod's Works and Days: How to Teach Self-Sufficiency*, Oxford: Oxford University Press.

Canevaro, L. G. (2015b), 'Witches and wicked objects', *New Voices in Classical Reception Studies*, 10: 27–41.

Canevaro, L. G. (2018a), 'Anticipating audiences: Hesiod's *Works and Days* and cognitive psychology', in J. Lauwers, H. Schwall and J. Opsomer (eds), *Psychology and the Classics: A Dialogue of Disciplines*, Berlin: De Gruyter, 142–57.
Canevaro, L. G. (2018b), *Women of Substance in Homeric Epic: Objects, Gender, Agency*, Oxford: Oxford University Press.
Canevaro, L. G. (2019a), 'Materiality and Classics: (Re)turning to the material', *Journal of Hellenic Studies*, 139: 1–11.
Canevaro, L. G. (2019b), 'Think for yourself: Hesiod's *Works and Days* and cognitive training', in L. G. Canevaro and D. O'Rourke (eds), *Didactic Poetry of Greece, Rome and Beyond: Knowledge, Power, Tradition*, Swansea: The Classical Press of Wales, 53–74.
Canevaro, L. G. (2019c), 'Women and memory: the *Iliad* and the *Kosovo Cycle*', in L. Castagnoli and P. Ceccarelli (eds), *Greek Memories: Theories and Practices*, Cambridge: Cambridge University Press, 53–67.
Canevaro, L. G. (forthcoming a), 'Hesiod's Pandora: animal, vegetable, mineral', in S. Bär and A. Domouzi (eds), *Ancient Epic and Artificial Intelligence*, New York: Bloomsbury.
Canevaro, L. G. (forthcoming b), 'Intertextuality through objects: An archaic Tupperware party', in A. Kelly and H. Spelman (eds), *Texts and Intertexts in Archaic and Classical Greece*, Cambridge: Cambridge University Press.
Chesi, G. M., and G. Sclavi (2020), 'Pandora and robotic technology today', in G. M. Chesi and F. Spiegel (eds), *Classical Literature and Posthumanism*, London: Bloomsbury, 301–8.
Chesi, G. M., and F. Spiegel (eds) (2020), *Classical Literature and Posthumanism*, London: Bloomsbury.
Clay, J. S. (1974), '*Demas* and *aude*: The nature of divine transformation in Homer', *Hermes*, 102: 129–36.
Clay, J. S. (2003), *Hesiod's Cosmos*, Cambridge: Cambridge University Press.
Clay, J. S. (2016), 'Homer's epigraph: *Iliad* 7.87–91', *Philologus*, 160.2: 185–96.
Cleland, L., G. Davies and L. Llewellyn-Jones (2007), *Greek and Roman Dress from A to Z*, Abingdon and New York: Routledge.
Cohen, J. J. (1996a), 'Monster culture (seven theses)', in J. J. Cohen (ed.), *Monster Theory: Reading Culture*, Minneapolis, MN: University of Minnesota Press, 3–25.
Cohen, J. J. (ed.) (1996b), *Monster Theory: Reading Culture*, Minneapolis, MN: University of Minnesota Press.
Cohen, J. J. (2015), *Stone: An Ecology of the Inhuman*, Minneapolis, MN: University of Minnesota Press.
Cohen, J. J., and J. Yates (eds) (2016), *Object Oriented Environs*, Santa Barbara, CA: Punctum Books.

Coole, D., and S. Frost (eds) (2010), *New Materialisms: Ontology, Agency, and Politics*, Durham, NC: Duke University Press.

Coxe, R. C. (1844), *The Mercy at Marsden Rocks: A True Tale*, Newcastle.

De Landa, M. (1997), *A Thousand Years of Nonlinear History*, New York: Zone Books.

Deleuze, G., and F. Guattari (1980), *Mille plateaux*, Paris: Les Editions de Minuit.

Detienne, M. (1972), *Les jardins d' Adonis: La mythologie des aromates en Grece*, Paris: Gallimard.

DuBois, P. (1988), *Sowing the Body: Psychoanalysis and Ancient Representations of Women*, Chicago, IL: University of Chicago Press.

Dukes, H. (2017), 'Beckett's vessels and the animation of containers', *Journal of Modern Literature*, 40.4: 75–89.

Edgeworth, M. (2011), *Fluid Pasts: Archaeology of Flow*, Bristol: Bristol Classical Press.

Edmonds, J. M. (1912), *Greek Bucolic Poets* (Loeb Classical Library), Cambridge, MA: Harvard University Press.

Elmer, D. F. (2005), 'Helen *Epigrammatopoios*', *CA*, 24.1: 1–39.

Ercolani, A. (2010), *Esiodo Opere e Giorni: Introduzione, Traduzione e Commento*, Rome: Carocci.

Estok, S. C. (2014), 'Painful material realities, tragedy, ecophobia', in S. Iovino and S. Oppermann (eds), *Material Ecocriticism*, Bloomington, IN: University of Indiana Press, 130–40.

Fanfani, G. (2017), 'Weaving a song: Convergences in Greek poetic imagery between textile and musical terminology: An overview on archaic and Classical literature', in S. Gaspa, C. Michel and M. L. Nosch (eds), *Textile Terminologies from the Orient to the Mediterranean and Europe, 1000 BC to 1000 AD*, Lincoln, NE: University of Nebraska Press, 421–36.

Fantuzzi, M., and R. Hunter (2004), *Tradition and Innovation in Hellenistic Poetry*, Cambridge: Cambridge University Press.

Faraone, C. (1999), *Ancient Love Magic*, Cambridge, MA: Harvard University Press.

Fränkel, H. (1946), 'Man's ephemeral nature according to Pindar and others', *TAPhA*, 77: 131–45.

Gaifman, M., and V. Platt (2018), 'Introduction: from Grecian urn to embodied object', in M. Gaifman, V. Platt and M. Squire (eds), *The Embodied Object in Greek and Roman Art, Art History*, 41.3: 403–19.

Gaifman, M., V. Platt and M. Squire (eds) (2018), *The Embodied Object in Greek and Roman Art, Art History*, 41.3 (special issue).

Garcia, L. F. Jr (2013), *Homeric Durability: Telling Time in the Iliad*, Cambridge, MA: Harvard University Press.

Gell, A. (1998), *Art and Agency: An Anthropological Theory*, Oxford: Oxford University Press.
Gibson, J. (1979), *The Ecological Approach to Visual Perception*, Boston: Houghton Mifflin.
Goldhill, S. (1987), 'An unnoticed allusion in Theocritus and Callimachus', *Illinois Classical Studies*, 12.1: 1–6.
Goldhill, S. (1990), *The Poet's Voice: Essays on Poetics and Greek Literature*, Cambridge: Cambridge University Press.
Goldhill, S. (2020), 'Conclusions', in G. M. Chesi and F. Spiegel (eds), *Classical Literature and Posthumanism*, London: Bloomsbury, 331–42.
Gow, A. S. F. (1950), *Theocritus. Edited with a Translation and Commentary*, 2 vols. Vol. I: *Introduction, Text, and Translation*, Vol. II: *Commentary, Appendix, Indexes, and Plates*, Cambridge: Cambridge University Press.
Greenwell, B. (2020), *A History of Marsden Rock and Marsden Grotto*, Sunderland.
Gutzwiller, K. J. (1986), 'The plant decoration on Theocritus' ivy cup', *AJPh*, 107.2: 253–5.
Hall, E. (2008), 'Putting the class into classical reception', in L. Hardwick and C. Stray (eds), *A Companion to Classical Receptions*, Malden, MA: Wiley-Blackwell, 386–97.
Hall, E. (2018), 'Materialisms old and new', in M. Telò and M. Mueller (eds), *The Materialities of Greek Tragedy: Objects and Affect in Aeschylus, Sophocles, and Euripides*, New York: Bloomsbury, 203–17.
Hall, E., and H. Stead (2020), *A People's History of Classics: Class and Greco-Roman Antiquity in Britain and Ireland 1689 to 1939*, Abingdon/New York: Routledge.
Halperin, D. M. (1983), *Before Pastoral. Theocritus and the Ancient Tradition of Bucolic Poetry*, New Haven, CT: Yale University Press.
Haraway, D. (1992), 'Otherworldly conversations; Terran topics; local terms', *Science as Culture*, 3.1: 64–98.
Harder, M. A., R. F. Regtuit and G. C. Wakker (eds) (1998), *Genre in Hellenistic Poetry*, Groningen: Forsten.
Harich-Schwarzbauer, H. (ed.) (2015), *Weben und Gewebe in der Antike: Materialität – Repräsentation – Episteme – Metapoetik*, Oxford/Philadelphia: Oxbow Books.
Harlizius-Klück, E., and G. Fanfani (2016), '(B)orders in ancient weaving and archaic Greek poetry', in G. Fanfani, M. Harlow and M.-L. Nosch (eds), *Spinning Fates and the Song of the Loom*, Oxford/Philadelphia: Oxbow Books, 61–99.
Heffernan, J. A. (1993), *Museum of Words*, Chicago, IL: University of Chicago Press.

Heidegger, M. (1971), *Poetry, Language, Thought*, transl. A. Hofstadter, New York: Harper & Row.

Heidegger, M. [1927] (1996), *Being and Time*, transl. J. Stambaugh, Albany, NY: State University of New York Press.

Hekman, S. (2008), 'Constructing the ballast: an ontology for Feminism', in S. Alaimo and S. Hekman (eds), *Material Feminisms*, Bloomington, IN: University of Indiana Press, 85–119.

Hiltner, K. (2011), *What Else Is Pastoral? Renaissance Literature and the Environment*, Ithaca, NY: Cornell University Press.

Hodder, I. (2012), *Entangled: An Archaeology of the Relationships between Humans and Things*, Oxford: Wiley-Blackwell.

Hoffmeyer, J. (2008), *Biosemiotics: An Examination into the Signs of Life and the Life of Signs*, Scranton, PA: University of Scranton Press.

Hofinger, M. (1967), 'Hesiodea: Notes sur la traduction des adjectives τετράτρυφος et ὀκτάβλωμος (*Travaux*, v.442)', *AC*, 36: 457–60.

Hollis, D., and J. König (eds) (2021), *Mountain Dialogues from Antiquity to Modernity*, London: Bloomsbury.

Holmes, B. (2019), 'On Stoic sympathy: Cosmobiology and the life of nature', in E. Bianchi, S. Brill and B. Holmes (eds), *Antiquities Beyond Humanism*, Oxford: Oxford University Press, 239–70.

Holmes, B. (forthcoming), *The Tissue of the World: Sympathy and the Concept of Nature in Greco-Roman Antiquity*, Chicago, IL: University of Chicago Press.

Hopkinson, N. (2015), *Theocritus, Moschus, Bion*, Cambridge, MA: Harvard University Press.

Hunt, J. M. (2011), 'The politics of death in Theocritus' first *Idyll*', *AJPh*, 132.3: 379–96.

Hunter, R. (1999), *Theocritus: A Selection. Idylls 1, 3, 4, 6, 7, 10, 11 and 13*, Cambridge: Cambridge University Press.

Hunter, R. (2002), 'The sense of an author: Theocritus and [Theocritus]', in R. K. Gibson and C. Shuttleworth Kraus (eds), *The Classical Commentary: Histories, Practices, Theories*, Leiden: Brill, 89–108.

Ingate, J. (2019), *Water and Urbanism in Roman Britain: Hybridity and Identity*, Abingdon: Routledge.

Ingate, J. (2020), 'Two parts hydrogen, oxygen one? Re-evaluating the role of Roman urban water infrastructure', in I. Selsvold and L. Webb (eds), *Beyond the Romans: Posthuman Perspectives in Roman Archaeology*, Oxford: Oxbow Books, 93–108.

Ingold, T. (2011), *Being Alive. Essays on Movement, Knowledge and Description*, New York: Routledge.

Ingold, T. (2012), 'Introduction', in M. Janowski and T. Ingold (eds), *Imagining Landscapes: Past, Present and Future*, Abingdon: Routledge, 1–18.
Iovino, S. (2012), 'Steps to a material ecocriticism: The recent literature about the "New Materialisms" and its implications for ecocritical theory', *Ecozone*, 3.1: 134–45.
Iovino, S. (2016), 'Afterword' to C. Schliephake (ed.), *Ecocriticism, Ecology, and the Cultures of Antiquity*, Lanham, MD: Lexington Books, 309–16.
Iovino, S., and S. Oppermann (eds) (2014), *Material Ecocriticism*, Bloomington, IN: University of Indiana Press.
Janko, R. (1994), *The Iliad: A Commentary. Vol. IV, Books 13–16*, General editor G. S. Kirk, Cambridge: Cambridge University Press.
Janowski, M., and T. Ingold (eds) (2012), *Imagining Landscapes: Past, Present and Future*, Abingdon: Routledge.
Johnson, M. H., and J. Morton (1991), *Biology and Cognitive Development: The Case of Face Recognition*, Oxford: Blackwell Scientific Publications.
Johnston, S. I. (1995), 'The song of the *iynx*: Magic and rhetoric in *Pythian* 4', *TAPhA*, 125: 177–206.
König, J. (2022), *The Folds of Olympus: Mountains in Ancient Greek and Roman Culture*, Princeton, NJ: Princeton University Press.
Lakoff, G., and M. Johnson (1980), *Metaphors We Live By*, Chicago, IL: University of Chicago Press.
Lamb, J. (2011), *The Things Things Say*, Princeton, NJ: Princeton University Press.
Lambert, M. (2002), 'Desperate Simaetha: Gender and power in Theocritus *Idyll 2*', *Acta Classica*, 45: 71–88.
Lardinois, A. (1998), 'How the Days fit the Works in Hesiod's *Works and Days*', *AJPh*, 119.3: 319–36.
Larson, J. (2001), *Greek Nymphs: Myth, Cult, Lore*, Oxford: Oxford University Press.
Lather, A. (2021), *Materiality and Aesthetics in Archaic and Classical Greek Poetry*, Edinburgh: Edinburgh University Press.
Latour, B. (2005), *Reassembling the Social: An Introduction to Actor-Network Theory*, Oxford: Oxford University Press.
LeVen, P. (2014), *The Many-Headed Muse: Tradition and Innovation in Late Classical Greek Lyric Poetry*. Cambridge: Cambridge University Press.
LeVen, P. (2021), *Music and Metamorphosis in Graeco-Roman Thought*, Cambridge: Cambridge University Press.
Macfarlane, R. (2003), *Mountains of the Mind: A History of a Fascination*, London: Granta.

McSweeney, J. (2014), *The Necropastoral: Poetry, Media, Occults*, Ann Arbor, MI: University of Michigan Press.

Maran, T. (2014), 'Semiotization of matter: A hybrid zone between biosemiotics and material ecocriticism', in S. Iovino and S. Oppermann (eds), *Material Ecocriticism*, Bloomington, IN: University of Indiana Press, 141–54.

Martindale, C. (1997), 'Green politics: the *Eclogues*', in C. Martindale (ed.), *The Cambridge Companion to Virgil*, Cambridge: Cambridge University Press, 107–24.

Mauss, M. [1923] (1967), *The Gift: Forms and Functions of Exchange in Archaic Societies*, transl. I. Gunnison, New York: Routledge.

Mayor, A. (2018), *Gods and Robots: Myths, Machines and Ancient Dreams of Technology*, Princeton, NJ: Princeton University Press.

Miles, G. B. (1977), 'Characterization and the ideal of innocence in Theocritus' *Idylls*', *Ramus*, 6.2: 139–64.

Mitchell, W. J. T. (1994), *Picture Theory: Essays on Visual and Verbal Representation*, Chicago, IL/London: University of Chicago Press.

Morton, T. (2008), 'John Clare's dark ecology', *Studies in Romanticism*, 47.2: 179–93.

Morton, T. (2012), *The Ecological Thought*, Cambridge, MA: Harvard University Press.

Morton, T. (2013), *Hyperobjects: Philosophy and Ecology after the End of the World*, Minneapolis, MN: University of Minnesota Press.

Morton, T. (2016), *Dark Ecology: For a Logic of Future Coexistence*, New York: Columbia University Press.

Morton, T. (2017), *Humankind: Solidarity with Nonhuman People*, London: Verso Books.

Most, G. (2006), *Hesiod: Theogony, Works and Days, Testimonia*, Harvard Loeb, Cambridge, MA and London: Harvard University Press.

Moyo, M. (2019), 'Fauna and erotic didactics in archaic Greek and Kalanga oral wisdom literatures', in L. G. Canevaro and D. O'Rourke (eds), *Didactic Poetry of Greece, Rome and Beyond: Knowledge, Power, Tradition*, Swansea: Classical Press of Wales, 225–48.

Mueller, M. (2016), *Objects as Actors: Props and the Poetics of Performance in Greek Tragedy*, Chicago, IL: University of Chicago Press.

Mueller, M. (forthcoming), *Sappho and Homer: A Reparative Reading*, Cambridge: Cambridge University Press.

O'Rourke, D. (2019), 'Knowledge is power: dynamics of (dis)empowerment in didactic poetry', in L. G. Canevaro and D. O'Rourke (eds), *Didactic Poetry of Greece, Rome and Beyond: Knowledge, Power, Tradition*, Swansea: Classical Press of Wales, 21–52.

Pache, C. O. (2011), *A Moment's Ornament: The Poetics of Nympholepsy in Ancient Greece*, Oxford/New York: Oxford University Press.
Paley, F. A. (1861), *The Epics of Hesiod*, London: Whittaker.
Panofsky, D., and E. Panofsky (1956), *Pandora's Box: The Changing Aspects of a Mythical Symbol*, New York: Pantheon Books.
Pantelia, M. C. (1993), 'Spinning and weaving: Ideas of domestic order in Homer', *AJPh*, 114.4: 493–501.
Payne, M. (2001), 'Ecphrasis and song in Theocritus' *Idyll* 1', *GRBS*, 42: 263–87.
Payne, M. (2007), *Theocritus and the Invention of Fiction*, Cambridge: Cambridge University Press.
Payne, M. (2014), 'The natural world in Greek literature and philosophy', in G. Williams (ed.), *Oxford Handbooks Online in Classical Studies*, https://doi.org/10.1093/oxfordhb/9780199935390.013.001.
Payne, M. (2019), 'Shared life as chorality in Schiller, Hölderlin, and Hellenistic poetry', in E. Bianchi, S. Brill and B. Holmes (eds), *Antiquities Beyond Humanism*, Oxford: Oxford University Press, 141–57.
Peperzak, A. T., S. Critchley, R. Bernasconi (eds) (1996), *Emmanuel Levinas: Basic Philosophical Writings*, Bloomington, IN: University of Indiana Press.
Petropoulos, J. C. B. (1994), *Heat and Lust: Hesiod's Midsummer Festival Scene Revisited*, Lanham, MD: Rowman & Littlefield.
Petrovic, A. (2016), 'Archaic funerary epigram and Hector's imagined *epitymbia*', in A. Efstathiou and I. Karamanou (eds), *Homeric Receptions Across Generic and Cultural Contexts*, Berlin: De Gruyter, 45–58.
Petrovic, A. (2019), 'The materiality of text: An introduction', in A. Petrovic, I. Petrovic and E. Thomas (eds), *The Materiality of Text: Placement, Perception, and Presence of Inscribed Texts in Classical Antiquity*, Leiden: Brill, 1–28.
Petrovic, A., and I. Petrovic (2022), 'Hesiod's religious norms in context: on *Works & Days* 724–760', *Kernos*, 35: 185–232.
Petrovic, A., I. Petrovic and E. Thomas (eds) (2019), *The Materiality of Text: Placement, Perception, and Presence of Inscribed Texts in Classical Antiquity*, Leiden: Brill.
Porter, J. I. (2019), 'Hyperobjects, OOO, and the eruptive classics – field notes of an accidental tourist', in E. Bianchi, S. Brill and B. Holmes (eds), *Antiquities Beyond Humanism*, Oxford: Oxford University Press, 189–209.
Purves, A. (2010), *Space and Time in Ancient Greek Narrative*, Cambridge and New York: Cambridge University Press.
Purves, A. (2015), 'Ajax and other objects: Homer's vibrant materialism', *Ramus*, 44.1–2: 75–94.
Rajewsky, I. O. (2005), 'Intermediality, intertextuality, and remediation: A literary perspective on intermediality', *Intermédialités*, 6: 43–64.

Rayor, D. J. (2005), 'The power of memory in Sappho and Erinna', in E. Greene (ed.), *Women Poets in Ancient Greece and Rome*, Norman, OK: University of Oklahoma Press, 59–71.

Reid, V. M., K. Dunn, R. J. Young, J. Amu, T. Donovan and N. Reissland (2017), 'The human fetus preferentially engages with face-like visual stimuli', *Current Biology*, 27: 1825–8 + e1–3.

Renfrew, C. (2005), 'Archaeology and commodification: The role of things in societal transformation', in W. M. J. van Binsbergen and P. Geschiere (eds), *Commodification: Things, Agency, and Identities ('The Social Life of Things' Revisited)*, Münster: Lit Verlag, 85–98.

Renfrew, C. (2012), 'Towards a cognitive archaeology: Material engagement and the early development of society', in I. Hodder (ed.), *Archaeological Theory Today*, 2nd edn, Cambridge and Malden, MA: Polity Press, 124–46.

Richardson, E. (ed.) (2018), *Classics in Extremis*, London: Bloomsbury.

Saunders, T. (2018), *Bucolic Ecology: Virgil's Eclogues and the Environmental Literary Tradition*, London: Bloomsbury.

Schama, S. (1995), *Landscapes and Memory*, London: Harper Perennial.

Schliephake, C. (ed.) (2016), *Ecocriticism, Ecology, and the Cultures of Antiquity*, Lanham, MD: Lexington Books.

Shryock, A., and D. L. Smail (2018), 'On containers: A forum. Introduction and concluding remarks', *History and Anthropology*, 29.1: 1–6, 49–51.

Segal, C. (1973), 'Simaetha and the iynx (Theocritus, Idyll II)', *Quaderni Urbinati di Cultura Classica*, 15: 32–43.

Segal, C. (1981), *Poetry and Myth in Ancient Pastoral: Essays on Theocritus and Virgil*, Princeton, NJ: Princeton University Press.

Segal, C. (1984), 'Underreading and intertextuality: Sappho, Simaetha, and Odysseus in Theocritus' second Idyll', *Arethusa* 17.2: 201–9.

Sissa, G. (2022), 'Τί θαυμαστόν? Intentional objects and erotic materialism in Greek culture', in H. Harich-Schwarzbauer and C. Scheidegger Lammle (eds), *Gender Studies in den Altertumswissenschaften: Women and Objects in Antiquity*, Trier: WVT Wissenschaftlicher Verlag, 15–62.

Skinner, M. B. (2001), 'Ladies Day at the Art Institute: Theocritus, Herodas, and the gendered gaze', in A. Lardinois and L. McClure (eds), *Making Silence Speak: Women's Voices in Greek Literature and Society*, Princeton, NJ: Princeton University Press, 201–22.

Snell, B. (1953), *The Discovery of the Mind*, New York: Angelico Press.

Squire, M. (2013), 'Ekphrasis at the forge and the forging of ekphrasis: The "shield of Achilles" in Graeco-Roman word and image', *Word and Image*, 29.2: 157–91.

Stavropoulou, E. (2021), 'Metal materiality and divine agency: Towards a new reading of Aeschylus' *Seven Against Thebes*'. PhD thesis, University of Warwick.
Steiner, D. (2010), *Homer Odyssey Books XVII and XVIII*, Cambridge: Cambridge University Press.
Stephens, S. (2006), 'Ptolemaic pastoral', in M. Fantuzzi and T. Papanghelis (eds), *Brill's Companion to Greek and Latin Pastoral*, Leiden: Brill, 91–117.
Svenbro, J. (1993), *Phrasikleia*, Ithaca, NY: Cornell University Press.
Tavenner, E. (1933), 'Iynx and rhombus', *TAPhA*, 64: 109–27.
Taylor, J. C. (2020), 'Plumbing the depths: Geological processes, deep time, and the shaping of landscapes in classical literature'. Doctoral dissertation, Harvard University, Graduate School of Arts & Sciences.
Telò, M. (forthcoming), *The Titular Object: Pregnancy and Props in Plautus and Beyond*.
Telò, M., and M. Mueller (eds) (2018), *The Materialities of Greek Tragedy: Objects and Affect in Aeschylus, Sophocles, and Euripides*, New York: Bloomsbury.
Thomas, R. (1996), 'Genre through intertextuality: Theocritus to Virgil and Propertius', in M. A. Harder, R. F. Regtuit and G. C. Wakker (eds), *Theocritus*, Groningen: Egbert Forsten, 227–46.
Thompson, E. P. (1966), 'History from below', *Times Literary Supplement*, 7 April.
Tueller, M. A. (2019), 'Writing, women's silent speech', in A. Petrovic, I. Petrovic and E. Thomas (eds), *The Materiality of Text: Placement, Perception, and Presence of Inscribed Texts in Classical Antiquity*, Leiden: Brill, 187–204.
van der Tuin, I. (2008), 'Deflationary logic: Response to Sara Ahmed's Imaginary prohibitions: Some preliminary remarks on the founding gestures of the "New Materialism"', *European Journal of Women's Studies*, 15.4: 411–16.
Wallace, E. K. (2018), 'The things things don't say: *The Rape of the Lock*, Vitalism, and New Materialism', *The Eighteenth Century*, 59.1: 105–22.
Webb, R. (2009), *Ekphrasis, Imagination and Persuasion in Ancient Rhetorical Theory and Practice*, Farnham and Burlington, VT: Ashgate.
Webb, R. (2018), 'Odysseus' bed: between object and action', in 'Dossier: Place aux objets! Présentification et vie des artefacts en Grèce ancienne', *Mètis*, 16: 65–83.
Weiner, A. B. (1992), *Inalienable Possessions: The Paradox of Keeping while Giving*, Berkeley, CA: University of California Press.
West, M. L. (1966), *Hesiod: Theogony*, Oxford: Clarendon Press.
West, M. L. (1978), *Hesiod Works and Days*, Oxford: Clarendon Press.
Westling, L. (2006), 'Darwin in Arcadia: Brute being and the human animal dance from Gilgamesh to Virginia Woolf', *Anglia* 124.1: 11–43.

Wheeler, W. (2011), 'The biosemiotic turn: Abduction; or, The nature of creative reason in nature and culture', in A. Goodbody and K. Rigby (eds), *Ecocritical Theory: New European Approaches*, Charlottesville: University of Virginia Press, 270–82.

Wheeler, W. (2014), 'Natural play, natural metaphor, and natural stories: biosemiotic realism', in S. Iovino and S. Oppermann (eds), *Material Ecocriticism*, Bloomington, IN: University of Indiana Press, 67–79.

Whitley, J. (2013), 'Homer's entangled objects: narrative, agency and personhood in and out of Iron Age texts', *Cambridge Archaeological Journal*, 23.3: 395–416.

Worman, N. (2018), 'Electra, Orestes and the sibling hand', in M. Telò and M. Mueller (eds), *The Materialities of Greek Tragedy: Objects and Affect in Aeschylus, Sophocles, and Euripides*, New York: Bloomsbury, 185–202.

Worman, N. (2021), *Tragic Bodies: Edges of the Human in Greek Drama*, London/New York: Bloomsbury.

Zapf, H. (2014), 'Creative matter and creative mind: Cultural ecology and literary creativity', in S. Iovino and S. Oppermann (eds), *Material Ecocriticism*, Bloomington, IN: University of Indiana Press, 51–66.

Zeitlin, F. I. (1996), *Playing the Other: Gender and Society in Classical Greek Literature*, Chicago, IL: University of Chicago Press.

Index Locorum

Aristotle
  Poetics
    1452a7–11: 130n

Erinna
  G-P 3.1–4: 176–7

Hesiod
  Theogony
    27–8: 94
    573–84: 51–3, 62, 176–7
  Works and Days
    25–6: 93
    41–2: 147
    43–4: 103
    57: 68
    61: 52, 53, 177
    67: 53–4
    97: 122
    117–18: 103
    170–3: 103
    373–5: 83
    382: 82–3
    442: 147
    475: 187
    505–60: 49–50, 83n
    582–4: 147–8
    586: 68
    705: 68

Homer
  Homeric Hymns
    7.40–1: 13n
  Iliad
    3.60: 121
    6.460–1: 126–7, 129, 173–4, 175
    7.89–91: 127, 129
    16.34: 183
    16.406–8: 116
    19.245: 162
    22.511: 85, 86, 162
    23.30: 183
  Odyssey
    4.219–30: 70
    5.231: 85
    9.108: 179
    9.125: 179
    9.190–2: 179–80
    9.233–5: 179
    9.240–3: 179
    9.319–28: 185
    9.480–6: 179
    9.537–42: 179

Homer (*cont.*)
  Odyssey (*cont.*)
    10.222–3: 84
    10.236: 70
    10.276: 70
    10.287: 70
    15.126: 162
    16.35: 187
    18.356–9: 137–8, 139
    18.360: 137–8
    18.364: 137–8
    19.494: 124
    23.103: 123–4
    23.183–204: 64
    24.222–5: 138–39

Pindar
  Pythian Odes
    4.213–19: 66–8, 69, 70
    12.5–6: 149

Plato
  Phaedrus
    258e–259d: 148, 151

Tatius, Achilles
  Leucippe and Clitophon
    8.6.10: 193–4

Telestes
  PMG 806: 149–50

Theocritus
  Idyll 1
    27–31: 11–14
    32–8: 48–50, 57, 58–62, 86, 91–2, 154
    39–44: 91, 110, 113–14, 115–17
    45–8: 113, 135–40
    48–54: 146–8, 149–52
    55–6: 13, 152–3
    57–8: 153–4
    59–60: 154–5
    55–60: 154–5

    139–41: 130–2
  Idyll 2
    15–17: 69–70
    28–31: 71–2, 78n
    38–40: 78
    79: 74
    82–3: 78–9
    88–90: 79
    106–7: 79
    110: 79, 80–1
    126: 80
    156: 77
    165: 74
  Idyll 3
    15–16: 123
    18: 123–4
  Idyll 4
    26–8: 187–8
  Idyll 6
    11–12: 184
    27: 183–4
    35–8: 184
    39–40: 184
  Idyll 7
    18–19: 94
    25–6: 111–13, 135n
    43–4: 93–4
    45–8: 92–3, 94
    78–85: 99–101
    91–3: 94–5, 96
    128–9: 95
    135–46: 102–3
    148–57: 104–5
  Idyll 8
    18–24: 188–9
  Idyll 11
    17–18: 180–1
    38: 179, 186
    43: 183
    45–8: 181
    50–3: 179, 182

56–9: 182
60–2: 179, 182–3
79: 179, 183
80–1: 179
Idyll 15
15–20: 82–3
21: 86–7
27–40: 83
45: 83
69–71: 84
72–3: 83, 84n
79: 84–7
80–1: 87–8
82–3: 88–90
84–6: 90
Idyll 17
64–5: 168–9
Idyll 21
6–13: 105–8
17–18: 108
22–6: 111
31: 108
34–5: 109–10
41–3: 116–17
44–5: 108–9
48–9: 110
52–7: 110
59–66: 110–11

Idyll 23
6: 121–2
7–10: 123
17–18: 122
19–21: 123–4
27–32: 126
37–8: 128
41: 122
46–8: 126–8
49–53: 124–5
57–60: 129–30, 132
63: 132
Idyll 28
1–4: 156, 158
5: 164–5
8–11: 158–9, 160, 161–2
12–13: 160, 163
14: 162
15–18: 157
22–5: 157–8, 160, 172, 173–5
[Theocritus]
Syrinx
1–20: 190–3, 195

Subject Index

Note: 'n' indicates note, italic indicates a figure

acanthus, 13, 152, 153, 155
Achilles, 162, 183 *see also* shields, shield of Achilles
Adonis, 87, 90
aetia, 66–9, 71, 75, 192, 193–4
affect, 12–13, 14–15, 18, 72, 78, 101, 119, 120, 130, 153, 155, 195, 209
allusions, 6, 13n, 32, 50, 57, 69, 84–5, 94–5, 163, 191–2, 195
Amaryllis, 122, 123–4
Andromache, 85, 86, 126–7, 129, 162, 173, 175
animals, humans and, 50, 52–4, 57, 66, 68, 72, 83, 93, 108–9, 147, 164–5, 180, 192 *see also* birds; cicadas; fish; foxes
animated objects, 17, 52, 62, 64, 65, 100, 119, 169–70, 177, 194
Anthropocene, 6, 16–17, 42
anthropocentrism, 3–4, 18, 20–2, 25, 28, 65, 98, 119, 166–7, 168–9, 178
anthropomorphism, 9, 18, 76, 118–19, 130, 133, 165–9, 206, 209
armour *see* weaponry

Asphalion, 110–11, 117, 182
assemblages, 13, 19, 37, 60, 63, 65, 129, 140, 148, 151, 155, 161–2, 163, 186, 187, 194–5, 198–9, 204–5
Athena, 52, 53, 121, 149, 162
Atwood, Margaret, 133–4
auloi, 149–50, 186
authorship, 30–2, 36, 132, 189, 191
autobiographical fallacy, 95–7, 191

Barad, Karen, 4–5, 15, 45, 99
beds, 8, 105, 106 *see also* Odysseus, bed of
bees, 101, 102, 192
Bennett, Jane, 9, 19, 21, 45, 47, 76, 119, 165, 167
bi-directionality, 17, 29
biosemiotics, 34–6, 38–40, 164–5
birds, 93, 147 *see also* iunx
bodies, human, 47–8, 52–3, 55, 66–81, 129, 173–4, 175, 193–4 *see also* hands
Brown, Bill, 7, 57–8, 62–3, 64, 85, 89, 150–1, 169, 171

SUBJECT INDEX | 227

Callimachus, 86, 92, 168
Calypso, 85, 86, 149
chisels, 13, 187, 205
cicadas, 102, 148, 151
Circe, 69–70, 84–5, 86, 149
class, 19, 22–3, 29, 41, 73–4, 87, 186
clothing *see* textiles
Cohen, Jeffrey Jerome, 36–7, 113–14, 117, 118–20, 123, 125, 130, 133, 179, 180, 184, 186
collaboration, 107, 110, 129, 155–69, 174
Comatas, 99–101, 192, 204
constitutive symbols, 9, 77, 183–4, 187, 189
containers, 99–101
   chests, 83, 99, 100–1, 192, 204
   storage jars, 54–5, 57, 122, 187
Cos, 96, 168–9
creativity, 34–8, 64–5, 87–90, 146–55 *see also* collaboration; *ekphrasis tropou*
Cyclopes, 179, 183
Cyclops *see* Polyphemus

Daphnis, 9, 42, 101, 130–2, 178, 186, 189
dark ecology, 6–7, 9, 40–3, 54, 55, 73, 78, 93, 125, 178–9, 180–6, 188, 208, 210
deep time, 34–5, 37, 101, 113–14, 119, 121
Delphis, 71, 72–5, 77–8, 79–80
diadems, 51–2, 53, 57, 59, 62, 177
distaffs, 9, 155–63, 164–5, 167–8, 171–2, 173–6
distributed agency, 18, 63, 87, 183, 184, 186
doors, 116n, 122, 129, 179

ekphrasis tropou, 64, 151–2
ekphrasis, 14–15, 33, 57–61, 62–5, 81–2, 84–90, 135–7, 151–5, 176–7, 195
embodiment, 75–80, 100–1, 134, 162, 164, 176–7, 199
entanglements, 18, 24, 37, 47, 49–50, 53, 81, 83–4, 88, 97–9, 100–1, 106–9, 113–14, 119, 120, 128–9, 149–50, 151, 155–7, 160, 161–2, 163, 170, 192, 201, 207
epigrams, 126–9, 132, 158, 172–6, 189–92, 195
Erinna, 173, 174–7, 192
Eros, 123, 129–30, 132, 133,
Eurymachus, 137–8, 379

fire, 53, 68–9, 77, 78–9, 181–2
fishermen, 7–8, 32, 41, 80, 105–11, 113–17, 185, 201
flowers, 126, 182 *see also* garlands
foxes, 147, 150–1, 200

Galatea, 178, 181, 183–4
garlands, 51–2, 124
garments *see* textiles
gender, 7, 22, 46–50, 60–1, 72–4, 76–7, 79, 81–3, 86–8, 89–90, 158–9, 173–4
Gorgo, 82, 83, 84–7, 88
Gorgons, 134, 149

hammers, 27, 75n, 112n, 189
hands, 20, 83, 86, 88, 107, 110, 143, *143*, 161–2, 168, 184, 189, 199
Hector, 85, 126–7, 129, 175
Heidegger, Martin, 9, 26–7, 189
Helen, 70, 162
Hephaestus, 53, 57, 64, 65
Hesiod
   and autobiography, 94, 95, 96, 97
   and *oiko*-criticism, 37–43, 55, 92–3, 103, 106–7, 112, 118, 125, 147, 148, 187

Hesiod (*cont.*)
  and women, 49–50, 68, 82–3
  see also Pandora
Homer, 24, 29, 36–8, 92, 120
  and landscape, 116–17, 123–4, 135–9
  and material memory, 70, 126–7, 128–9, 162, 173–5, 187–8, 173, 174
  and textiles, 84–5, 89, 158–60, 162
  see also Odysseus; Polyphemus; shield of Achilles
homunculus effect, 100–1
Hope, 55n, 57, 122
houses, 8, 50, 57, 93, 105, 106, 108, 111, 139 *see also* doors; walls
hybrid agency, 32, 107, 109, 110, 161–2, 184, 189, 192, 198–9, 201
hyperobjects, 106–7, 125, 131

intermediality, 32–4, 54, 57, 81, 85–7, 100, 115, 137–9, 186
intertextuality, 31, 32, 34, 50–4, 57, 69, 84–5, 91–2, 100, 115, 121, 135–7
intra-action, 4–5, 15, 75, 99, 115, 204
isomorphism, 9, 76, 119, 133, 165–7, 206, 209
it-narratives, 170–1
iunx, 66–70, 71, 72, 74, 75
ivy, 12–14, 153, 155

Jason, 62, 66–7, 69, 71n
John Mandeville, The Book of, 36–7

labour, 19–20, 23, 63, 82–4, 88–9, 91–2, 105–6, 107, 137–9, 148, 160–2
Laertes, 139
landscape, 8, 25, 28–9, 39, 41–2, 178, 179–82, 184, 185–6, 202–10
  imagined, 91–113, 135–40
  see also locus amoenus; mountains; plants; sea; stone

lithic agency, 32, 36–7, 41, 112–14, 125, 128, 129–30, 132, 178, 192, 201
Liverpool cup, *196*, 197–201
locus amoenus, 28, 41, 102–4, 139, 148, 181, 186, 210
looms, 149, 159, 160
Lycidas, 92, 94, 95, 96–7, 99, 102, 111–13

magic, 66–74, 77–8, 90
Marsden Bay, 202–10, *203, 206*
Marxist theory, 6n, 20–1, 63, 210
material-discursive narrative, 14–15, 44–6, 65–6, 81, 86, 89, 143, 170–1, 193, 195, 204, 210
material feminism(s), 7, 20n, 22, 44–8, 65–6, 74–6
Medea, 20, 68–70
memory, 34–5, 70, 77, 127–9, 131–2, 133, 158, 162, 174–6
metals, 64, 87, 110–11, 121, 136, 197–9
metamorphoses, 34–5, 36, 54, 193–4, 207
metaphor, 36–7, 68, 79, 93, 94, 100, 112, 116n, 122, 134, 149, 165–6, 209
moon, 74
Morton, Timothy, 3n, 20–1, 27, 40, 41n, 54, 93, 107, 125
mountains, 93, 94, 114–15, 179–80, 181
MP5 (artist), 55, *56*, 57
Muses, 93, 94–5, 111, 132, 148, 149

Nausicaa, 76
nets, 113, 185, 200–1
networks, 29, 66, 125, 129–30, 135, 140, 156, 161, 162
Nikias, 156, 161, 178
nooses, 124–5, 129
nymphs, 94–5, 168–9 *see also* Cos; Galatea

SUBJECT INDEX | 229

Odysseus, 69n, 70, 76, 89, 137–9, 150n, 187
   bed of, 64, 151, 187
   and Polyphemus, 179, 181, 182–3, 184–5
Orpheus relief, 200
othering, 33, 41, 72, 179–80, 184–5

Pan, 186, 191, 192–4
Pandora, 50–5, *56*, 57, 62, 68, 122, 176–7
panpipes *see* syrinx
pastoral genre, 5–6, 22–5, 27–9, 35, 39, 41–3, 103–5, 153–4, 198
Patroclus, 116, 183
Penelope, 124
personification, 74, 95, 156, 166–7, 169
persuasive analogies, 67n, 71–2, 74, 77–8, 79
petromorphism, 118–19, 123–4, 130, 134, 183, 206–7
plaiting, 20, 105, 106, 108, 149–50, 151–2, 155
plants *see* acanthus; flowers; ivy; reeds; vines
poetry, and weaving, 147–51, 155–6, 158–61
Polyphemus, 9, 20, 41, 178–86
Pope, Alexander, 47–8, 76, 170–1
Praxinoa, 82, 83–4, 87–9, 90
Prometheus, 52, 57, 176, 192, 193
proximity, human-nonhuman, 53–4, 71, 72, 76, 106, 108, 157, 161, 166, 181, 192, 209–10
Ptolemy II Philadelphus, 96, 168

quasi-objects, 63, 151

reeds, 149–50, 189, 193–4
reification, 9, 75–6, 116n, 189, 195, 197–8, 200
rocks *see* stone

San Sperate, Sardinia, 140–5
Sappho, 32n, 69n, 175
Sciola, Pinuccio (artist), 140–4, *143*
sea, 78, 108, 110, 113, 116n, 131n, 181–5 *see also* water
seasons, 41, 50, 111, 118, 182
senses, 13, 14, 59, 86, 98–9, 101, 102, 154–5, 186–7, 195, 199
shields, 191
   shield of Achilles, 8, 57–8, 59–60, 62–5, 85, 89, 115–17, 151, 191, 197–9 *see also* ekphrasis
Simaetha, 7, 68–70, 71, 72–5, 76–81
Simichidas, 92, 94–7, 103, 105, 111–12, 191
similes, 50, 64, 79, 108–9, 116, 120
spinning, 158–60, 161n *see also* distaffs, weaving
staffs, 94, 95, 111, 185
statues, 60–1, 124, 129–30, 132, 133–4
stone, 8, 13, 32, 36–7, 41, 112–21 123–6, 143–5, *144*, 178, 183, 191–2, 198, 201 *see also* lithic agency; Marsden Bay; petromorphism; statues; walls
Strife, 93, 118
sympathy, 18, 90, 102
syrinx, 9, 186–9, 190–5
systems, 15, 19–20, 115, 139, 163

tapestries, 7, 50, 69n, 81–2, 84–90
Telemachus, 123–4, 162, 187, 191
text, materiality of, 33, 36–7, 149, 172–3, 191, 195 *see also* poetry; epigram
textiles, 20, 58–9, 83, 84–7, 87–9, 149, 158–9, 161–3 *see also* tapestries; veils; weaving
Theugenis, 9, 158, 160, 161–3, 167–8, 174
Thyrsis, 12, 14, 131, 154–5

tools, 106, 107, 110, 116–17, 179 *see also* chisels; distaffs; hammers; nets; syrinx; traps; weaponry
trans-corporeality, 31, 79–80, 209
traps, 107–8, 151–2

veils, 52, 53, 59, 62
vibrant (vital) matter, 12–13, 53–4, 57, 58, 60–1, 62, 76, 88–9, 90, 135–7, 152, 170–1, 176–7, 187, 193–5, 198–9, 207 *see also* vital materialism
vines, 147, 150, 151, 199, 200
vineyards, 8, 135–7, 139n, 151, 200
Virgil, 5, 24, 27–8
vital (vibrant) materialism, 19, 21, 23, 47–8, 88–9 *see also* vibrant matter
voices, inanimate, 113, 144, 168, 176–7, 184, 193–4

walls
 drystone, 8, 20, 135–40, 197, 201
 building of, 8, 126, *56*, 57, 127–8, 133, 140–3, *141–2, 143*
water, 42, 52–3, 130–2 *see also* sea
weaponry, 63, 118n, 198–9 *see also* shields
weaving, 82–3, 84, 147–50, 151, 159–61 *see also* plaiting; poetry; spinning; woven objects
winds, 50, 78, 83n, 164–5
witches, 72–3
woven objects, *see* tapestries; textiles; trap

xenia, 70, 95, 156, 158, 175–6, 182, 185

Zeus, 57, 66, 94, 96, 191